BLACKOUT

The
GOSNELL
Grand Jury Report
THE MEDIA DOESN'T WANT YOU TO READ

✜✜✜✜✜✜✜✜✜✜✜

INTRODUCTION BY
JONAH GOLDBERG

The Official Grand Jury Report
First Judicial District of PA

Introduction Copyright © 2013 by Jonah Goldberg

FIRST EDITION

This introduction may not be reproduced in any form or by any electronic or mechanical means, including information storage and retrieval systems, without permission in writing from the publisher, except by a reviewer who may quote brief passages in a review.

Library of Congress Cataloging-in-Publication Data on File

For inquiries about volume orders, please contact:

Beaufort Books
27 West 20th Street, Suite 1102
New York, NY 10011
sales@beaufortbooks.com

Published in the United States by Beaufort Books
www.beaufortbooks.com

Distributed by Midpoint Trade Books
www.midpointtrade.com

Printed in the United States of America

Interior and Cover Design by United Writers Press
www.unitedwriterspress.com

TABLE OF CONTENTS

Introduction: The Banality of Evil	1
Section I: Overview	13
Murder in plain sight	15
Butcher of women	18
See no evil	20
Names	26
What to do	29
Section II: The Raid	31
Section III: Gosnell's Illegal Practice	35
Section IV: The Intentional Killing of Viable Babies	109
Section V: The Death of Karnamaya Mongar	127
Section VI: How Did This Go On So Long?	147
Who Could Have Prevented All This Death and Damage?	229
Section VII: The Criminal Charges	231
Section VIII: Recommendations of the Grand Jury	263
Appendix A: Anesthesia Chart	281
Appendix B: Anesthesia for Surgery	282
Appendix C: Price List	283
Appendix D: K. Mongar file	284

INTRODUCTION:
"THE BANALITY OF EVIL"

"The banality of evil." The phrase itself has become a bit banal as it is used so often in some circles. For those unfamiliar with it, the journalist-philosopher Hannah Arendt, author of *Eichmann in Jerusalem*, coined the phrase. Arendt covered the trial of Adolph Eichmann, an SS bureaucrat who organized the nuts and bolts of Hitler's "Final Solution." Eichmann didn't man the gas chambers or guard the camps; he moved paper around. He was simultaneously a dull everyman, and an architect of unspeakable evil. Arendt's point was that we have a natural human desire to turn those who do monstrous things into un-human monsters. We want the bad man to be a boogey man. But, as she argued, Eichmann was not an evil mastermind, nor a bloodthirsty ghoul. Rather, he was simply a cog in the machine. He was chosen for his job not because he had a special taste for death and genocide, but because he was a reliable party man who got the job done. An evil system may attract evil men, but it also turns weak men evil. The banality of Eichmann's evil was that while his deeds were horrendous and inhuman, he himself was all too human.

Which brings us to the case of Kermit Gosnell. A commentator on Fox News said of Dr. Gosnell, "He is the face of evil." No. He isn't. He's the face of just another guy. He's not a comic book villain. He looks like a grandfather. And while his alleged crimes are unspeakable he is, like Eichmann, the product of a system. Specifically, the system that made Gosnell possible was established by two 1973 Supreme Court decisions—Roe v. Wade and Doe v. Bolton—and subsequently sustained by a tapestry of court cases and a political and media culture that have entrenched the view that a fetus isn't a human until, in the words of California Senator Barbara Boxer, "you bring your baby home" from the hospital. Until then, the mother and the doctor have complete sovereignty over the child.

Kermit Gosnell is, in a very real sense, an Eichmann in that system. But unlike Eichmann, Gosnell literally, not just figuratively, had blood on his hands—lots of it. When the FBI raided his clinic, he was having dinner. "He was still wearing his bloody latex gloves. They had some holes in them," testified FBI agent Jason Huff. Gosnell kept eating during the interview. During his trial—still underway as of this writing—Gosnell sat silently as witness after witness reported seeing crying babies decapitated, drowned in the toilet, or left to suffer in shoeboxes as they waited to have their spinal cords "snipped." One journalist in the courtroom reported that Gosnell "just calmly watched and occasionally took notes with a vague hint of a smile on his face from time to time."

Such confident nonchalance is learned over a lifetime. In a sense, you can understand why Gosnell would feel unfairly picked on. Under the system created by Roe and Doe the worst that can be said of his efforts is that he cut too many corners, was sloppy and fudged some paperwork (I am overlooking charges that he was also a drug dealer). As Claremont McKenna College professor Jon A. Shields notes, under Roe and Doe Gosnell's only "clear legal violation[s]" are "relatively minor ones." Under Pennsylvania law, for instance, an abortionist needs a second opinion from another doctor to perform a third trimester abortion. "Is that failure really a capital crime?" Shields archly asks. "Had Gosnell performed

Introduction

the same late term abortions across the river in Cherry Hill, New Jersey—or in 40 other states—he would not have committed even a procedural offense."

The attacks on Gosnell from the feminist left are revealing. They are rightly outraged that Gosnell's "charnel house" (the Grand Jury's term) was a fetid and barbaric dungeon, with cat feces in the procedure rooms and unsterilized instruments on the surgical tray (Gosnell gave some patients STDs, his tools were so rarely sanitized). The feminists are justifiably aghast that patients were given the wrong anesthesia, with (at least) one woman dying as a result. They are understandably mortified by the casual racism that inspired Gosnell (an African-American) to provide a clean waiting room for white customers only. What they are not offended by is the fact that he was killing late-term fetuses or fully delivered babies. "These particular charges involve late-term abortion," feminist columnist Amanda Marcotte wrote for Slate magazine in 2011, "and all I could think upon reading the news story was, "I wish these women could have gone to Dr. George Tiller,' because he was renowned for the quality of care provided at his Kansas clinic." In other words, it's not the killing that offends, but the unsanitary and sloppy killing.

What endures is the idea that these babies are not really babies. As Gosnell's defense attorney said in court, "If we...say a baby is born alive because it moves one time without any other movement, that is ludicrous." And it is true, the idea that a baby moving independently of its mother is alive is ludicrous under the system of Roe and Doe. It is not ludicrous according to the more basic worldviews of common sense, basic decency, Judeo-Christian morality, and, not inconsequentially, our Constitution. But it is ludicrous when seen through the eyes of a worldview that thinks a baby isn't a baby until you bring it home from the hospital.

It's worth noting that this is the position President Barack Obama took when he was a state legislator. He not only opposed, but actively fought against, a bill that would have treated babies accidentally delivered during an abortion as human beings. Intriguingly, then state senator Obama's primary reason for opposing the bill was that he believed the location of the baby should not determine its moral or legal status. He recognized a key weakness of the pro-abortion position. If the only thing which distinguishes a "born alive baby" — with full constitutional rights — from "uterine contents" — is its location, then the Supreme Court might recognize a viable developing human as a "baby" wherever it may be — in or out of the womb. Recognizing the rights of a fully-delivered-but-unwanted-baby might force the Court to recognize the rights of a viable baby still in the womb. And, as a good liberal, Barack Obama couldn't have that.

And that is what is at the core of the Gosnell case. The doctor was charged with murdering babies. If he'd killed them in utero or partially delivered, he would have been slapped on the wrist or charged with nothing at all. This isn't merely a disconnect in legal logic, but a moral chasm that is not easily bridged. Whatever opinion one may have about where life begins and what that means about the sanctity of that life, there is no debate at the other end of the spectrum. A baby one minute before it is separated from its mother is no more of a human being a minute later. A baby with a toe still in the birth canal cannot by any legitimate standard be seen as mere "uterine contents" but a fully recognized human once its toehold is lost. And, surely, a baby still at the hospital isn't just a "viable fetus"

Introduction

(*The New York Times'* term for fully delivered babies) until you carry it over the transom into your home.

Governments that get into the business of using convenient political standards for who is or who is not a human invariably lead their people into grave evil. Slavery was a system whereby the state arbitrarily decided that some people are persons with God-given rights and other people are not. The Holocaust came about when arguably the most legalistic society in the world suddenly decided that some people did not count as humans on account of some ancient grievance or pseudoscientific theory. Under Roe and Doe, we have a system whereby some humans don't count as humans because they are inconvenient to the mother, and mere uterine contents to the doctor.

This is the darkness the Gosnell trial illuminates. Strip away the horrors—Gosnell's collection of baby feet, his fondness for cutting the spines of already dead babies for no apparent reason—and you are left with not merely a logical disconnect, but a moral chasm that cannot be bridged or obscured by medicinal buzz phrases or politically correct euphemisms.

Nor can it be ignored, though the press tried mightily. On April 10, my friend and fellow Fox News contributor Kirsten Powers wrote a column for USA Today on the de facto media blackout of the trial. The three major networks hadn't covered it in three months. *The New York Times* ran one story on page A17. *The Washington Post* ran no original stories on it. "You don't have to oppose abortion rights to find late-term abortion abhorrent or to find the Gosnell trial eminently newsworthy," she admonished. "This is not about being "pro-choice' or "pro-life.' It's about basic human rights."

BLACKOUT: The Official GOSNELL Grand Jury Report

Powers' finger-wagging paid off. A riot of stammered explanations that never rose to the level of acceptable excuses poured forth. Mollie Hemingway of the website "Get Religion" — who had been following the story all along — joined the frenzy. She started asking one reporter after another, "Why haven't you covered the trial?" The answers were revealing. Sarah Kliff, a *Washington Post* reporter who'd covered the alleged travails of Sandra Fluke as if the "reproductive rights activist" were a martyr for all of our patriarchal sins, explained that she didn't report on the Gosnell case because it was a "local crime" story. Megan McCardle, an insightful writer for *The Atlantic* honestly spoke for many. "To start, it makes me ill. I haven't been able to bring myself to read the grand jury inquiry. I am someone who cringes when I hear a description of a sprained ankle."

Both answers are true but not sufficient. Of course it is a local crime story. So was the O.J. Simpson murder trial. So is the Boston bombing. The JonBen Ramsay case was a local affair, too. If the mere fact that something occurred in a specific place justifies ignoring it, then almost nothing would ever get covered. As for the story being too gruesome to touch, as someone who has read the Grand Jury Report, I can sympathize. But the Newtown shootings were horrible to contemplate, too.

The Newtown massacre — a wholly legitimate news story to be sure — got plenty of coverage for a simple reason: it was a convenient story for liberals. It put guns in the dock. It's sickening to think about, but if Gosnell had used a gun instead of a pair of scissors, you can be sure he would have elicited far more outrage from the mainstream media.

Introduction

Relatedly, the reason the Gosnell case received so little attention is that it was so inconvenient for liberalism. "Let's just state the obvious," David Weigel, a liberal writer at Slate declared. "National political reporters are, by and large, socially liberal. There is a bubble. Horror stories of abortionists are less likely to permeate the bubble than, say, a story of about a right-wing pundit attacking an abortionist who then claims to have gotten death threats."

I would go further. It's not just that the media is liberal—even more liberal than Weigel is willing to concede. It is not simply that they are in a bubble. For decades, the press has been trying to build a Potemkin village, a friendly façade, to mask the reality of the system of Roe and Doe. For years, to the extent the mainstream media would cover partial birth abortion, they always insisted on referring to it as "so-called partial birth abortion," as if it was all just a right-wing hoax. Every pro-lifer is a pro-life "extremist" but no pro-choicer is ever an extremist, because even abortion-on-demand in the eighth month is a reasonable position, according to the press. I can't tell you how many editors at mainstream media outlets have insisted to me that the restrictions on abortion in this country are grave and draconian despite the fact that, going by the Supreme Court, they are in fact among the most lax in the Western world (far more lax than in most of Europe). And the fact that some states have regulations banning or limiting late term abortions is far less consequential than either the pro-life or pro-choice movements claim. Violations of such laws are virtually never prosecuted, because attorneys general understand they would not withstand Supreme Court review.

In 2000, when Republicans tried to pass a bill that would protect the lives of accidentally delivered live babies, Democrats, NARAL, and the press protested vociferously. "The purpose of this bill" lamented noted pro-choice extremist Rep. Jerrold Nadler (D-NY), "is only to get the pro-choice members to vote against it so [Republican pro-lifers] can slander us and say we are for infanticide." Nadler was largely right. But then again so were the Republicans; it *is* infanticide.

The mainstream media ignored the Gosnell case because the last thing they wanted to do was to walk through one of the fake doors of their Potemkin village to the reality that lurks behind. It is the same reason why, starting with a Republican governor in Pennsylvania, Gosnell's clinic wasn't inspected for seventeen years. It is why the Abortion Federation of America refused to report Gosnell to the Department of Health, even though it was the first abortion clinic to ever be denied accreditation by the AFA, according to an inspector interviewed by the Grand Jury. It is why Planned Parenthood of Pennsylvania admitted that it heard many complaints about Gosnell's abattoir but never once opted to report it. Bearing witness against the system is something that must not be done.

Obviously, the squalor at 3801 Lancaster Street is an outlier, far worse than what you would find at a typical abortion mill or "family planning" center. But it is not a moral outlier. The moral chasm between the triviality of killing a fetus inside the mother and a baby of the same age just outside of the mother is the same there as it is at any other facility. The Gosnell case causes supporters of the system to focus on that moral chasm. The monstrousness of Gosnell's actions force us all to contemplate the monstrousness that the system demands. "Battle not with monsters," Nietzsche advised, "lest ye become a monster, and if you gaze into the abyss, the abyss gazes into you."

§

Introduction

I wasn't asked to write the introduction to this rather unconventional book because I am a famous pro-life crusader, or because I have written a great deal on the subject of abortion in general, or the Gosnell case in particular. I was asked to write about this because I had posted a small item on *National Review Online* about how well-written this Grand Jury report is. I am not a great student of the genre, but I've read a few. And this report struck me as equal to some of the greatest reportorial journalism I have ever read.

I have long argued that opinion journalism is often the best kind of journalism. I don't necessarily mean mere punditry—of which I am a part time purveyor. I mean the sort of journalism where the author makes a sustained and serious argument. Unlike the allegedly objective reporter, the opinion journalist makes his preferences and biases known so that the reader can't account for them. The result is that you know where the opinion journalist is coming from. With the "objective reporter" you're left to guess (though it's not necessarily hard to guess) where he has let his biases tilt his coverage. Did he pick this legal expert because he makes the best case or simply makes the case the reporter wants to hear? Did she choose that statistic because it illuminates the facts or did she pick it because it skews them?

I am not some post-modernist who thinks there is no truth. Rather, I believe that the truth is best discovered through adversarial debate. A good opinion journalist anticipates his opponent's best arguments and objections and tries to deal with them honestly. The "objective" reporter pretends that there are no valid objections to what he provides. How could there be? The objective reporter is merely describing reality. Well, reality is complicated.

BLACKOUT: The Official GOSNELL Grand Jury Report

We recognize this fact in the most crucial fact-finding institution in our collective lives: the legal system. Everyone understands that the prosecution is biased in favor of conviction and the defense is biased in favor of the defendant. If the prosecution doesn't anticipate the defense's best arguments, it will lose—and vice versa. But in the process, both sides must tell the truth. There are agreed-upon rules of evidence.

This Grand Jury report is an important part of that process. I do not know if all of the legal arguments in it will be upheld by the judge. In fact, I very much doubt they will (already three of the baby-murder charges have been dismissed by the judge). But the facts of the report remain utterly and entirely undisputed. District Attorney R. Seth Williams and his team have put forward a truly compelling and thoroughly horrifying narrative about how a figurative butcher charged his patients the way a literal butcher would: by the pound. "The bigger the baby, the more he charged," the report explains plainly. At times it reads like a screenplay, at others like a transcript of a medieval torture chamber. Stripped of legalese and utterly clear in its biases, it rescues horrors from disposal down the media's memory hole.

According to the law, Gosnell's crimes may not add up to much. Then again, to paraphrase Dickens, the law is an ass. As with slavery and myriad other instances, man's law and morality can be at cross-purposes. Under the system of Roe and Doe, Gosnell's crimes may in fact end up being minor. But the facts are anything but minor. They are simply the facts. And however this case turns out, the Grand Jury has served an invaluable purpose: it has born witness.

Jonah Goldberg

BLACKOUT

SECTION I: OVERVIEW

This case is about a doctor who killed babies and endangered women. What we mean is that he regularly and illegally delivered live, viable, babies in the third trimester of pregnancy—and then murdered these newborns by severing their spinal cords with scissors. The medical practice by which he carried out this business was a filthy fraud in which he overdosed his patients with dangerous drugs, spread venereal disease among them with infected instruments, perforated their wombs and bowels—and, on at least two occasions, caused their deaths. Over the years, many people came to know that something was going on here. But no one put a stop to it.

Let us say right up front that we realize this case will be used by those on both sides of the abortion debate. We ourselves cover a spectrum of personal beliefs about the morality of abortion. For us as a criminal grand jury, however, the case is not about that controversy; it is about disregard of the law and disdain for the lives and health of mothers and infants. We find common ground in exposing what happened here, and in recommending measures to prevent anything like this from ever happening again. The "Women's Medical Society"

That was the impressive-sounding name of the clinic operated in West Philadelphia, at 38th and Lancaster, by Kermit B. Gosnell, M.D. Gosnell seemed impressive as well. A child of the neighborhood, Gosnell spent almost four decades running this clinic, giving back— so it appeared—to the community in which he continued to live and work.

BLACKOUT: The Official GOSNELL Grand Jury Report

But the truth was something very different, and evident to anyone who stepped inside. The clinic reeked of animal urine, courtesy of the cats that were allowed to roam (and defecate) freely. Furniture and blankets were stained with blood. Instruments were not properly sterilized. Disposable medical supplies were not disposed of; they were reused, over and over again. Medical equipment—such as the defibrillator, the EKG, the pulse oximeter, the blood pressure cuff— was generally broken; even when it worked, it wasn't used. The emergency exit was padlocked shut. And scattered throughout, in cabinets, in the basement, in a freezer, in jars and bags and plastic jugs, were fetal remains. It was a baby charnel house.

The people who ran this sham medical practice included no doctors other than Gosnell himself, and not even a single nurse. Two of his employees had been to medical school, but neither of them were licensed physicians. They just pretended to be. Everyone called them "Doctor," even though they, and Gosnell, knew they weren't. Among the rest of the staff, there was no one with any medical licensing or relevant certification at all. But that didn't stop them from making diagnoses, performing procedures, administering drugs.

Because the real business of the "Women's Medical Society" was not health; it was profit. There were two primary parts to the operation. By day it was a prescription mill; by night an abortion mill. A constant stream of "patients" came through during business hours and, for the proper payment, left with scripts for Oxycontin and other controlled substances, for themselves and their friends. Gosnell didn't see these "patients"; he didn't even show up at the office during the day. He just left behind blank, pre-signed prescription pads, and had his unskilled, unauthorized workers take care of the rest. The fake

Section I: Overview

prescriptions brought in hundreds of thousands of dollars a year. But this drug-selling operation is the subject of separate investigation by federal authorities.

Our focus was on the other side of the business.

Murder in plain sight

With abortion, as with prescriptions, Gosnell's approach was simple: keep volume high, expenses low — and break the law. That was his competitive edge.

Pennsylvania, like other states, permits legal abortion within a regulatory framework. Physicians must, for example, provide counseling about the nature of the procedure. Minors must have parental or judicial consent. All women must wait 24 hours after first visiting the facility, in order to fully consider their decision. But Gosnell's compliance with such requirements was casual at best. At the Women's Medical Society, the only question that really mattered was whether you had the cash. Too young? No problem. Didn't want to wait? Gosnell provided same-day service.

The real key to the business model, though, was this: Gosnell catered to the women who couldn't get abortions elsewhere — because they were too pregnant. Most doctors won't perform late second-trimester abortions, from approximately the 20th week of pregnancy, because of the risks involved. And late-term abortions after the 24th week of pregnancy are flatly illegal. But for Dr. Gosnell, they were an opportunity. The bigger the baby, the more he charged.

There was one small problem. The law requires a measurement of gestational age, usually done by an ultrasound. The ultrasound film would leave documentary proof that the abortion was illegal.

Gosnell's solution was simply to fudge the measurement process. Instead of hiring proper ultrasound technicians, he "trained" the staff himself, showing them how to aim the ultrasound probe at an angle to make the fetus look smaller. If one of his workers nonetheless recorded an ultrasound measurement that was too big, it would just be redone. Invariably these second ultrasounds would come in lower. In fact, almost every time a second ultrasound was taken, the gestational age would be recorded as precisely 24.5 weeks — slightly past the statutory cutoff. Apparently Gosnell thought he would get away with abortions that were just a little illegal. In reality, of course, most of these pregnancies were considerably more advanced.

But the illegal abortion business also posed an additional dilemma. Babies that big are hard to get out. Gosnell's approach, whenever possible, was to force full labor and delivery of premature infants on ill-informed women. The women would check in during the day, make payment, and take labor-inducing drugs. The doctor wouldn't appear until evening, often 8:00, 9:00, or 10:00 p.m., and only then deal with any of the women who were ready to deliver. Many of them gave birth before he even got there. By maximizing the pain and danger for his patients, he minimized the work, and cost, for himself and his staff. The policy, in effect, was labor without labor.

There remained, however, a final difficulty. When you perform late-term "abortions" by inducing labor, you get babies. Live, breathing, squirming babies. By 24 weeks, most babies born prematurely will survive if they receive appropriate medical care. But that was not what the Women's Medical Society was about. Gosnell had a simple solution for the unwanted babies he delivered: he killed

Section I: Overview

them. He didn't call it that. He called it "ensuring fetal demise." The way he ensured fetal demise was by sticking scissors into the back of the baby's neck and cutting the spinal cord. He called that "snipping."

Over the years, there were hundreds of "snippings." Sometimes, if Gosnell was unavailable, the "snipping" was done by one of his fake doctors, or even by one of the administrative staff. But all the employees of the Women's Medical Society knew. Everyone there acted as if it wasn't murder at all.

Most of these acts cannot be prosecuted, because Gosnell destroyed the files. Among the relatively few cases that could be specifically documented, one was Baby Boy A. His 17-year-old mother was almost 30 weeks pregnant—seven and a half months—when labor was induced. An employee estimated his birth weight as approaching six pounds. He was breathing and moving when Dr. Gosnell severed his spine and put the body in a plastic shoebox for disposal. The doctor joked that this baby was so big he could "walk me to the bus stop." Another, Baby Boy B, whose body was found at the clinic frozen in a one-gallon spring-water bottle, was at least 28 weeks of gestational age when he was killed. Baby C was moving and breathing for 20 minutes before an assistant came in and cut the spinal cord, just the way she had seen Gosnell do it so many times.

And these were not even the worst cases. Gosnell made little effort to hide his illegal abortion practice. But there were some, "the really big ones," that even he was afraid to perform in front of others. These abortions were scheduled for Sundays, a day when the clinic was closed and none of the regular employees were present. Only one person was allowed to assist with these special cases—Gosnell's wife. The files for these patients were not kept at the office; Gosnell took them home with him and disposed of them. We may never know the details of these cases. We do know, however, that, during the rest of the week, Gosnell routinely aborted and killed babies in the sixth and seventh month of pregnancy. The Sunday babies must have been bigger still.

Butcher of women

Dr. Gosnell didn't just kill babies. He was also a deadly threat to mothers. Not every abortion could be completed by inducing labor and delivery. On these occasions, Gosnell would attempt to remove the fetus himself. The consequences were often calamitous — though that didn't stop the doctor from trying to cover them up.

One woman, for example, was left lying in place for hours after Gosnell tore her cervix and colon while trying, unsuccessfully, to extract the fetus. Relatives who came to pick her up were refused entry into the building; they had to threaten to call the police. They eventually found her inside, bleeding and incoherent, and transported her to the hospital, where doctors had to remove almost half a foot of her intestines.

On another occasion, Gosnell simply sent a patient home, after keeping her mother waiting for hours, without telling either of them that she still had fetal parts inside her. Gosnell insisted she was fine, even after signs of serious infection set in over the next several days. By the time her mother got her to the emergency room, she was unconscious and near death.

A nineteen-year-old girl was held for several hours after Gosnell punctured her uterus. As a result of the delay, she fell into shock from blood loss, and had to undergo a hysterectomy.

Section I: Overview

One patient went into convulsions during an abortion, fell off the procedure table, and hit her head on the floor. Gosnell wouldn't call an ambulance, and wouldn't let the woman's companion leave the building so that he could call an ambulance.

Undoubtedly there were many similar incidents, but even they do not demonstrate Gosnell at his most dangerous. Day in and day out, the greatest risks came when the doctor wasn't even there. Gosnell set up his practice to rely entirely on the untrained actions of his unqualified employees. They administered drugs to induce labor, often causing rapid and painful dilation and contractions. But Gosnell did not like it when women screamed or moaned in his clinic, so the staff was under instruction to sedate them into stupor. Of course his assistants had no idea how to manage the powerful narcotics they were using. Gosnell prepared a list of preset dosage levels to be administered in his absence. But no allowances were made for individual patient variations, or for any monitoring of vital signs. All that mattered was the money. The more you paid, the more pain relief you received. It was all completely illegal, and completely unsafe.

Only in one class of cases did Gosnell exercise any real care with these dangerous sedatives. On those rare occasions when the patient was a white woman from the suburbs, Gosnell insisted that he be consulted at every step. When an employee asked him why, he said it was "the way of the world."

Karnamaya Mongar was not one of the privileged patients. She was a 41-year-old refugee who had recently come to the United States from a resettlement camp in Nepal. When she arrived at the clinic, Gosnell, as usual, was not there. Office workers had her sign various forms that she could not read, and then began doping her up. She received repeated unmonitored, unrecorded intravenous injections of Demerol, a sedative seldom used in recent years because of its dangers. Gosnell liked it because it was cheap.

After several hours, Mrs. Mongar simply stopped breathing. When employees finally noticed, Gosnell was called in and briefly attempted to give CPR. He couldn't use the defibrillator (it was broken); nor did he administer emergency medications that might have restarted her heart. After further crucial delay, paramedics finally arrived, but Mrs. Mongar was probably brain dead before they were even called. In the meantime, the clinic staff hooked up machinery and rearranged her body to make it look like they had been in the midst of a routine, safe abortion procedure.

Even then, there might have been some slim hope of reviving Mrs. Mongar. The paramedics were able to generate a weak pulse. But, because of the cluttered hallways and the padlocked emergency door, it took them over twenty minutes just to find a way to get her out of the building. Doctors at the hospital managed to keep her heart beating, but they never knew what they were trying to treat, because Gosnell and his staff lied about how much anesthesia they had given, and who had given it. By that point, there was no way to restore any neurological activity. Life support was removed the next day. Karnamaya Mongar was pronounced dead.

See no evil

Pennsylvania is not a third-world country. There were several oversight agencies that stumbled upon and should have shut down Kermit Gosnell long ago. But none of them did, not even after

Section I: Overview

Karnamaya Mongar's death. In the end, Gosnell was only caught by accident, when police raided his offices to seize evidence of his illegal prescription selling. Once law enforcement agents went in, they couldn't help noticing the disgusting conditions, the dazed patients, the discarded fetuses. That is why the complete regulatory collapse that occurred here is so inexcusable. It should have taken only one look.

The first line of defense was the Pennsylvania Department of Health. The department's job is to audit hospitals and outpatient medical facilities, like Gosnell's, to make sure that they follow the rules and provide safe care. The department had contact with the Women's Medical Society dating back to 1979, when it first issued approval to open an abortion clinic. It did not conduct another site review until 1989, ten years later. Numerous violations were already apparent, but Gosnell got a pass when he promised to fix them. Site reviews in 1992 and 1993 also noted various violations, but again failed to ensure they were corrected.

But at least the department had been doing something up to that point, however ineffectual. After 1993, even that pro forma effort came to an end. Not because of administrative ennui, although there had been plenty. Instead, the Pennsylvania Department of Health abruptly decided, for political reasons, to stop inspecting abortion clinics at all. The politics in question were not anti-abortion, but pro. With the change of administration from Governor Casey to Governor Ridge, officials concluded that inspections would be "putting a barrier up to women" seeking abortions. Better to leave clinics to do as they pleased, even though, as Gosnell proved, that meant both women and babies would pay.

BLACKOUT: The Official GOSNELL Grand Jury Report

The only exception to this live-and-let-die policy was supposed to be for complaints dumped directly on the department's doorstep. Those, at least, would be investigated. Except that there were complaints about Gosnell, repeatedly. Several different attorneys, representing women injured by Gosnell, contacted the department. A doctor from Children's Hospital of Philadelphia hand-delivered a complaint, advising the department that numerous patients he had referred for abortions came back from Gosnell with the same venereal disease. The medical examiner of Delaware County informed the department that Gosnell had performed an illegal abortion on a 14-year-old girl carrying a 30-week-old baby. And the department received official notice that a woman named Karnamaya Mongar had died at Gosnell's hands.

Yet not one of these alarm bells — not even Mrs. Mongar's death — prompted the department to look at Gosnell or the Women's Medical Society. Only after the raid occurred, and the story hit the press, did the department choose to act. Suddenly there were no administrative, legal, or policy barriers; within weeks an order was issued to close the clinic. And as this grand jury investigation widened, department officials "lawyered up," hiring a high-priced law firm to represent them at taxpayer expense. Had they spent as much effort on inspection as they did on attorneys, none of this would have happened to begin with.

But even this total abdication by the Department of Health might not have been fatal. Another agency with authority in the health field, the Pennsylvania Department of State, could have stopped Gosnell single-handedly. While the Department of Health regulates facilities, the Department of State, through its Board of Medicine, licenses and oversees individual physicians. Like their colleagues at Health,

Section I: Overview

however, Department of State officials were repeatedly confronted with evidence about Gosnell, and repeatedly chose to do nothing.

Indeed, in many ways State had more damning information than anyone else. Almost a decade ago, a former employee of Gosnell presented the Board of Medicine with a complaint that laid out the whole scope of his operation: the unclean, unsterile conditions; the unlicensed workers; the unsupervised sedation; the underage abortion patients; even the over-prescribing of pain pills with high resale value on the street. The department assigned an investigator, whose investigation consisted primarily of an offsite interview with Gosnell. The investigator never inspected the facility, questioned other employees, or reviewed any records. Department attorneys chose to accept this incomplete investigation, and dismissed the complaint as unconfirmed.

Shortly thereafter the department received an even more disturbing report—about a woman, years before Karnamaya Mongar, who died of sepsis after Gosnell perforated her uterus. The woman was 22 years old. A civil suit against Gosnell was settled for almost a million dollars, and the insurance company forwarded the information to the department. That report should have been all the confirmation needed for the complaint from the former employee that was already in the department's possession. Instead, the department attorneys dismissed this complaint too. They concluded that death was just an "inherent" risk, not something that should jeopardize a doctor's medical license.

The same thing happened at least twice more: the department received complaints about lawsuits against Gosnell, but dismissed them as meaningless. A department attorney said there was no "pattern of conduct." He never bothered to check a national litigation database, which would have shown that Gosnell had paid out damages to at least five different women whose internal organs he had punctured during abortions. Apparently, the missing piece in the "pattern" was press coverage. Once that began, after the raid, the department attorney quickly managed to secure a license suspension against Gosnell.

Similar inaction occurred at the municipal level. The Philadelphia Department of Public Health does not regulate doctors or medical facilities; but it is supposed to protect the public's health. Philadelphia health department employees regularly visited the Women's Medical Society to retrieve blood samples for testing purposes, but never noticed, or more likely never bothered to report, that anything was amiss. Another employee inspected the clinic in response to a complaint that dead fetuses were being stored in paper bags in the employees' lunch refrigerator. The inspection confirmed numerous violations of protocols for storage and disposal of infectious waste. But no follow-up was ever done, and the violations continued to the end.

A health department representative also came to the clinic as part of a citywide vaccination program. She promptly discovered that Gosnell was scamming the program; more importantly, she was the only employee, city or state, who actually tried to do something about the appalling things she saw there. By asking questions and poking around, she was able to file detailed reports identifying many of the most egregious elements of Gosnell's practice. It should have been enough to stop him. But instead her reports went into a black hole, weeks before Karnamaya Mongar walked into the Woman's Medical Society.

Section I: Overview

Ironically, the doctor at CHOP who personally complained to the Pennsylvania Department of Health about the spread of venereal disease from Gosnell's clinic, the doctor who used to refer teenage girls to Gosnell for abortions, became the head of the city's health department two years ago. But nothing changed in the time leading up to Mrs. Mongar's death. And it wasn't just government agencies that did nothing. The Hospital of the University of Pennsylvania and its subsidiary, Penn Presbyterian Medical Center, are in the same neighborhood as Gosnell's office. State law requires hospitals to report complications from abortions. A decade ago, a Gosnell patient died at HUP after a botched abortion, and the hospital apparently filed the necessary report. But the victims kept coming in. At least three other Gosnell patients were brought to Penn facilities for emergency surgery; emergency room personnel said they have treated many others as well. And at least one additional woman was hospitalized there after Gosnell had begun a flagrantly illegal abortion of a 29-week-old fetus. Yet, other than the one initial report, Penn could find not a single case in which it complied with its legal duty to alert authorities to the danger. Not even when a second woman turned up virtually dead.

So too with the National Abortion Federation. NAF is an association of abortion providers that upholds the strictest health and legal standards for its members. Gosnell, bizarrely, applied for admission shortly after Karnamaya Mongar's death. Despite his various efforts to fool her, the evaluator from NAF readily noted that records were not properly kept, that risks were not explained, that patients were not monitored, that equipment was not available, that anesthesia was misused. It was the worst abortion clinic she had ever inspected. Of course, she rejected Gosnell's application. She just never told anyone in authority about all the horrible, dangerous things she had seen.

Bureaucratic inertia is not exactly news. We understand that. But we think this was something more. We think the reason no one acted is because the women in question were poor and of color, because the victims were infants without identities, and because the subject was the political football of abortion.

Names

Obviously, Kermit Gosnell is the man with the clearest criminal culpability for what happened here. But many of the people who worked for the Women's Medical Society should also be charged with criminal offenses; and many of the people who worked for the public, while not criminally liable, should be called out.

We group the criminal charges into three categories: charges arising from the baby murders and illegal abortions; charges in connection with the death of Karnamaya Mongar; and charges stemming generally from the ongoing operation of a criminal enterprise.

We were able to document seven specific incidents in which Gosnell or one of his employees severed the spine of a viable baby born alive. We charge Gosnell, Lynda Williams, Adrienne Moton, and Steven Massof with murder in the first degree. Along with Sherry West, they are also charged with conspiracy to commit murder in relation to the hundreds of unidentifiable instances in which they planned to, and no doubt did, carry out similar killings. We also charge Gosnell with various violations of the Abortion Control Act,

Section I: Overview

including infanticide and performing illegal late-term abortions. Charged as co-conspirators with him in this regard are Williams, West, and Pearl Gosnell, his wife.

Two employees were Gosnell's accomplices in the administration of the drugs that killed Karnamaya Mongar. We charge Gosnell, Lynda Williams, and Sherry West with third-degree murder, drug delivery resulting in death, violations of the controlled substance act and conspiracy. Gosnell, West, and Elizabeth Hampton are charged with hindering apprehension (and Hampton also with perjury) for lying to the police, to the hospital, and to us about how this woman died.

Illegality was so integral to the operation of the Women's Medical Society that the business itself was a corrupt organization. We charge Gosnell, Lynda Williams, Sherry West, Adrienne Moton, Maddline Joe, Tina Baldwin, Pearl Gosnell, Steven Massof, and Eileen O'Neill with running that organization or conspiring to do so. We charge Massof and O'Neill, in conspiracy with Gosnell, with theft by deception for pretending to be doctors, and billing for their services as if they were licensed physicians. Gosnell should also be charged with obstruction and tampering for altering his patient files to hide illegality, and for destroying or removing other files entirely. As a final note, we charge Gosnell and Tina Baldwin, his employee, with corrupting the morals of a minor. Gosnell hired Tina's 15-year-old daughter as a staff member. She was required to work 50-hour weeks, starting after school until past midnight, during which she was exposed to the full horrors of Gosnell's practice. Bad enough that he expected grown-ups to do it.

That leaves the government employees whose job was to make sure that things like this don't happen. Worth special mention is Janice

BLACKOUT: The Official GOSNELL Grand Jury Report

Staloski of the Pennsylvania Department of Health, who personally participated in the 1992 site visit, but decided to let Gosnell slide on the violations that were already evident then. She eventually rose to become director of the division that was supposed to regulate abortion providers, but never looked at Gosnell despite specific complaints from lawyers, a doctor, and a medical examiner. After she was nonetheless promoted, her successor as division director, Cynthia Boyne, failed to order an investigation of the clinic even when Karnamaya Mongar died there. Senior legal counsel Kenneth Brody insisted that the department had no legal obligation to monitor abortion clinics, even though it exercised such a duty until the Ridge administration, and exercised it again as soon as Gosnell became big news. The agency's head lawyer, chief counsel Christine Dutton, defended the department's indifference: "People die," she said.

Lawyers at the Pennsylvania Department of State behaved in the same fashion. Attorneys Mark Greenwald, Charles Hartwell, David Grubb, Andrew Kramer, William Newport, Juan Ruiz, and Kerry Maloney were confronted with a growing pile of disquieting facts about Gosnell, including a detailed, inside account from a former employee, and a 22-year-old dead woman. Every time, though, they managed to dismiss the evidence as immaterial. Every time, that is, until the facts hit the fan.

We want better from our public servants. We trust that their actions will be reviewed, and that they will be held accountable.

Section I: Overview

What to do

If oversight agencies expect to prevent future Dr. Gosnells, they must find the fortitude to enact and enforce the necessary regulations. Rules must be more than words on paper.

We recommend that the Pennsylvania Department of Health plug the hole it has created for abortion clinics. They should be explicitly regulated as ambulatory surgical facilities, so that they are inspected annually and held to the same standards as all other outpatient procedure centers. Inspectors should review patient files, including ultrasound images, on site. Equipment, and employees' licenses, should be scrutinized. Second-trimester abortions should be performed or supervised by physicians board-certified in obstetrics and gynecology.

The Pennsylvania Department of State must repair its review process. Complaints should be taken by internet and telephone, and patients should be assured of confidentiality and a response when the investigation is completed. No complaint should be dismissed until the subject's full history of prior complaints has been considered, and malpractice databases have been examined. Reports about individual doctors should be cross-checked against reports about the medical offices where they have worked, and vice versa.

The Philadelphia Department of Public Health should do at least as much to control infectious medical waste as it does to inspect swimming pools and beauty parlors.

Statutory changes are necessary as well. Infanticide and third-trimester abortion are serious crimes. The two-year statute of limitations currently applicable for these offenses is inadequate to their severity. The limitations period for late abortion should be

BLACKOUT: The Official GOSNELL Grand Jury Report

extended to five years; infanticide, like homicide, should have none. Impersonating a physician is also a serious, and potentially very dangerous, act. Yet under current law it is not a crime at all. An appropriate criminal provision should be enacted. There may also be other statutory and regulatory revisions that we, as lay people, have not thought to consider. Legislative hearings may be appropriate to further examine these issues.

We recognize that these relatively technical recommendations will be unsatisfying to those fighting the abortion battle. "Pro-choice" advocates will argue that the real solution is government-funded abortion. "Pro-lifers" will see the case as an indictment of all legalized abortion.

We must leave these broader questions to others; our authority as a grand jury is more limited. But we exercise its full extent by recommending the maximum response available under the criminal law: murder charges. If you willfully disregard a deadly risk to the mother's life, and kill her, you will be charged with murder. If you deliver a viable baby, born alive, and kill it, you will be charged with murder. That prospect may make doctors more careful about performing abortions, especially abortions approaching the legal limit. We hope so.

SECTION II:
THE RAID

On February 18, 2010, the Federal Bureau of Investigation and detectives from the Philadelphia District Attorney's Office executed search warrants at the Women's Medical Society, a clinic operated by Dr. Kermit Barron Gosnell at 3801-05 Lancaster Avenue in Philadelphia. The federal Drug Enforcement Administration (DEA), the Philadelphia Police Department, and the District Attorney's Dangerous Drug-Offender Unit had been investigating Gosnell and his clinic for months, based on reports of illegal prescription drug activity.

During the drug-trafficking investigation, District Attorney's Detective James Wood learned from one of the clinic employees that a woman had died in November 2009, following an abortion procedure. Detective Wood discovered other disturbing details about Gosnell's medical practice. The premises were dirty and unsanitary. Gosnell routinely relied on unlicensed and untrained staff to treat patients, conduct medical tests, and administer medications without supervision. Even more alarmingly, Gosnell instructed unlicensed workers to sedate patients with dangerous drugs in his absence.

Based on this information, Detective Wood believed that further investigation of the woman's death the previous November was warranted. The detective searched for a police report on the incident, but finding none, he went to the Philadelphia Medical Examiner's Office to try to identify the woman and to find out more about her death. Detective Wood learned that the dead woman was Karnamaya

Mongar, and that her toxicology report revealed an extremely high level of Demerol, a drug Gosnell used at the clinic to anesthetize patients.

In light of this suspicious death and the other significant health and medical concerns, DEA Agent Stephen Dougherty invited personnel from the Pennsylvania Department of State (which regulates doctors and the practice of medicine) and the Pennsylvania Department of Health (which regulates health care facilities) to accompany law enforcement officers on the February 18 raid. No one from these agencies had visited the clinic in more than 15 years, even after the Department of Health had been informed of Mrs. Mongar's death months earlier.

The search team waited outside until Gosnell finally arrived at the clinic, at about 8:30 p.m. When the team members entered the clinic, they were appalled, describing it to the Grand Jury as "filthy," "deplorable," "disgusting," "very unsanitary, very outdated, horrendous," and "by far, the worst" that these experienced investigators had ever encountered.

There was blood on the floor. A stench of urine filled the air. A flea-infested cat was wandering through the facility, and there were cat feces on the stairs. Semi-conscious women scheduled for abortions were moaning in the waiting room or the recovery room, where they sat on dirty recliners covered with blood-stained blankets.

All the women had been sedated by unlicensed staff—long before Gosnell arrived at the clinic—and staff members could not accurately state what medications or dosages they had administered to the waiting patients. Many of the medications in inventory were past their expiration dates.

Section II: The Raid

Investigators found the clinic grossly unsuitable as a surgical facility. The two surgical procedure rooms were filthy and unsanitary—Agent Dougherty described them as resembling "a bad gas station restroom." Instruments were not sterile. Equipment was rusty and outdated. Oxygen equipment was covered with dust, and had not been inspected. The same corroded suction tubing used for abortions was the only tubing available for oral airways if assistance for breathing was needed. There was no functioning resuscitation or even monitoring equipment, except for a single blood pressure cuff in the recovery room.

Ambulances were summoned to pick up the waiting patients, but (just as on the night Mrs. Mongar died three months earlier), no one, not even Gosnell, knew where the keys were to open the emergency exit. Emergency personnel had to use bolt cutters to remove the lock. They discovered they could not maneuver stretchers through the building's narrow hallways to reach the patients (just as emergency personnel had been obstructed from reaching Mrs. Mongar).

The search team discovered fetal remains haphazardly stored throughout the clinic—in bags, milk jugs, orange juice cartons, and even in cat-food containers. Some fetal remains were in a refrigerator, others were frozen. Gosnell admitted to Detective Wood that at least 10 to 20 percent of the fetuses were probably older than 24 weeks in gestation—even though Pennsylvania law prohibits abortions after 24 weeks. In some instances, surgical incisions had been made at the base of the fetal skulls.

The investigators found a row of jars containing just the severed feet of fetuses. In the basement, they discovered medical waste piled high. The intact 19-week fetus delivered by Mrs. Mongar three months earlier was in a freezer. In all, the remains of 45 fetuses were recovered at the clinic that evening and turned over to the Philadelphia medical examiner, who confirmed that at least two of them, and probably three, had been viable.

A simultaneous search of Gosnell's house found patient files that he had taken from the clinic. In a filing cabinet in his 12-year-old daughter's closet, they found $240,000 in cash and a gun.

On February 22, 2010, the Pennsylvania Board of Medicine suspended Gosnell's medical license, citing "an immediate and clear danger to the public health and safety." On March 12, the state Department of Health filed papers to begin the process of shutting down the clinic.

The Philadelphia District Attorney submitted this case, pertaining to criminal wrongdoing at Gosnell's clinic, to the Grand Jury on May 4, 2010. We, the jurors, have reviewed thousands of pieces of evidence and heard testimony from 58 witnesses. The squalid spectacle that greeted investigators when they raided the clinic last February was awful, to say the least. Yet even their descriptions of the scene could not prepare the Grand Jurors for the shocking things we have since learned about Gosnell, his medical practice, and the way abortion clinics are regulated in Pennsylvania.

SECTION III:
GOSNELL'S ILLEGAL PRACTICE

Gosnell's "medical practice" was not set up to treat or help patients. His aim was not to give women control over their bodies and their lives. He was not serving his community. Gosnell ran a criminal enterprise, motivated by greed.

Some 40,000 abortions are performed across the Commonwealth each year. Abortion is normally one of the simplest and safest medical procedures. But not in Gosnell's clinic. Employing unlicensed, untrained workers in a facility that was grossly inadequate and unsanitary, his operation made a pretext of providing health care. In the absence of any regulatory oversight, Gosnell recklessly cut corners, allowed patients to choose their medication based on ability to pay, and provided abysmal care—all to maximize his profit.

We estimate that Gosnell took in as much as $10,000 to $15,000 a night, mostly in cash, for a few hours of work performing abortions. And this amount does not include the money he made as one of the top Oxycontin prescribers in the state. The Women's Medical Society stands as a monument to an absolute disdain for the health and safety of women, and in many cases of babies who were born alive in this filthy clinic.

BLACKOUT: The Official GOSNELL Grand Jury Report

> **The deaths of women and of countless viable babies were a direct and foreseeable consequence of the reckless and illegal manner in which Gosnell operated his clinic.**

Employees at the Women's Medical Society who testified before the Grand Jury were not surprised when a lethal overdose of drugs killed one of Gosnell's patients in November 2009. They had seen many close calls and at least one other patient's death caused by Gosnell's careless and criminal practices. They knew that Gosnell chose unlicensed, untrained, and unsupervised workers to anesthetize his abortion patients, and that the drugs, in accordance with his office procedure, were administered in the doctor's absence.

None of Gosnell's employees were licensed or properly trained. Gosnell's staff warned him that two of his employees, Lynda Williams and Sherry West, were not only unlicensed and unqualified, but sloppy and unconcerned as well. They presented an obvious danger to the clinic's patients, whom they routinely over-medicated and failed to monitor.

But while Williams and West were perhaps slightly more careless than other workers, their actions were consistent with the corner-cutting practice that Gosnell had operated for decades. Every aspect of that practice reflected an utter disregard for the health and safety of his patients, a cruel lack of respect for their dignity, and an arrogant belief that he could forever get away with the slovenly and careless treatment of the women who came to his clinic. The only thing Gosnell seemed to care about was the cash he raked in from his illegal operation.

Section III: Gosnell's Illegal Practice

The fact that the doctor staffed his facility with unlicensed and indifferent workers, and then let them practice medicine unsupervised, was only one factor that made his clinic such a dangerous place for its patients. Dirty facilities; unsanitary instruments; an absence of functioning monitoring and resuscitation equipment; the use of cheap, but dangerous, drugs; illegal procedures; and inadequate emergency access for when things inevitably went wrong, all put patients at grave risk—every day.

When two of Gosnell's staff members sought abortions, they knew better than to go to him. They went to other clinics, where they marveled that physicians actually counseled patients, the facilities appeared sanitary, and a doctor was in the room when they were medicated.

Mrs. Mongar was just one of many patients victimized by Gosnell's depravity. There were scores more. At least one other mother died following an abortion in which Gosnell punctured her uterus and then sent her home. He left an arm and a leg of a partially aborted fetus in the womb of another woman, and then told her he did not need to see her when she became sick days later, having developed a temperature of 106 degrees. He perforated bowels, cervixes, and uteruses. He left women sterile.

He also killed live, viable, moving, breathing, crying babies. He killed them by cutting their spinal cords after their mothers had delivered them after receiving excessive amounts of medication designed to induce active labor. This report documents multiple murders of viable babies. The evidence makes a compelling case that many others were also murdered.

BLACKOUT: The Official GOSNELL Grand Jury Report

Gosnell and his employees performed abortions long after the legal limit. The doctor's unorthodox methods, especially with late second-trimester and third-trimester pregnancies, virtually mandated the premature delivery of live babies—whose spinal cords he would then routinely slit. These practices persisted for many years without interruption by any regulatory body.

The pain, suffering, and death that he and his employees perpetrated were not the result of accidentally botched procedures. It was Gosnell's standard business practice, to slay viable babies. The women who died, or whose health he recklessly endangered or irreparably harmed, were simply collateral damage for the doctor's corrupt and criminal enterprise.

> **Gosnell set up his practice so that, in his absence, excessively medicated patients went into labor and often delivered live babies.**

Latosha Lewis, who worked for Gosnell for over eight years, explained to the Grand Jury how the doctor ran the clinic. According to Lewis and other staff members who testified, the office was actually split into two practices—the abortion clinic, which was mostly on the first floor, and a family practice on the second floor. (Witnesses testified that the family practice had devolved in the last several years into mainly a "pain management" practice.) The office opened at approximately 10:00 a.m., with family practice patients coming only in the evenings. Abortion patients arrived throughout the day. Gosnell, who was the only licensed doctor, did not usually arrive to see patients or perform procedures until after 8:00 p.m.

Section III: Gosnell's Illegal Practice

Abortions were generally scheduled four days a week—on Mondays, Tuesdays, Thursdays, and Saturdays. Gosnell did not see patients on Wednesdays, but some were seen by his unlicensed staff. According to his staff, the doctor and his wife, Pearl, performed extremely late-term procedures on Sundays. First-trimester abortions at the Women's Medical Society were generally one-day procedures and were performed all four days. Second-trimester abortions were performed usually over a two-day period. Questionable late-term and suspected third-trimester procedures took three days.

When Latosha Lewis began work at the clinic in 2000, the practice would perform approximately 20 first-trimester and 5 or 6 second-trimester abortions every procedure night. By 2009, however, the practice's first-trimester abortions had dropped off significantly. Lewis explained that Gosnell had a bad reputation in the Philadelphia community, and local referral agencies would not recommend his clinic to women seeking abortions. This assertion was confirmed by representatives of Philadelphia community organizations that provide referrals and information on sexual health services.

As a result, Gosnell began to rely much more on referrals from other areas where abortions as late as 24 weeks are unavailable. More and more of his patients came from out of state and were late second-trimester patients. Many of them were well beyond 24 weeks. Gosnell was known as a doctor who would perform abortions at any stage, without regard for legal limits. His patients came from several states, including Delaware, Maryland, Virginia, and North Carolina, as well as from Pennsylvania cities outside the Philadelphia area, such as Allentown. He also had many late-term Philadelphia patients because most other local clinics would not perform procedures past 20 weeks.

While there was no doctor on the premises during the day, the clinic's unlicensed assistants saw abortion patients beginning at about 10:00 a.m. Women could walk in for ultrasounds and for what the clinic staff called "pre-exams." During the pre-exam, which cost $125, one of the clinic's workers would ask the patient about her past medical history, allergies, and last menstrual period. The staff member would also draw blood, take the woman's blood pressure, and perform an ultrasound to determine the age of the fetus—even though none of the staff was properly trained to do ultrasounds. The clinic worker would have the patient sign the facility's consent form (rarely if ever reviewing it with the client), and then schedule the procedure.

Lewis testified that when she first went to work for Gosnell, he usually complied with at least part of a Pennsylvania law that requires doctors to wait 24 hours after counseling patients before performing an abortion. She said that Gosnell might wait a day after the patient's initial pre-exam, even if he did not provide the counseling.

By 2008, as the number of women and girls seeking first-trimester abortions from Gosnell shrank, the doctor disregarded the law to attract more patients. Lewis said that a lot of times patients would not return after their first visit to the clinic. The doctor had his staff offer procedures the same day that patients walked in the door—as long as the patient paid in full, typically in cash.

If first-trimester patients wanted to proceed right away, the doctor would complete the abortion that night using a five-minute suction procedure with an instrument called a curette. Two patients present in the facility during the February 2010 raid told a state Department of Health surveyor, "that it was the only clinic in town that you call

Section III: Gosnell's Illegal Practice

the day of and get an appointment and have the procedure done that day."

Second-trimester procedures were more complicated because the woman's cervix had to be dilated sufficiently to extract the fetus. If the woman was between 15 and 24 weeks pregnant, a worker would usually schedule her to come back on a Monday or a Friday night for the first step of a two- or three-day procedure. If, however, the pregnancy was 24 weeks or more—and the patient had her money ready—dilation would often begin that night.

The dilation procedure involved placing synthetic or seaweed rods called laminaria into the woman's cervix. The rods would expand as they absorbed moisture and would slowly push the cervix open. Although Gosnell usually performed this delicate procedure himself, it was not uncommon for him to have unlicensed employees pry open the patient's vagina with a speculum and insert the laminaria. After the laminaria were placed, the patient would be sent home with pain medicine and Cytotec to soften the cervix. Patients would be instructed to return the next day to complete the abortion or to have laminaria replaced if the fetus was really large. Sometimes, if a patient had come from out of state, the doctor would allow the woman to sleep in the facility. No personnel stayed with these patients; they were left alone and unsupervised in the clinic.

Inserting laminaria is a standard procedure followed by doctors who perform second-trimester abortions. Thereafter, Gosnell's procedure was not only grossly out of compliance with accepted medical standards, it was ghoulish, dangerous, and criminal. Patients returned to the clinic the next day (if they hadn't spent the night). The person at the front desk, usually the unlicensed and untrained longtime employee Tina Baldwin, would start medicating the patients by giving them more Cytotec to induce labor and temazapan (Restoril) to make them sleepy. The doctor did not arrive before 8:00 pm or later, despite the fact that patients frequently began arriving at noon.

For hours after they came to the clinic, patients were left naked from the waist down (the clinic provided no robes, only blankets that were washed once a week). Women sat in bloodstained lounge chairs in the "recovery room" while unlicensed, unsupervised workers gave them large doses of various drugs.

Cytotec was administered hourly, or whenever the staff got around to it. Pills of either 100 mg. strength or 200 mg. — the workers were unclear what they were giving — were administered both buccally, that is, by placing them in the patient's cheek or lip, or vaginally. These frequent doses of Cytotec made the women's uteruses contract and cramp, throwing them into active labor and causing severe pain. Kareema Cross, a co-worker of Lewis's, testified that as the patients got "bigger and bigger" over the years, the workers would give more and more Cytotec.

To make the patients "comfortable" — and keep them quiet — the clinic's unlicensed and untrained workers used butterfly needles for IV access and injected several different strong, sedative drugs into the women and girls in order to, as Latosha Lewis and Kareema Cross put it, "knock them out."

All afternoon and evening, as patients woke and complained of pain, workers would continue to medicate them with injections of sedatives. Between doses, the staff would leave patients largely untended. This would go on until the doctor arrived, some six or more hours after the patient did, or until the woman delivered.

Section III: Gosnell's Illegal Practice

Very often, the patient delivered without Gosnell being present. Lewis testified that one or two babies fell out of patients each night. They dropped out on lounge chairs, on the floor, and often in the toilet. If the doctor was not there, it was not unusual for no one to tend to the mother or the baby. In fact, several of the clinic's workers refused to deal with the expelled babies or the placenta. So, after delivering babies, women and girls would have to just sit and wait—sometimes on a toilet for hours—for Gosnell to arrive. Lewis acknowledged that she would not do anything but wait with the women:

> A lot of times this happened when [Gosnell] wasn't there. If … a baby was about to come out, I would take the woman to the bathroom, they would sit on the toilet and basically the baby would fall out and it would be in the toilet and I would be rubbing her back and trying to calm her down for two, three, four hours until Dr. Gosnell comes. She would not move.

James Johnson, who supposedly cleaned the clinic and bagged its infectious waste, confirmed Lewis's account. He testified that sometimes patients "miscarried or whatever it was" into the toilet and clogged it. He described how he had to lift the toilet so that someone else—he said it was too disgusting for him—could get the fetuses out of the pipes.

Amazingly, these premature deliveries—what Gosnell called "precipitations"—were routine. The doctor's customary practice called for intense and painful labor, accompanied by heavy doses of potent drugs, all while he was absent from the clinic. Lewis said Gosnell told her that he preferred it when women precipitated, often before he got to the clinic, because it made his job easier. A surgical procedure to remove fetuses, Lewis explained, could take half an hour. Whereas there was little to do—just suctioning the placenta—when babies were already expelled. In addition, by avoiding surgical abortions, Gosnell was less likely to perforate the women's uteruses with surgical instruments—something he had done, and been sued for, many times.

If fetuses had not precipitated, Gosnell would often have his staff physically push them out of their mothers by pressing on the mothers' abdomens.

According to a board-certified gynecologist and obstetrician who testified as a medical expert, Gosnell's labor-induction method of performing second-trimester abortions—as opposed to a standard surgical procedure—entails significant risks, including hemorrhage and debilitating pain that leaves patients unable to care for themselves. The pain suffered by women in full labor requires careful supervision and appropriate sedation. Thus, according to the expert, labor induction should be performed only in a hospital setting, where medical professionals can monitor the women throughout their labor. Gosnell had neither the staff nor the facility to perform this type of abortion safely. He did it routinely anyway.

Gosnell staffed his abortion clinic with unlicensed and unqualified workers.

Gosnell deliberately hired unqualified staff because he could pay them low wages, often in cash. Most of Gosnell's employees who worked with patients had little or no remotely relevant training or education. Nor did they have any certifications or licenses to treat patients. Yet they did so regularly, and without supervision—in violation of Pennsylvania's medical practice standards and the law.

Section III: Gosnell's Illegal Practice

Tina Baldwin testified that certification did not matter to Gosnell. He told his workers that there was a "grandfather clause where if you—since he's a doctor and he taught you, you could be automatically whatever it is he taught you to be. You could be certified because he taught you to do that."

Gosnell had several employees who lasted just a short time at his clinic, but the following were his principal employees after 2000:

Latosha Lewis worked at the clinic for approximately eight years, beginning in 2000 and ending on February 18, 2010. (She left to work at another facility for a year in 2002, and took two maternity leaves.) Although she completed an eight-month program at the Thompson Institute, a for-profit vocational training institution in Philadelphia, she received no certificate or license that qualified her for her responsibilities at the abortion clinic. She was not trained or certified to perform ultrasounds, to administer medication, or to deliver babies—all jobs that Gosnell assigned to her.

Lewis's duties included conducting pre-exams and ultrasounds, drawing blood, administering Cytotec and intravenous anesthesia, putting patient charts together, assisting the doctor with procedures, and attending to patients in the recovery room. She performed almost all of these tasks—except assisting with procedures—without supervision from the doctor, and usually while he was absent from the facility.

For most of the time Lewis was employed at the clinic, she worked from about 10:00 a.m. until the night's procedures were completed—sometimes as late as 2:00 or 3:00 a.m. In the beginning, Gosnell paid her $7 an hour, plus time-and-a-half overtime for anything over 40 hours and $20 cash for every second-trimester abortion. He later revised his pay scale, raising her base rate to $12 an hour, but not paying overtime. In 2008, Lewis stopped assisting with procedures and cut back her hours to 9:00 a.m.-5:00 p.m.

Lewis was working at the clinic on November 18, 2009, and conducted the pre-exam of Karnamaya Mongar. She was also present the next day when Mrs. Mongar returned, but left for the day before Mrs. Mongar began to have any troubles. Lewis remained at the clinic until law enforcement raided it on February 18, 2010.

Tina Baldwin worked at the clinic for nine years, beginning in February 2001 and continuing until the practice closed in February 2010. She had the same training from the Thompson Institute as Lewis, but did not get certified as a medical assistant until 2009, when she started to look for another job. From 2001 to 2005, Baldwin performed the same duties at the clinic as Lewis—assisting with surgeries, anesthetizing patients, performing ultrasounds, drawing blood, and working in the recovery room.

After 2005 Baldwin stopped working nights and instead staffed the reception desk from about 9:00 a.m. to 5:00 p.m. She described her job as supervising the medical assistants and "making sure everybody else did what they were supposed to do." She also dispensed Cytotec and Restoril for second-trimester patients, and collected the money for their abortions.

Baldwin was at the front desk when Karnamaya Mongar came to the clinic for her procedure on November 19, 2009. Baldwin gave her Cytotec and Restoril, but left the clinic before paramedics were summoned.

Baldwin acknowledged that she was not trained—except by Gosnell—to perform ultrasounds, and that she knew that she was

Section III: Gosnell's Illegal Practice

not supposed to administer IV medication. Yet she performed these duties and supervised other untrained workers, including her teenage daughter Ashley, as they performed these duties, all in violation of standards of professional conduct and Pennsylvania law.

Kareema Cross worked at the clinic for four and a half years, beginning in August 2005, as another uncertified "medical assistant." She performed the same duties as Latosha Lewis—conducting pre-exams, assisting with surgeries, performing ultrasounds, drawing blood, and administering IV medications. In 2008, when another unlicensed worker, Steve Massof, left and Tina Baldwin and Latosha Lewis stopped working nights, Cross's responsibilities increased. She began to administer Cytotec vaginally, and gave IV medication more frequently. She also had to staff the front desk at times. Cross stopped assisting Gosnell with procedures in July 2009.

Ashley Baldwin was a 15-year-old high school sophomore when she started working at Gosnell's clinic in 2006. Tina Baldwin is her mother. Although Ashley was just a teenager and still in high school, Gosnell had her assisting with procedures, performing ultrasounds, intravenously sedating patients, and assisting patients as they delivered in Gosnell's absence. Gosnell claimed to her mother that allowing the teen to essentially practice medicine was legal, through a "grandfather clause" which permitted him to train workers and avoid certification requirements. Ashley worked as much as 50 hours a week, into the early morning hours, while a full-time high school student. She was present on November 19, 2010, when Karnamaya Mongar went into cardiac arrest.

Sherry West was hired by Gosnell in October 2008. She had known Gosnell as a patient for 35 years. She had recently been diagnosed with hepatitis C. The doctor hired her to perform the same duties as his other "medical assistants." Like them, she had no training or certificate that would qualify her to do ultrasound examinations, administer anesthesia, monitor patients in the recovery room, or do any of the other duties that she performed. No precautions were taken to protect patients from exposure to hepatitis C.

West worked at the clinic every day except Wednesday and Sunday. She was paid strictly in cash, at a rate of between eight and ten dollars an hour. Her hours were supposed to be 3:00 p.m. to closing. She was present on the night that Karnamaya Mongar died and was still working at the clinic on February 18, 2010, when the facility was raided.

Lynda Williams was hired to work full-time in 2008. She had previously worked with Gosnell at Atlantic Women's Medical Services in Delaware, and had filled in from time to time at 3801 Lancaster Avenue. Gosnell originally hired Williams to clean instruments, but very soon had her anesthetizing abortion patients, performing ultrasounds, administering Cytotec vaginally, and dealing with babies born alive while he was not at the clinic. The way Williams dealt with the babies was the way the doctor showed her—she cut their spinal cords with scissors. She was not certified or licensed to perform any of these duties.

Williams commuted to work with Sherry West and kept the same hours. She and West were supposedly attending to Karnamaya Mongar in the recovery room throughout the afternoon of November 19, 2009. It was Williams who actually administered the lethal mixes of Demerol, promethazine, and diazepam that killed Karnamaya Mongar. When the clinic was raided in February 2010, she was still employed and still administering anesthetics to patients.

Section III: Gosnell's Illegal Practice

Elizabeth (Liz) Hampton is Gosnell's sister-in-law, his wife's sister. She is also the common-law wife of James Johnson, who was the clinic's janitor and was in charge of disposing of the medical waste. Hampton worked on and off at the clinic. Her duties included cleaning instruments and answering phones. Although the evidence indicates that Hampton did not usually administer medication, her initials "L.H." appear on Karnamaya Mongar's file and seem to indicate that she gave Cytotec to Mrs. Mongar at 6:30 p.m.

Hampton was in fact present when Karnamaya Mongar was at the clinic on November 19, 2009. She was also present when the clinic was raided three months later.

Adrienne Moton knew Gosnell through his niece and spent time with his family. She worked evenings to assist with abortions, but, like the others, had no relevant training or license. She assisted with procedures and cut the spinal cords of aborted babies.

Randy Hutchins was the only licensed medical provider, other than Gosnell, to work with any regularity at the clinic in the last several years. However, it was not lawful for him to perform the duties assigned by Gosnell because Gosnell did not obtain the State Board of Medicine's approval, as required. Hutchins testified that he worked for Gosnell for a year in the 1980s but left after he stole money from the doctor. Hutchins explained that he had a cocaine problem at the time. He returned to work at the clinic in July 2009 partially because Gosnell was willing to allow him to work off the debt. From August until the middle of September, Hutchins said, "I really didn't get paid."

Hutchins normally worked Mondays, Tuesday, and Fridays. His primary job was to see "pain management" patients. However, his name also appeared on Karnamaya Mongar's records on Wednesday,

November 18, 2009. Her chart shows that Hutchins inserted laminaria the night before her procedure.

Hutchins quit in February 2010, before the raid, because Gosnell never filed the paperwork required to allow him to work legally.

Maddline Joe worked for 17 years as the receptionist at Women's Medical Society. In 2007, she became the office manager. She was responsible for payroll, insurance forms, and filing the reports on all abortions that were mandated by the Abortion Control Act.

Anna Keith was Gosnell's aunt. She was the office manager until she retired in 2007.

Jennifer Leach is a 28-year-old woman who had a time card as if she were an employee of the clinic. She testified that Gosnell paid her $300 a week to provide "psycho-social counseling" one day a week to non-abortion patients, even though she had no training as a counselor. She acknowledged that she often did not show up to work at the clinic.

Leach saw Gosnell as a patient when she was 17 years old. She said that she and Gosnell had a "fling" on and off for a couple of years, ending the week before she testified. Leach has an 11-year-old child.

Pearl Gosnell, the doctor's third wife, also helped out in the office. Pearl assisted with abortion procedures on Sundays and days the clinic was normally closed. She worked at the clinic as a full-time medical assistant from 1982 until she married Gosnell in 1990. After that, she said, she worked there "maybe every other day," bringing "paper towels, toilet paper, cleaning supplies, soap." On Sundays, she assisted in the procedure room and monitored the patients in the recovery room.

Section III: Gosnell's Illegal Practice

Pearl claimed that she was certified to take temperatures and blood pressure by Lyons Technical Institute, but could not produce any records because, she said, the school had closed. She is licensed in cosmetology.

Kermit Gosnell himself was not qualified. Under Pennsylvania law, an abortion facility must have at least one doctor certified by the American Board of Obstetrics and Gynecology, either on staff or as a consultant. Gosnell, the only licensed physician associated with the Womens' Medical Society, is not an obstetrician or gynecologist, much less a board-certified one. In fact, 40 years ago, he started but failed to complete a residency in obstetrics and gynecology.

Just as his clinic bore no resemblance to a bona fide medical facility, the image of himself that Gosnell promoted had no truth to it. In newspaper and television interviews, he portrayed himself as a hard-working, conscientious doctor doing the best he could for his community. In fact, he left his clinic and his patients untended all day while he was at home, relaxing or exercising. Any contributions he may have made to the community are undermined by the substandard treatment that he passed off as medical care for the indigent.

Gosnell routinely cracked jokes about babies whose necks he had just slit. He treated his patients with condescension—slapping them, providing abysmal care, and often refusing even to see or talk to them—unless they were Caucasian, or had money. He yelled at and intimidated his staff. And he took advantage of poor women in desperate situations.

BLACKOUT: The Official GOSNELL Grand Jury Report

Gosnell presented two of his unlicensed workers as doctors in his practice, and allowed them to treat, diagnose, and prescribe medicine for patients.

Gosnell hired unlicensed medical school graduates Steve Massof and Eileen O'Neill to practice as doctors at his clinic. They were presented to patients and staff as "Dr. Steve" and "Dr. O'Neill," and Massof was listed on a sign inside the office door as "Dr. Steve Massof, Medical Intern." Both saw, diagnosed, and treated patients when Gosnell was not at the clinic. And both prescribed medicine to patients who never saw Gosnell—even though their prescriptions bore Gosnell's signature. (Massof admitted writing on pre-signed prescription pads; O'Neill insisted that Gosnell signed the prescriptions after she wrote them.)

Massof was a 1998 graduate of St. George's University Medical School in Grenada. He had taken and passed some of the tests necessary to become a doctor in the United States, but was never accepted into a residency program. Massof worked as a bartender and cook in Pittsburgh after graduating from medical school. In 2003, Gosnell hired Massof to work as a doctor at the clinic despite the fact that he knew that Massof was not licensed to treat patients.

Massof testified that he had an "ECFMG" (Educational Commission for Foreign Medical Graduates) certificate that qualified him to enter a residency program. But Gosnell's clinic had no residency program, and Massof's certificate did not allow him to practice medicine without the supervision of such a program. Massof was never registered with Pennsylvania's Board of Medicine as a graduate medical trainee, as is required to practice medicine in the Commonwealth.

Section III: Gosnell's Illegal Practice

Nevertheless, Gosnell directed Massof to perform as the facility's only "doctor" daily from noon until Gosnell (or O'Neill, the other unlicensed doctor) arrived at the clinic for the night — frequently some eight or nine hours later. Kareema Cross testified that, while Massof was working at the clinic, Gosnell felt comfortable arriving as late as 9:00 or 10:00 p.m. During that time, Massof treated medical patients for conditions including diabetes, asthma, pain, and infectious diseases; prescribed drugs; anesthetized abortion patients; performed ultrasounds; delivered babies; removed placentas; cut umbilical cords; and, in accordance with Gosnell's practice, severed the spinal cords of the late second-trimester and the third-trimester babies that precipitated.

Massof began working at the clinic in July 2003 and left in June 2008. His work schedule was erratic. He normally worked six days a week from noon until 2:00 to 3:00 a.m. when the abortion procedures were completed. Gosnell paid him in cash: $300 a week and an additional $30 for each second- or third-trimester abortion patient.

Eileen O'Neill testified that she graduated in 1995 from a medical school in Texas. She described an odd course of residency in which she seemingly worked simultaneously in Texas and at a Louisiana abortion clinic and then spent a month at Gosnell's clinic, where she said she "just stood around and did nothing pretty much."

Louisiana Board of Medicine records show that O'Neill was licensed to practice medicine in Louisiana from 1996 to 2000 (she testified, incorrectly, that she was licensed from 1995 to 1998). She testified that she worked at the Delta abortion clinic in Baton Rouge from 1998 to 2000, even though she also testified that she moved to Texas in 1998. She said that she worked at the Louisiana abortion clinic as a "side job." During that same time period, in 1998 or 1999, she said she was licensed to practice in Texas, but obtained "special dispensation" to finish her residency at Reading Hospital in Pennsylvania. She spent one month of her residency at Gosnell's clinic.

O'Neill briefly held a "graduate medical training license" in Pennsylvania, but let it expire in 2001. After her residency stints, she never held a medical license in Pennsylvania. (She asserted that she has a license application pending now.)

O'Neill relinquished her Louisiana medical license in 2000 — she claimed because of "post traumatic stress syndrome" — and has not been licensed to practice medicine in any capacity since 2001. Despite being fully aware that she was not licensed, Gosnell hired her to work at his clinic in 2002. O'Neill testified that she met Gosnell through Leroy Brinkley, the owner of both the Baton Rouge abortion clinic and Atlantic Women's Services, the Delaware abortion clinic where Gosnell worked one day a week.

In her testimony, O'Neill tried to minimize her hours, her pay, and her responsibilities at Gosnell's clinic. She said that she commuted from Phoenixville to work four hours a night (8:00 p.m. to midnight), three nights a week (Mondays, Thursdays, and Fridays). She testified, under oath, that she was really a volunteer, and that Gosnell just provided her with gas money. She testified:

> A: He gave me travel money every now and then, just whenever he had cash. He always said he never had any money.
> Q: So how much did you make?
> A: For 15 hours a week, sometimes he give me 200 every couple of weeks and sometimes 200 a month. Sometimes 400 every two months.

Section III: Gosnell's Illegal Practice

Gosnell, she said, paid her in cash.

O'Neill acknowledged that she saw patients and that they called her Dr. O'Neill. But she claimed that her responsibilities were mainly paperwork, tasks such as composing hardship letters, doing referrals, and filling out forms for disability and family medical leave. She insisted that she saw patients only when Gosnell was at the clinic, a claim refuted by her co-workers and disproved by her own files. Steve Massof testified that every day she worked, O'Neill saw patients before Gosnell arrived for the night. And Kareema Cross confirmed that O'Neill was regularly at the clinic before Gosnell came in.

O'Neill tried to assert that she did not treat patients, based on a fiction that the doctor was always there supervising her. But her own testimony belied this sham:

> Q: What do you mean that you didn't treat patients?
> A: Well, I never decide what the treatment is. That's up to him.
> Q: What would you do —
> A: Because I'm there with him all night. So I can talk to him about patients.
> Q: Okay. So your testimony is that he was with — that every time you saw patients, where was he, the doctor?
> A: Well, it depends, he would be in and out sometimes. I mean the deal was, he was supposed to be seeing them with me, but I'm sure there's times when he didn't. Sometimes he just stuck his head in, you know.

Later, she qualified her claim further:

> Q: ...you're saying all the services that you provided to the patient was in the company of Dr. Gosnell.
> A: No. I didn't say that. I said I would like it to be. He was always on the premises. Sometimes he'd just poke his head in. Whatever he tells me to do, I would do.

BLACKOUT: The Official GOSNELL Grand Jury Report

Massof testified that O'Neill worked alone and unsupervised, that she treated patients, and that she prescribed drugs. Latosha Lewis described O'Neill as "basically the doctor that saw family practice patients." Files found at the clinic show O'Neill signing post-procedure pelvic exams as the "clinician." Gosnell introduced O'Neill to an evaluator from the National Abortion Federation (NAF), an association of abortion providers, as the doctor who performed the first-trimester medical abortions (performed with pills, not surgery) — and O'Neill confirmed to the NAF evaluator that she did treat these patients.

Gosnell also introduced O'Neill to another one-time clinic worker, Randy Hutchins, as a physician. Hutchins believed O'Neill was a licensed doctor because he saw her treat patients at the clinic. Hutchins personally knew one of the patients — Della Mann, a registered nurse who had worked at the clinic years earlier (and, again, for four days in December 2009, when the NAF evaluator was present).

Mann told the Grand Jury that she had been a "patient" of O'Neill's for several years and a patient of Gosnell's for over 20 years before O'Neill joined his practice. She explained that she started seeing O'Neill when she arrived for an appointment with Gosnell one night and was told by the person at the front desk that she would be seen by "Dr. O'Neill" instead. Mann testified that for approximately seven years, until 2009, she saw "Dr. O'Neill" for "each and every one of my visits." She said that she saw Gosnell only four or five times during that period. Mann listed a number of conditions for which she had seen O'Neill. O'Neill had diagnosed her conditions, prescribed medication, and signed her charts. Mann could not say

Section III: Gosnell's Illegal Practice

whose signature was on the prescriptions, but she saw O'Neill write them.

Mann never saw or talked to Gosnell about these conditions. He did not pop his head in, and he did not consult with O'Neill. As far as Mann knew, O'Neill was her doctor. And she always assumed that O'Neill was licensed. She certainly never suspected that Gosnell allowed her to be treated by a "volunteer" at his clinic. Mann told the Grand Jurors: "If I knew that she was not licensed, I wouldn't have let her touch me."

Mann did eventually stop seeing O'Neill, but it was not because she was not licensed. Mann said that in 2008, she decided to stop going to Gosnell's office because of its reckless handling of patient files. She said that the files were left all over the place and that anyone, including other patients, could have access to them.

O'Neill was in the clinic on February 18, 2010, when law enforcement conducted the raid. She fled, however, before being interviewed — even though she had been told not to leave.

The Women's Medical Society was filthy and totally unsuitable as a medical office or a surgical facility.

The Grand Jury toured the facility at 3801 Lancaster Avenue. It is unbelievable to us that the Pennsylvania Department of Health approved this building as an abortion facility. We were stunned to learn that, between 1978 and 1993, the department sporadically inspected and approved the clinic, and then never inspected it again until February 2010, when health department employees entered the facility at the request of law enforcement officials who were investigating allegations of the illegal sale of drugs and prescriptions.

BLACKOUT: The Official GOSNELL Grand Jury Report

The physical layout of the clinic, a confusing maze of narrow hallways and multiple twisting stairways, should have been an obvious bar to its use for surgical procedures. The three-story structure, created by joining two buildings, had no elevator. Access from procedure rooms to the outside by wheelchair or stretcher was impossible, as was evident the night Karnamaya Mongar died.

According to former staff members, the facility had been substantially cleaned up by the time the Grand Jury visited it. Between late February 2010, when the practice was closed, and our tour of the clinic in August, significant efforts had been made to make the facility look and smell cleaner. Despite such efforts, it remained a wretched, filthy space. The walls appeared to be urine-splattered. The procedure tables were old and one had a ripped plastic cover. Suction tubing, which was used for abortion procedures—and doubled as the only available suction source for resuscitation—was corroded. A large, dirty fish tank stood in the waiting room, filled with turtles and fish. The dirt-floored basement was stuffed with patient files, plants, junk, and boxes of un-disposed-of medical waste. The entire facility smelled foul.

These were the conditions after the facility had been shut down and cleaned. Former employees, including Latosha Lewis and Kareema Cross, testified to the abhorrent conditions when the clinic was operating. They described the odor that struck one immediately upon entering—a mix of smells emanating from the cloudy fish tank where the turtles were fed crushed clams and baby formula; and from boxes of medical waste that sat around for weeks at a time, leaking blood, whenever Gosnell failed to pay the bill to the disposal company.

They described blood-splattered floors, and blood-stained chairs

Section III: Gosnell's Illegal Practice

in which patients waited for and then recovered from abortions. Even the stirrups on the procedure table were often caked with dried blood that was not cleaned off between procedures. There were cat feces and hair throughout the facility, including in the two procedure rooms. Gosnell, they said, kept two cats at the facility (until one died) and let them roam freely. The cats not only defecated everywhere, they were infested with fleas. They slept on beds in the facility when patients were not using them.

Kareema Cross testified about the procedure rooms: "The rooms were dirty. Blood everywhere. Dust everywhere. Nothing was clean." The bathrooms, according to Lewis, were cleaned just once a week despite the fact that patients were vomiting in the sinks and delivering babies in the toilets.

Medical waste and fetal remains were supposed to be picked up weekly by a licensed disposal provider. Gosnell, however, did not pay his bills in a timely manner, and the disposal provider would not pick up—sometimes for months. In the interim, and as the search team discovered during the February 18 raid, freezers at the clinic were full of discarded fetuses, and medical waste was piled up in the basement.

Sometimes, according to Tina Baldwin, fetal remains were left out overnight. "You knew about it the next day when you opened the door … Because you could smell it as soon as you opened the door." According to a plan that Gosnell filed with the Philadelphia Health Department in 2004, waste was to be stored in the basement for once-a-week pickup by a waste disposal company. But he didn't follow the plan. He failed to pay his bills. Weeks went by without a pickup, and the containers in the basement leaked.

BLACKOUT: The Official GOSNELL Grand Jury Report

> **Gosnell used and reused unsanitary instruments to perform abortions.**

The instruments that were inserted into women's bodies were also unsanitary, according to the workers. Kareema Cross showed the Grand Jury a photograph she had taken, showing how the instruments were purportedly sterilized. The photo shows a pan on the floor. In it are the doctor's tools, supposedly soaking in a sterilizing solution. But the photo shows that the instruments cannot get clean because they do not fit in the pan, and are not submerged. Gosnell would nonetheless pluck instruments from this pan on the floor and use them for procedures. Cross said that she saw Gosnell insert into a woman's vagina a speculum that was still bloody from a previous patient. She testified about how Gosnell would ignore her complaints about his unsanitary practices:

> The instruments were dirty. It was plenty of times that I had complained. He'll — it would be a spec, a speculum and he'll use it. I would complain — I'll leave the speculum on his tray, so he can see it. So he can say something to whoever is cleaning them. It'll have blood on it. And he would still use it and it was a lot of girls that was complaining about getting infections ... trichonomas, chlamydia because of the instruments not being cleaned.

Several workers testified that Gosnell insisted on reusing plastic curettes, the tool used to remove tissue from the uteruses, even though these were made for single use only. Latosha Lewis testified that Gosnell would make his staff reuse the curettes until they broke. Like Cross, Lewis believed it was the unsanitary instruments that were causing patients to become infected with chlamydia and gonorrhea.

Section III: Gosnell's Illegal Practice

When inspectors from Pennsylvania's Departments of Health and State surveyed the facility in February 2010, they corroborated much of what the former staff members described. Department of Health workers found that the suction source used by the doctor to perform abortions was the only one available to resuscitate patients. They found the tubing attached to the suction source was "corroded." They also described the suction source's vacuum meter as "covered with a brown substance making the numbers on the meter barely readable." An oxygen mask and its tubing were "covered in a thick gray layer of a substance that appeared to be dust."

The inspector from the Department of State reported: "The clinic conditions are deplorable and unsanitary ... There was blood on the floor and parts of aborted fetuses were displayed in jars."

> **Gosnell had unlicensed and unsupervised staff routinely administer potent and dangerous drugs when he was not present at the clinic.**

As bad as the physical condition of the facility was, the practice that Gosnell conducted inside of it was even worse. It was not a mistake or an exceptional circumstance that forced Lynda Williams and Sherry West to sedate Mrs. Mongar when Gosnell was absent from his clinic. According to multiple staff members, that was routine procedure. In fact, Gosnell, the clinic's only licensed medical provider, rarely arrived at all before 8:00 p.m. Abortion patients, on the other hand, began arriving as early as noon.

It was Gosnell's intention and instruction that his untrained and unlicensed staff administer drugs—both to initiate labor and to sedate patients—before he arrived.

BLACKOUT: The Official GOSNELL Grand Jury Report

Patients, meanwhile, did not receive individual medical consideration. Drugs were administered without regard to a patient's weight, medical condition, potential risk factors, or any other relevant factors that physicians need to weigh in determining appropriate medication. Gosnell ordered his untrained and inexperienced staff to administer drugs to patients even when they protested, as 16-year-old Ashley Baldwin did, that they were not qualified. Gosnell told Ashley and other employees that if they were not willing to administer medication and anesthetize patients, procedures that Pennsylvania law requires a medical license to perform, they could not work at the clinic.

As Kareema Cross explained it, Gosnell told her when she was first hired that it was her job to medicate the patients when they were in pain. But after assigning this as one of her job responsibilities, he did not oversee what she did on individual patients. Indeed, he couldn't oversee his workers as they anesthetized patients, because he was usually not at the clinic when they did so. His practice was to leave it to the untrained workers to decide when to medicate and re-medicate the patients. He also left the precise medication mixture to the judgment of his unlicensed, untrained staff.

Gosnell disliked it when workers disturbed him by calling for medication advice. Ashley told us that he complained that they were "rushing him." According to Lewis, "You had to rely on your own. If you felt like they were in pain and you wanted to administer medication, you would just administer the medication yourself."

Williams was known by other staff members to improvise her own drug cocktails. She would give a patient "[w]hat she thought she needed," according to Ashley. "She used what she wanted."

Section III: Gosnell's Illegal Practice

West would do the same. Other staff members repeatedly reported this dangerous practice to Gosnell, yet he continued to give Williams responsibility for drugging his second-trimester patients. Cross warned Gosnell in 2008 that Williams gave too much medication, but "Gosnell didn't care what she did." Cross would tell Williams that she was giving too much medication; Williams would respond, "well, that is what Dr. Gosnell told me to give."

Gosnell's practice of having unqualified personnel administer anesthesia began years before the death of Mrs. Mongar. We heard from a former employee, Marcella Stanley Choung, who told us that her "training" for anesthesia consisted of a 15-minute description by Gosnell and reading a chart he had posted in a cabinet. She was so uncomfortable medicating patients, she said, that she "didn't sleep at night." She knew that if she made even a small error, "I can kill this lady, and I'm not jail material." One night in 2002, when she found herself alone with 15 patients, she refused Gosnell's directives to medicate them. She made an excuse, went to her car, and drove away, never to return.

Choung immediately filed a complaint with the Department of State, but the department never acted on it. She later told Sherilyn Gillespie, a Department of State investigator who participated in the February raid, that she has worked at seven different abortion clinics and "she has never experienced an illegally run, unsanitary, and unethical facility such as the Women's Medical Society operated by Dr. Gosnell." She has never reported any other provider or facility to state authorities.

Gosnell knew that using unlicensed and uncertified staff was wrong. He had testified in the criminal trial of a man charged with illegally practicing medicine by assisting Gosnell with abortion procedures in 1972. In 1996, he was censured and fined in two states—Pennsylvania and New York—for employing unlicensed personnel in violation of laws regulating the practice of medicine. As far back as 1989, and again in 1993, the Pennsylvania Department of Health cited him for not having any nurses in the recovery room. Gosnell ignored the warnings and the law. He just paid his fines and knowingly continued the dangerous practice of employing unqualified personnel to administer dangerous drugs. It was his modus operandi.

Patients were allowed to choose any level of sedation, as long as they paid for it.

Gosnell did not actually prescribe the amount of medicine, if any, to be used on a particular patient. Instead, he had his staff offer patients a list of medications that could be bought a la carte, in differing quantities, for first-trimester abortions. This practice demonstrates that he was not really practicing medicine; he was running a money-making racket, cutting corners and endangering patients to maximize his profits.

Second-trimester patients always received the highest level of sedation—usually after being administered multiple lesser doses—as part of their package price. The age, size, health, and other characteristics of the individual patient were immaterial to the dosage. Often clinic staff would begin administering medicine chosen by the patient before the doctor ever saw the patient. It was routine for the unlicensed workers to heavily sedate second-trimester patients hours before the doctor arrived at the clinic.

Section III: Gosnell's Illegal Practice

Even when Gosnell was in the clinic, he did not give written or oral orders for medication. Rather, the unlicensed workers determined the mix of drugs they would administer by referring to, although not always following, a chart that was posted in the recovery room. The chart—a "cheat sheet" of the clinic's sedation cocktails—was handwritten by high-school-student Ashley Baldwin, who worked every night except Sunday at the clinic, performing a variety of medical procedures for which she had no training.

Ashley's color-coded chart described the various levels of sedation that Gosnell provided, and the mix of drugs that comprised them, as follows:

(1) Local (10 mg. of nalbuphine and 12.5 mg. of promethazine);
(2) Heavy (50 mg. Demerol, 12.5 mg. promethazine, and 5mg. diazepam);
(3) Twilight (75 mg. Demerol, 12.5 mg. promethazine, and 7.5 mg. diazepam); and
(4) Custom (75 mg. Demerol, 12.5 mg. promethazine, and 10 mg. diazepam).

Latosha Lewis described how she and the other unlicensed staff members presented the choice of medication to the clinic's patients:

> You can pick which anesthesia you want to receive, whether you want to be up, half asleep, if you want to be knocked out, and it's additional to your procedure, but local anesthesia is included in the smaller cases and custom anesthesia, which is the highest, to be put to sleep in the bigger cases.

An "Anesthesia for Surgery" form (Appendix B) presented to patients for their signature—and payment—did not identify or describe the drugs to be administered. However, it suggested:

BLACKOUT: The Official GOSNELL Grand Jury Report

It will probably be best to pay the extra money and be more comfortable if some of the following conditions are true for you.
1. The decision to have the procedure is a difficult decision.
2. Medication is usually necessary for your menstrual cramps.
3. Your decision has been forced by your parents or partner.
4. Your family members or friends "don't like pain."

The "Custom" mix of medications is described on the form as follows:

> Most women who choose CUSTOM SLEEP want to feel <u>ABSOLUTELY NO CRAMPS OR PAIN</u> during their procedure. A needle with an anticlotting medication is inserted prior to the procedure and sedation is repeatedly administered until the patient is comfortable throughout the procedure.

The form has a place to sign next to "I choose CUSTOM SLEEP" and a blank where the price of the "Custom" option is handwritten in. The price of the "Custom" sedation is $150. The form explains the effects of the "Twilight Sleep" concoction in this way:

> Most women who choose TWILIGHT SLEEP want to feel <u>VERY FEW OR VERY SLIGHT CRAMPS</u> during their procedure.

The cost listed is $90, which was in addition to the cost of the procedure. The form describes the clinic's "Heavy Sedation" option:

> Most women who choose HEAVY SEDATION feel <u>SLIGHT TO MODERATE CRAMPS</u> during their procedure.

"Heavy sedation" costs $50 extra.

Section III: Gosnell's Illegal Practice

All of the drugs listed on the chart, including those that put patients into a deep sleep and could be considered general anesthesia, were offered to patients undergoing first-trimester abortions—a procedure that usually takes only a few minutes and is relatively pain-free even without medication. Legitimate abortion clinics give no medication for these procedures, or small doses of a local anesthetic such as lidocaine to numb the immediate area—an entirely different medication from the clinic's misnamed "local," which includes a combination of narcotics given intravenously.

Even if the strong sedatives offered by Gosnell were being administered by licensed professionals—which they were not—the implications of the clinic's "Anesthesia for Surgery" form are troubling for several reasons. First, decisions on medication dosages were left totally up to patients, and were almost always made without any consultation with a doctor. Even worse, the patients were encouraged to make these decisions based on factors that have nothing to do with medicine—factors as irrelevant to their health as their friends' feelings about pain.

Probably most dangerous of all, Gosnell's form offered patients a choice among varying levels of pain, without any explanation of the risks presented by the various drugs or the effects of increased dosages of the drugs. No legitimate medical practice allows patients to choose their levels of anesthesia, especially when their choices are uninformed and based solely on a description of cost and how much pain the patients wish to feel.

We were particularly appalled by the reference in the form to a decision being "forced" on a patient by a partner or parents. A legitimate practitioner would never perform forced abortions.

BLACKOUT: The Official GOSNELL Grand Jury Report

Gosnell would and did. As long as he was paid, the patient's wishes or circumstances were not his concern.

> **Patients received multiple, heavy doses of sedatives that kept them anesthetized for several hours with no licensed medical professional on the premises.**

In addition to revealing the mercenary, rather than medical, nature of Gosnell's practice, the anesthesia form confirms what Latosha Lewis and Kareema Cross told the Grand Jury: the "custom" medication administered to second-trimester patients was not just a single dose that was administered to keep the patients asleep through a surgical procedure of limited duration. Rather, the medication was first "inserted prior to the procedure" and sedation was "repeatedly administered" until the procedure was completed.

Cross testified that she and the other workers would administer the "custom" dose of medication just before the doctor performed the procedure. But all day long, the staff had been administering powerful "twilight" levels of the sedating drugs:

> Q: And what about if the patient was 20 to 24 weeks?
> A: 20 to 24 weeks, [Dr. Gosnell] will do dilation for two days. For 23 to 24, he'll do dilation for two days and ... he'll go in. We'll give them the medication to put them to sleep. At that time we give them custom.
> Q: What's that?
> A: More medication. It's higher than twilight because all day we give them twilight to put them to sleep and make them comfortable.
> Q: So all day you're putting people to sleep?
> A: Yes.
> Q: And they are waking up sometimes?
> A: Yes.
> Q: And then you're putting them back to sleep?

Section III: Gosnell's Illegal Practice

A: Yes.

Q: How many times would a patient wake up and go back to sleep?

A: About three or four times.

Q: Before they're going in for their procedure?

A: Yes.

Q: So, if a patient is between 20 and 24 weeks, she would get even more additional medication?

A: Yes.

Q: So, she would have already been awake and asleep three or four times throughout the day —

A: Yes.

Q: because she was given drugs throughout the day?

A: Yes.

Q: By either yourself or Ashley or Sherry or Lynda?

A: Yes.

Q: And then when [Dr. Gosnell] arrives on site, on the premises, and he's getting ready to take care of it, to terminate the pregnancy, he would put the patient to sleep again?

A: Yes.

Q: With a heavier dosage of medication?

A: Yes.

Q: Who would give that heavier dosage of medication?

A: Me, Sherry. Sherry would be in recovery at that time. Me, Lynda, or Ashley.

Q: And would he tell you at that point how much to give or would you just give what you knew to give?

A: Just give what I knew to give.

Q: How did you know what to give?

A: Just from looking at the sign...

Cross stated that she would check on patients every hour and give more medication if they were cramping.

Latosha Lewis described the same standard procedures as Cross. She testified that second-trimester patients would arrive at the clinic in the early afternoon. They would be given Cytotec and Restoril by whomever sat at the front desk. Cytotec was given to induce labor by softening the cervix and causing the uterus to contract. Restoril,

BLACKOUT: The Official GOSNELL Grand Jury Report

Lewis explained, was to calm the women's nerves. Women were then placed in the "recovery room" where any one of the several unlicensed workers placed an IV access in the women's hands. For the next several hours — sometimes as many as eight or nine — women sat, medicated and in labor until either the doctor, or their baby, arrived. Lewis testified:

> We would undress them eventually from waist down, cover them up, and just put a blanket over them and they would sit there for hours while we're — either every hour on the hour or whenever we got a chance, we're still giving them more Cytotec. If the IV is in, we're giving them pain meds through the IVs. And that's what we're doing the whole time until the doctor arrives, unless the baby comes out.

Gosnell, she testified, was at home while his patients went into labor and his workers repeatedly medicated them at will. The goal, according to the clinic's workers, was to keep the patients asleep.

According to Lewis, the workers would not document what she referred to as the "mini-doses" or "in-betweens" that the workers gave continuously to achieve their goal — a room full of comatose women.

Gosnell used medication—and slaps— to silence loud or complaining patients.

Tina Baldwin testified that, while the size and weight of the patients were immaterial to dosages, one factor that did influence the staff's use of medication was the temperament of the patient. Baldwin said that she would call Gosnell at home when she had a question about medicating a patient:

Section III: Gosnell's Illegal Practice

>A: ... He would ask you what her temperament was, you know.
>Q: Why did it matter what her temperament was?
>A: I don't know. He would just ask you what it was, you know, what she was doing.
>Q: For instance, if someone was carrying on, really crying out in pain —
>A: Oh, you would knock them out completely.
>Q: Why?
>A: Because he wouldn't want you — he didn't want to hear all that. He just didn't want to hear all that. He didn't want that in his office. He didn't like confrontation. He didn't like nobody calling the police or anything. He didn't like none of that stuff going on.
>Q: So he would just drug a girl in the back if she was complaining and carrying on?
>A: If she was out of hand, yeah, she would get put under.
>Q: How often would that happen?
>A: Any time somebody got out of hand.
>Q: How often would people get out of hand?
>A: Let's say 24 weeks and you're feeling all of it, I would say at least three a week, three or four a week, something like that.
>Q: And there's other patients there with her, right?
>A: Yeah. And when it gets like that, we try — they used to take the other patients upstairs through the back way or we would shut the front, shut the door before surgery and that girl that was being a problem, nine times out of ten — you would get her out of the way first. Put her in a room, put her in a room, let's give her her medication, quiet her up. She's upsetting everybody else. So usually she would get done first.

If Gosnell was present in the clinic, drugs might be the back-up plan for subduing unruly patients. Tina Baldwin testified that she saw Gosnell slap a woman on the thigh when she got "a little bit rowdy." Baldwin explained that when that did not quiet her, he used drugs: "I mean he slapped her and that didn't work, then he would medicate her and put her under." According to Baldwin, some women returned to complain and ask why they had slap or hand marks on their thighs.

BLACKOUT: The Official GOSNELL Grand Jury Report

Even when Gosnell was in the building, he did not oversee the administration of anesthesia— except when the patient was white.

Tina Baldwin told the Grand Jury that the untrained medical assistants, without supervision by Gosnell, routinely administered even the final dose of sedation just before the procedure—unless the patient was white. She testified:

> …it was two rooms back there. And if he was working on one person in one room, you were in the other room you were setting that patient up to be done when he's done because it was just a back and forth thing. You would go ahead and medicate this person before he gets in the room.
> Q: Okay. Was he present when you did that medication?
> A: No, no. And sometimes he asked them—but it was a race thing.
> Q: What do you mean?
> A: It was—he sometimes he used to—okay. Like if a girl—the black population was —African population was big here. So he didn't mind you medicating your African American girls, your Indian girl, but if you had a white girl from the suburbs, oh, you better not medicate her. You better wait until he go in and talk to her first. And one day I said something to him and he was like, that's the way of the world. Huh? And he brushed it off and that was it.

Tina Baldwin also testified that white patients often did not have to wait in the same dirty rooms as black and Asian clients. Instead, Gosnell would escort them up the back steps to the only clean office— Dr. O'Neill's—and he would turn on the TV for them. Mrs. Mongar, she said, would have been treated "no different from the rest of the Africans and Asians."

Section III: Gosnell's Illegal Practice

Gosnell employed a high school student to medicate and monitor abortion patients until he and other staff arrived at the clinic to perform abortions.

In September 2006, Gosnell hired Ashley Baldwin, Tina's daughter, to work at his clinic when she was just 15 years old. She was a sophomore in high school. She came to the clinic each day in the early afternoon. In the beginning, her job was to answer phones and do paperwork. But before the end of her sophomore year, Gosnell assigned her to attend to the abortion patients in the recovery room.

For about a year, she was working "in the back" with other unlicensed workers who knew Gosnell's customs and practices. Kareema Cross, Latosha Lewis, Adrienne Moton, and Steve Massof assisted Gosnell with the abortion procedures and were usually at the clinic during the afternoon and evening before the doctor arrived. But as those employees left, or cut back their hours, Ashley became responsible for more and more activities involving patients.

In addition to attending to the patients in the recovery room, the now high-school junior began to assist Gosnell in the smaller of the two procedure rooms—one the staff referred to as "O'Keefe." (The larger procedure room, where Gosnell performed later-term abortions, was named "Monet.") Gosnell showed Ashley how to operate the ultrasound machine—which he told her was old and didn't really work—and how to measure and record the size of the fetuses. This became a routine part of her job.

By her senior year, Ashley was doing just about everything in the clinic except performing surgeries. She testified that Gosnell was coming into the clinic later and later, and that when he came in later, so did Lynda Williams and Sherry West. Often, Ashley was the only person staffing the clinic from the time her mother left at 6:00 p.m. until whenever Williams and West, who drove to work together, arrived. Even when West and Williams were at the clinic, Ashley said, Sherry West preferred to hang around at the front desk instead of working.

Ashley testified:

> I was just supposed to be in the recovery room, and inside another small room. But since they weren't there, I had to bring the girls from the front to the back, set them up in both rooms, wait until he got there, if a precipitation happened, I had to handle it on my own.

By "precipitation," Ashley meant that women and girls actually delivered babies. They delivered babies when Ashley was the only person present in the clinic to take care of them, their babies, the placenta, and all of the other drugged patients waiting for procedures. By Ashley's own admission, the women and babies did not get any kind of standard medical care. She described doing the best she could:

> Q: Okay. You said that as a senior you would be working and the babies would precipitate and you would be left to take care of it; is that right?
> A: Yes.
> Q: How would you take care of it?
> A: I would usually tell the girl to go to the bathroom, and I would—there is a phone right by one of the bathrooms, and I would call his phone.
> Q: Call whose phone?
> A: Doc. Call his cell phone while he's running or doing something.
> Q: What do you mean by running?
> A: He go for a run before he come to work.
> Q: And that is why he would get there so late?

Section III: Gosnell's Illegal Practice

> A: ... Yes. Or go swimming. And I would wait until he got there, so I would have to sit in the bathroom with the girl.
> Q: How many times did you see babies precipitate when you were there?
> A: A lot. Mostly all the second tri's mostly.

Other staff members confirmed that it was standard procedure for women to deliver fetuses — and viable babies — into toilets while patients and staff waited for Gosnell to arrive at the clinic.

In addition to essentially delivering babies, Ashley medicated patients, performed ultrasounds, filled out patient charts, and diagnosed sexually transmitted diseases using a microscope that she said was not as good as the one in her high school chemistry lab. Gosnell trained Ashley to administer intravenous medication by having her insert an IV "butterfly needle" — once — into his hand and injecting a saline solution. She testified about how he trained her concerning the actual drugs that she would use to medicate patients:

> Q: Okay. So there were times when you also gave medication to patients when the doctor wasn't there?
> A: Yes.
> Q: What kind of medications did you give?
> * * *
> A: Doc gave me a chart of medication. I couldn't really read the chart, so I made the chart over on my own and color coded. And it was diazepam, nalbuphine, sometime Demerol if there was no nalbuphine, and I forgot the other one.
> Q: Promethazine?
> A: Promethazine, Yeah.
> Q: How do you know how much to give a patient?
> A: He gave me a book.
> Q: The doctor gave you a book?
> A: Yes.
> Q: This is right after you turned 18 as a senior in high school?
> A: Yes.

BLACKOUT: The Official GOSNELL Grand Jury Report

> Q: And did you read the book? Did you read the book?
> A: Yes.
> Q: What did it tell you?
> A: It was a whole lot of percentages and decimal points and stuff. He was just like: you have to focus on this part right here. So, I just read and understood the part that he told me.
> Q: Did you understand the book?
> A: The part that he told me to read, the math, yeah, but not the words.
> Q: Okay. And so how did you know how to mix up or draw up the medications?
> A: He—he did them first, and then he told me to do them in front of him.
> Q: How much training did you get?
> A: Just that twenty minutes.

Based on this "training," Ashley would draw up the medications for as many as 20 patients a night. Ashley testified that she also administered drugs to first-trimester patients who would go into the smaller procedure room where she worked. She said that sometimes she would telephone the doctor if one of the first-trimester patients was in pain and he was not at the clinic. He would tell her: "Well, med them, I'm on my way." Ashley would then administer the "local" or, as she referred to the mix, "the blue meds" that were included with the fee for first-trimester patients.

The Grand Jury noted that, while testifying, Ashley mixed up Demerol with diazepam when describing the drugs that constituted a "heavy" dose. She said the clinic's "heavy" mix of sedatives contained 50 mg. of diazepam and 12.5 mg. of promethazine. On the chart, however, a "heavy" is described as 50 mg. of Demerol, 12.5 mg. of promethazine, and 5mg. of diazepam. This mistake gave the jurors just a hint of how dangerous Gosnell's practice—its procedures and its staffing—was for his patients.

Section III: Gosnell's Illegal Practice

Ashley was working 50 hours a week at the clinic and Gosnell was paying her $8.50 an hour—in cash. On her high school "work roster," Gosnell wrote that she worked from noon to 6:00 p.m. Her title was "student." In truth, Ashley often worked until 2:00 a.m. and performed the duties of a registered nurse or a doctor. When asked who was in charge of the clinic before Gosnell arrived, Ashley testified: "Me."

> **The workers Gosnell hired were incompetent and uncaring in administering anesthesia to his patients—while he was not on the premises.**

Latosha Lewis and Kareema Cross testified that whatever they did know about medicating patients they had learned from other unlicensed, untrained workers who came before them. Lewis admitted that she was careless about medicating patients until she overmedicated a patient to the point that the patient's eyes rolled up into her head. She testified that, after that frightening experience, she was more careful to measure when she prepared injections and was more watchful when the patients were medicated.

In 2008, however, Lewis stopped assisting with the abortion procedures, and Cross stopped in July 2009. Sherry West and Lynda Williams, whom Gosnell hired to take over their duties, were not as conscientious. West had been a long-time patient of Gosnell's and, according to Cross, she and Lynda Williams both obtained narcotics— Xanax, Oxycontin, promethazine, and Percocet—through Gosnell.

According to Lewis, Gosnell hired Sherry West when she lost her job at the Philadelphia Veterans Administration Medical Center after contracting hepatitis C. Yet, despite her hepatitis, West regularly failed to wear gloves when treating patients. In fact, Cross testified that she never saw West wear gloves, even though West worked in the procedure room with the doctor and inserted patients' IV connections.

Cross also said that Williams and West did not know how to give injections correctly, and that patients regularly came in to complain because their arms swelled up after injections as a result of improper technique.

Even more dangerous was West and Williams's reckless attitude toward medicating patients. Cross, Lewis, and Ashley Baldwin all described West and Williams as incompetent. Although medicating patients based on a predetermined chart is in itself astonishingly reckless, West and Williams did not even follow the chart when medicating patients. Neither seemed to understand — or care about — the grave risk to patients that their haphazard approach posed. Latosha Lewis testified: "It was a game to them." Lewis said that when they were supposed to be administering medications, West and Williams were "just goofing off and playing around."

According to Kareema Cross, Williams was especially dangerous because she imagined that she was the doctor. Williams seemed to feel it didn't matter what she did, because Gosnell didn't care. Cross, Lewis, and Ashley Baldwin all testified that Williams routinely overmedicated patients. This happened because she paid no attention to the chart when she drew up the drugs in a syringe, and because she failed to keep track of or to record what she administered. West, who had told Gosnell that she wasn't comfortable medicating patients, ended up following Williams's lead.

Williams's habit of using too much medication was so serious that Cross reported it to Gosnell at least a year before Karnamaya

Section III: Gosnell's Illegal Practice

Mongar died. Cross got the doctor's attention by telling him that he was losing money because Williams was using so much medication. As a result, Gosnell put a logbook in the recovery room to keep better track of drugs. This solution, however, was designed to save money, not protect patients. Even if the staff wrote in the logbook, which they frequently did not, they still did not record dosages where it mattered—in the patients' files. Cross said that Williams did neither.

Cross testified that she could recall at least 15 times when she had medicated a second-trimester patient only to have Williams come along right behind her and medicate again. Lewis said that no one, including herself, recorded the repeated doses of sedation that the clinic's staff administered to second-trimester patients to keep them anesthetized throughout their—often six- or seven-hour—wait for the doctor.

Lewis was particularly concerned because Williams and West would medicate patients and then not watch them. Even though the clinic had no machines to monitor patients' breathing or heartbeat, West and Williams would just leave the sedated patients in the back and go out to the front desk to eat and do "other things." Without the benefit of machines, monitoring at a minimum would require physically watching the patients to make sure they were breathing. Neither Williams nor West did this. Even Kareema Cross admitted that she sometimes did not.

Indeed, given how the clinic's practice was set up—with multiple second-trimester patients sitting for hours in induced labor, crying in pain, and receiving repeated doses of sedation; with babies precipitating; with no doctor present, and unlicensed staff who showed up only when they felt like it; and with virtually no monitoring equipment—it would have been impossible even for a conscientious staff member to appropriately monitor the patients.

According to Ashley Baldwin, Williams medicated patients "whenever Sherry told her to," which was "whenever Sherry felt like somebody needed something." As for how Williams determined which drugs and how much to give, Ashley answered: "What she thought they needed. She used what she wanted to." Williams almost never referred to the chart of medications and rarely called the absent doctor for instructions. Ashley testified that Williams used a lot of diazepam and gave repeated doses. (As noted earlier, the high-schooler mixed up diazepam and Demerol elsewhere in her testimony.) Ashley explained that the workers did not usually call to consult with Gosnell because he frequently became angry when they called him.

In addition to administering drugs to sedate patients, Gosnell's unlicensed workers also gave second-trimester patients repeated doses of Cytotec to soften their cervixes, stimulate contractions, and induce labor. Most of the staff administered Cytotec by placing a tablet inside the patient's cheek or lip. But Williams administered it vaginally.

As Ashley described the situation: Second-trimester patients were in a lot of pain because of all the vaginal Cytotec Williams administered. Williams then administered repeated, heavy doses of sedating drugs to make them "comfortable." Cytotec causes labor to begin. Women who were given excessive Cytotec would suffer excessive pain as a result. According to Lewis and Cross, the goal of Gosnell's assistants was to keep the second-trimester patients knocked out during labor and delivery. The doctor was present, if at all, only at the very end of this drug-induced delivery process.

Section III: Gosnell's Illegal Practice

When something went wrong, Gosnell avoided seeking emergency assistance for patients.

If something went wrong during a procedure — and it inevitably did, given Gosnell's careless techniques and gross disregard for patient safety — he avoided seeking help. Sherilyn Gillespie, the Department of State investigator who participated in the raid, interviewed a number of former patients whose experiences illustrate Gosnell's alarming and self-serving practice of covering up life-threatening mistakes, no matter the risk to the patient.

Dana Haynes went to Gosnell for an abortion in November 2006. She called relatives just before her procedure to tell them that she should be ready to be picked up by 7:45 p.m. When Ms. Haynes's cousins arrived, clinic staff refused to admit them into the clinic and made excuses as to why Haynes was not ready. Finally, after hours of waiting, the cousins gained entry to the clinic by threatening to call the police. They found Ms. Haynes alone, incoherent, slumped over, and bleeding. There was no monitoring equipment, and there was blood on the floor.

Gosnell called an ambulance only after the cousins demanded that he do so. Kareema Cross testified that, after having problems performing Ms. Haynes's abortion and extracting only portions of her fetus, Gosnell had placed her in the recovery room while he performed abortions on other patients. Rather than call an ambulance, Gosnell kept Ms. Haynes waiting for hours after the unsuccessful procedure because he wanted to try to fix it himself. By the time Ms. Haynes's cousins rescued her from the recovery room, Gosnell had tried at least twice, unsuccessfully, to complete the abortion.

Ms. Haynes was transported to the Hospital of the University of Pennsylvania. There, doctors discovered that Gosnell had left most of the fetus inside her uterus and had perforated her cervix and bowel. Ms. Haynes required surgery to remove five inches of bowel, needed a large blood transfusion, and remained hospitalized for five days.

Similarly, Gosnell should have sent another patient, Marie Smith, to the hospital when he was unable to remove the entire fetus during her abortion in November 1999. But again, he just kept the patient waiting, sedated and bleeding in the recovery room while he proceeded with other patients. Again, it was an insistent relative — Marie's mother — who found her. In Marie Smith's case, Gosnell did not tell her that he had left parts of the fetus inside her uterus. (Doctors are required to inspect the extracted tissue to ensure they have removed it all.)

Instead, Gosnell allowed Marie Smith to go home. When her mother called days later to report that Marie's condition had worsened, he assured her that Marie would be fine. Fortunately, the mother ignored Gosnell's assurances and took her daughter to the emergency room. When they arrived at Presbyterian Hospital, Marie was unconscious. Doctors found that Gosnell had left fetal parts inside her and that she had a severe infection. They told her she was lucky to be alive.

Another patient, a 19-year-old, had to have a hysterectomy after Gosnell left her sitting in his recovery room for over four hours after perforating her uterus. Gosnell finished performing the abortion at 8:45 p.m. on April 16, 1996, but did not call fire rescue until 1:15 a.m. By the time emergency help arrived, the patient was not breathing. She arrived at the Hospital of the University of Pennsylvania in

Section III: Gosnell's Illegal Practice

shock, having lost significant blood. To save her life, doctors had to remove her uterus.

In at least one case, Gosnell prevented a patient's companion from summoning help. The patient, a recovering addict who was undergoing methadone treatment, started convulsing when Gosnell administered anesthesia. When she fell off the procedure table and hit her head, the staff summoned her companion who was waiting for her. The companion asked Gosnell to call an ambulance, but Gosnell refused. He also prevented the companion from leaving the clinic to summon help.

Tina Baldwin told us that she knew of two or three times that Gosnell perforated a woman's uterus and then tried to surgically repair these mistakes himself. According to Tina Baldwin, Gosnell did not even tell these patients that he had harmed them.

Gosnell took photographs of his patients' genitalia before procedures and collected fetuses' feet in jars.

Gosnell engaged in other practices with patients that defy any medical or even common-sense explanation. Steven Massof testified that the doctor would often photograph women's genitalia before he performed their abortions. According to Massof, Gosnell told him that he was photographing women from Liberia and other African countries who had undergone clitorodectomies, the surgical removal of the clitoris.

In his curriculum vitae, Gosnell described this activity as "clinical research: clitoral surgery patients—cultural and functional realities." There is no evidence, however, that the doctor obtained the necessary permissions to engage in human experimentation.

BLACKOUT: The Official GOSNELL Grand Jury Report

Massof said that Gosnell took pictures of women, and of fetuses, with a digital camera and with his phone. Gosnell told Massof that he was taking the photographs for "his teaching," but Massof said that he was unaware that Gosnell taught anywhere. Gosnell would often show the photographs to Massof and exclaim about the skill of the surgeons who had sewn the women's labia together, leaving only a small opening to allow menstrual flow.

Another of the doctor's practices that defies explanation was his habit of cutting the feet off of aborted fetuses and saving them in specimen jars in the clinic. Kareema Cross showed the Grand Jury photographs she had taken in 2008 of a closet where Gosnell stored jars containing severed feet. During the February 2010 raid, investigators were shocked to see a row of jars on a clinic shelf containing fetal parts. Ashley Baldwin testified that she saw about 30 such jars.

None of the medical experts who testified before the Grand Jury had ever heard of such a disturbing practice, nor could they come up with an explanation for it. The medical expert on abortions testified that cutting off the feet "is bizarre and off the wall." The experts uniformly rejected out of hand Gosnell's supposed explanation that he was preserving the feet for DNA purposes should paternity ever become an issue. A small tissue sample would suffice to collect DNA. None of the staff knew of any instance in which fetal feet were ever used for this purpose.

Gosnell operated his clinic with complete disregard for Pennsylvania laws that regulate abortion clinics, health care facilities, and the practice of medicine.

Section III: Gosnell's Illegal Practice

Gosnell flagrantly violated virtually every regulation and law Pennsylvania has relating to the operation of abortion facilities. He did not comply with the basic standards of his profession. Nor did he follow state regulations pertaining to health care facilities generally.

Gosnell violated Pennsylvania's Abortion Control Act in many ways. He failed to counsel patients, despite a requirement to provide counseling at least 24 hours before abortions. He performed abortions on minors without a parent's consent or a court order. He failed to take steps to ascertain accurate gestational ages and he intentionally falsified gestational ages. He did not report to the state Department of Health any of the second- and third-trimester abortions that he performed. Nor did he comply with the Act's requirement to send tissue from late-term abortions to a pathologist to verify that fetuses were not viable or born alive.

Many of Gosnell's violations directly endangered women and caused them serious harm. His contempt for laws designed to protect patients' safety resulted in the death of Karnamaya Mongar. For example, although Pennsylvania's abortion regulations, 28 Pa. Code §29.31 et seq., require abortion providers to have functional resuscitation equipment and drugs "ready for use," Gosnell had no such provisions. The clinic's one defibrillator, the device used to help revive cardiac arrest patients, had not worked for years. There was only one suction source—the one Gosnell used for the abortion procedures—and no equipment to assist with breathing. And on February 18, 2010, three months after Karnamaya Mongar had died of an overdose of anesthesia, there was no "crash cart" with the drugs necessary to reverse the effects of just such overdoses. Had any of these items been present in the clinic, as the law requires, Mrs. Mongar might be alive.

BLACKOUT: The Official GOSNELL Grand Jury Report

Gosnell's facility also lacked equipment legally mandated for monitoring sedated patients. According to Kareema Cross, the clinic owned one old electrocardiogram (EKG) machine to monitor heart rate and a pulse oximeter, an instrument that is attached to the patient's finger and measures oxygen saturation in the blood, but these had not worked for at least six years. These instruments are the minimum equipment required to monitor patients who are sedated, according to the certified gynecologist and obstetrician who shared his expertise with the Grand Jury. The Department of Health found only one blood pressure cuff in the clinic in February 2010.

Gosnell's failure to equip his clinic with functioning monitoring and resuscitation instruments was all the more dangerous because of his use of unlicensed workers to perform crucial jobs. State abortion regulations require that women in the recovery room be "supervised constantly" by a registered nurse or a licensed practical nurse under the direction of a registered nurse or a physician. From 2006 until the clinic closed in 2010, Gosnell's recovery room was often supervised — and not constantly, because she had several other duties — by a high school student, Ashley Baldwin. The state Department of Health documents that, as far back as 1989, Gosnell had no registered or licensed nurses to staff the clinic's recovery room.

The complete disregard for patient care was evident in every aspect of Gosnell's practice. The staff routinely discharged patients before they were fully alert or could even walk. Tina Baldwin described how staff members would discharge still-medicated patients when closing time came:

Section III: Gosnell's Illegal Practice

> A: Oh, I did see some people, they were so drugged. I mean you had to get them out, take them with a wheel chair—take them out in a wheelchair.
>
> Q: And you would just send them on their merry way out the door?
>
> A: If it got late, at the time when I was working there, if it got too late like 1:00, 2:00 in the morning and they had a family member, yeah they would go out.

The state law requires that a second doctor, or a nurse anesthetist, administer general anesthesia, if it is used. General anesthesia is defined by anesthesiologists as a drug-induced loss of consciousness during which patients cannot be aroused, even by painful stimulation, a definition that would include the clinic's "custom sleep" dosage administered to "knock [patients] out." Not only did the clinic not have a second doctor administer anesthesia, it did not have any doctor at all present when Ashley Baldwin, Lynda Williams, Sherry West, Tina Baldwin, Latosha Lewis, Kareema Cross, Adrienne Moton, and Steve Massof routinely administered mixtures of potentially lethal drugs to clinic patients.

Another violation of Pennsylvania law proved significant the night Karnamaya Mongar died: Clinics must have doors, elevators, and other passages adequate to allow stretcher-borne patients to be carried to a street-level exit. Gosnell's clinic, with its narrow, twisted passageways, could not accommodate a stretcher at all. And his emergency street-level access was bolted with no accessible key. Any chance Mongar had of being revived was hampered by the time wasted looking for keys to the door. Ashley Baldwin testified:

BLACKOUT: The Official GOSNELL Grand Jury Report

Q: How long was—were the paramedics on-site?
A: A long time, because I couldn't get the key to the lock.
Q: What happened? Tell the members of the jury what happened.
A: Doc told me to get the keys to the locks, but it was like six sets of locks with thirty keys on each one.

Gosnell routinely performed abortions past Pennsylvania's 24-week limit.

Several of the clinic's former staff told the Grand Jury that Gosnell performed many, many abortions beyond the legal limit in Pennsylvania—a gestational age of 24 weeks. Their testimony is confirmed by clinic files, by fetal remains found at the facility, by photographs of babies that Gosnell delivered and then killed, and by a 30-plus-weeks baby girl born dead at a hospital after Gosnell had inserted laminaria to begin a third-trimester abortion.

Steven Massof estimated that in 40 percent of the second-trimester abortions performed by Gosnell, the fetuses were beyond 24 weeks gestational age. Latosha Lewis testified that Gosnell performed procedures over 24 weeks "too much to count," and ones up to 26 weeks "very often." When Lewis started working at the clinic, 20 first-trimester abortions and five or six second-trimester abortions typically were performed per night. But in the last few years, she testified, Gosnell increasingly saw out-of-state referrals, which were all second-trimester, or beyond.

By these estimates, Gosnell performed at least four or five illegal abortions every week. When a detective asked the doctor what percentage of the fetuses —including the first- and second-trimester fetuses—found at the facility during the February 2010 raid were beyond 24 weeks, Gosnell himself estimated "ten or twenty percent at

Section III: Gosnell's Illegal Practice

the most." The Philadelphia medical examiner analyzed the remains of 45 fetuses seized from the clinic. Of these, 16 were first-trimester; 25 were second-trimester, ranging from 12 to 21 weeks; 2 were 22 weeks; 1 was 26 weeks; and 1 was 28 weeks. The raid took place on a Thursday, so the clinic's busiest day for late-term abortions — Saturday — was not included.

Gosnell's former employees testified that they knew many abortions were performed beyond 24 weeks because they had performed ultrasounds that established gestational ages greater than the 24-week legal limit. When this happened, they would tell Gosnell, and he would often redo the ultrasound, or staff members would be ordered to do so, to produce a different gestational age to record in the patient's file. Gosnell taught his employees how to manipulate the ultrasound machine to get a false reading — one that would make the fetus appear to be smaller, and younger, than it actually was. Latosha Lewis testified:

> Q: Did anybody ever show you how to manipulate an ultrasound?
> A: Yes.
> Q: Who did?
> A: Dr. Gosnell.
> Q: When did he do that?
> A: I'm not accurate with the dates, but I would say since I've been there maybe, the second time I came back '03, '04 maybe.
> ***
> Q: How were you instructed to manipulate the ultrasound and for what purpose?
> A: Basically to manipulate an ultrasound if the woman was laying flat, if you just want an accurate ultrasound, you would just place it on the patient's stomach and you would measure. If you want to adjust the measurements, you would just lift off the ultrasound a little bit, which you would just make the head look a little smaller. So you would want to measure it, the measurements would be smaller.

Q: Would that make the gestational age of the fetus younger?
A: Yes.
* * *
Q: For what purpose was that?
A: By state law we were only allowed to go up to 24 weeks in a procedure. And a lot of times we would have females that were past 24 and a half weeks. So we manipulate the measurement of the ultrasound, so that indeed that we would try to get the patient to be at the 24-week mark. So we could still perform the procedure even though we were past 24 weeks.
Q: How often would he do this?
A: Very often.

Lynda Williams told the FBI that "Gosnell dummies paperwork and he will redo ultrasounds over himself to manipulate the image to reflect fetuses at younger ages."

Kareema Cross and Tina Baldwin testified that they also manipulated ultrasound results at Gosnell's direction. They told of other instances in which Gosnell replaced ultrasound photos that they had put in patient files. If their photos showed a biparietal diameter, a measurement of the fetus's skull, corresponding to a gestational age above 24 weeks, Gosnell simply substituted a different photo showing a measurement consistent with a younger fetus. Ashley Baldwin testified that she saw Gosnell manipulate ultrasound results himself "a good ten times."

Tina Baldwin testified that sometimes Gosnell would manipulate ultrasounds for women who were within the 24-week legal limit so that he could charge them more. "From 15 weeks to 24 weeks then, you're talking about money and you're talking about making it, moving it to make it bigger and smaller." Gosnell charged his patients on a sliding scale based not on gestational age, with late-term abortions sometimes costing $2,500 or more.

Section III: Gosnell's Illegal Practice

Lewis and Massof both testified that they believed Gosnell dealt with some of the patients with the longest-term pregnancies on Sundays, when his staff was not at the clinic. When Massof came in on Monday mornings he would find bloody instruments in the sink even though they had all been cleaned before the facility closed on Saturday night. When Massof asked Gosnell if he had seen patients on Sunday, the doctor answered, according to Massof: "Oh, yes, I took care of it. I had my wife or somebody help me or whatever." Gosnell's wife Pearl confirmed that she assisted her husband with procedures on Sundays.

Steve Massof told the jurors that when the ultrasound showed that the fetus was beyond 24 weeks, the staff would give the chart to Gosnell for him to "counsel" the patient. It is not clear that Gosnell ever counseled these patients. However, he did negotiate the price, because he charged more for women with pregnancies beyond 24 weeks. Latosha Lewis testified that Gosnell would still perform abortions on these patients. She rarely, if ever, saw Gosnell decline to do a procedure because a woman was too far along. Massof said that even if the ultrasound showed a fetus was 24 weeks, it would often be a week or two older by the time the procedure was done because "they would have to get their money."

Kareema Cross told us, "If it's a big baby, he [Gosnell] never tell us the truth." Instead, "He'll always say the baby was 24.5." According to his workers, Gosnell recorded any fetus over 24 weeks as "24.5" weeks on their charts. The fetus could be 26 or 28 weeks, but on the chart, the doctor would always write 24.5. They testified that he told them 24.5 weeks was the legal limit. Yet, because Gosnell regularly recorded late-term abortions as 24.5 weeks, his own notations prove that he performed numerous illegal abortions in violation of Pennsylvania's 24-week limit.

Sometimes, where the gestational age exceeded the 24-week limit, Gosnell forgot—or did not bother—to include a manipulated ultrasound in the file. Instead, even where the only ultrasound established a gestational age greater than 24 weeks, Gosnell performed an abortion anyway, indicating, in the patient's file, that the patient was exactly 24.5 weeks pregnant.

Law enforcement officers seized some abortion patient files from Gosnell's clinic. Between the time that law enforcement raided Gosnell's office in February and the time that investigators returned with a warrant to seize patient files, many files had disappeared. The Grand Jurors viewed a videotape of the February 2010 raid and saw files on shelves outside the procedure rooms and along a hallway. Those shelves and that hallway were empty when investigators returned. Lewis and others told us that these were second-trimester files. Most of the second-trimester files from 2008, 2009, and 2010 remain missing.

The Grand Jury, reviewing just the fraction of Gosnell's abortion files seized by authorities, was still able to document numerous instances in which ultrasound readings were manipulated to disguise illegal late-term abortions. Our review, although limited by the disappearance of many patient files, revealed that Gosnell reported performing abortions on 24.5-week fetuses more than 80 times between 2007 and February 2010.

Clinic staff testified that Gosnell took patients files home and did not keep records of most of his late-term abortions at the clinic. Tina Baldwin explained that Gosnell took second-trimester files home

Section III: Gosnell's Illegal Practice

"if there were difficult cases or some cases where he thought they shouldn't be in there." Massof told us that Gosnell always took files home, so "I think he has them. If he hasn't destroyed them, he has them." A subsequent search of Gosnell's home and car turned up only some of these files. One of the files seized from Gosnell's car was partially shredded.

Gosnell caused a 30-week baby to be stillborn.

The vast majority of Gosnell's post-24-week abortions we learned of from files. But there were some that came to the attention of other doctors and hospitals that were called on to treat his patients. This is how the Grand Jury learned of one third-trimester viable fetus that Gosnell caused to die before it was born. He did so by initiating an abortion on a 14-year-old girl who is estimated to have been 30 weeks pregnant. The teenager came to Gosnell for an abortion in September 2007.

Although most post-first-trimester procedures took two days to complete — one day for insertion of laminaria and dilation of the cervix, with the patient returning the next day for extraction — a woman we will call "Nancy" was scheduled for a three-day procedure because her pregnancy was so advanced. On the first day, Gosnell inserted laminaria to begin dilation. Two days later, Nancy returned to have the laminaria replaced for further dilation. She was scheduled to return the following day, a Sunday, for the abortion procedure.

At home at 3:00 a.m. Sunday morning, however, her membranes ruptured after several hours of labor. She attempted to contact the clinic, but was unsuccessful and went instead to Crozer-Chester

Hospital. There, she delivered a stillborn baby girl weighing 2 lbs., 1 oz. Because the fetus was clearly beyond Pennsylvania's 24-week limit for abortions, the hospital reported the stillbirth to the Delaware County Medical Examiner, Dr. Frederick Hellman.

Dr. Hellman's autopsy established that the baby's gestational age was at least 29 to 30 weeks, and perhaps as much as 34 weeks. This conclusion was corroborated by a neonatologist who testified before the Grand Jury. The expert witness told the jury that the average weight of a baby born at 29 weeks is a little over two pounds.

In response to a subpoena, Gosnell sent Nancy's file and a letter to Dr. Hellman on September 28, 2007. In the letter, Gosnell stated that an ultrasound showed that the pregnancy was 24.5 weeks on September 7 (three days before the scheduled abortion). Gosnell's own file, however, contained an ultrasound indicating that Nancy was more than 25 weeks pregnant, based on a measurement of the fetus's head. Dr. Hellman testified that even that ultrasound appeared to have been manipulated to make the fetus's head appear smaller. Dr. Hellman's measurement of the skull during the autopsy showed that Nancy was almost 30 weeks pregnant.

Gosnell also wrote in his letter to Dr. Hellman that he had injected the fetus with Digoxin the day before the birth, in order to cause fetal demise before the intended abortion procedure. The medical examiner, however, testified that he found no indication that the fetus had, in fact, been injected with Digoxin. The autopsy did not reveal any puncture wound from an injection, nor was Digoxin evident in the toxicology screen.

Based on scalp hemorrhage, the medical examiner concluded that the fetus had died during labor, possibly from the strong

Section III: Gosnell's Illegal Practice

contractions that would have resulted from the heavy doses of labor-inducing medications. Dr. Hellman opined that Nancy's baby was viable. The neonatologist told us that the survival rate for babies born at 29 weeks is 95 percent; at 30 weeks, the survival rate is nearly 100 percent.

Based on his findings, the medical examiner reported Gosnell's violations of the Abortion Control Act to the Pennsylvania Department of Health. It took no action.

Gosnell began an abortion on a 29-week pregnant woman and then refused to take dilators out when the woman changed her mind.

We learned of another illegal, third-trimester abortion only because the mother changed her mind. In 2004, a 27-year-old woman went to Gosnell, pregnant with her first child. She testified that she was surprised when Gosnell told her she was 21 weeks pregnant. On the first day of what was to be a two-day procedure, Gosnell inserted dilators in the woman's cervix. After Gosnell had finished inserting the laminaria, the woman asked him what happened to the babies after they were aborted. She testified that Gosnell told her they were burned.

At home, thinking over how Gosnell disposed of the fetuses, the woman had a change of heart. She called her cousin and the cousin called Gosnell to tell him that they wanted him to take the laminaria out. Gosnell said that he could not do that once the procedure was started. And he did not want to return the $1,300 that the patient had already paid. The pregnant woman ended up going to the Hospital at the University of Pennsylvania to have the laminaria removed. It was

BLACKOUT: The Official GOSNELL Grand Jury Report

determined at the hospital that she was 29 weeks pregnant. A few days later, the 27-year-old delivered a premature baby girl. She was treated at Children's Hospital of Philadelphia and is today a healthy kindergartener.

Either a doctor or a nurse at the hospital told the woman that what Gosnell had done was illegal. Gosnell recorded in the woman's chart that she was 24.5 weeks pregnant.

Gosnell's illegal practice was a huge moneymaker.

Clinic workers' testimony gave the jurors an idea of how profitable Gosnell's abortion business was. Maddline Joe, an employee of Gosnell's for nearly 20 years and office manager for the last two and a half, said that in the early years, the clinic averaged 20 first-trimester and 5 or 6 second-trimester patients a night. In the last few years, she said, the first-trimester business was down to 10 to 15 patients a night. As the first-trimester business dropped off, according to Latosha Lewis, Gosnell began to do more very late-term abortions, often on out-of-state patients. These, Lewis said, brought in a lot of money.

Lynda Williams provided the FBI with a handwritten chart listing what Gosnell charged for abortions at various gestational ages:

6 weeks - 12 weeks	$330
13 weeks - 14 weeks	$440
15 weeks - 16 weeks	$540
17 weeks - 18 weeks	$750
19 weeks - 20 weeks	$950
21 weeks - 22 weeks	$1,180
23 weeks - 24 weeks	$1,625

Section III: Gosnell's Illegal Practice

But other employees said that what he charged was often more. They said he charged as much as $3,000 for a single late-term abortion. The great aunt of another patient testified that she paid $2,500.

Even using conservative estimates, the amount of money that Gosnell took in every procedure night is staggering. If he did 20 first-trimester abortions at $330 a piece, and five 19- to 20-week abortions at $950, he would take in $11,350 a night. Similarly, in the later years, if he performed 10 first-trimester and 5 late-second-trimester (23 to 24 weeks) abortions a night, Gosnell would still take in $11,425. And that does not include any of the illegal abortions past 24 weeks for which he charged much more, or the profits he made by selling additional anesthesia a la carte to first-trimester patients.

This amounts to nearly $1.8 million a year — almost all of it in cash — assuming just three procedure nights a week. (Testimony indicated that he performed abortions from about 8:00 p.m. to 1:00 a.m., three nights a week — for a total of 15 hours.) In light of the testimony we heard that Gosnell performed the really late third-trimester abortions on Sundays, his take was likely much higher. And none of this includes his income from writing prescriptions — according to one law enforcement agent, Gosnell was one of the top three Oxycontin prescribers in the state of Pennsylvania.

Gosnell's criminal enterprise was not limited to illegal late-term abortions; he also conspired to defraud patients, insurance companies, and a nonprofit that provides financial assistance for abortions.

Gosnell committed a variety of frauds. He defrauded his patients by charging them for appointments with Steve Massof and Eileen O'Neill under the pretense that they were real doctors. Kareema

Cross testified that this sometimes caused confusion with patients and hospitals. She said that the clinic would receive calls when patients reported to a hospital that they had been treated or sent to the hospital by "Dr. O'Neill." When no one at the hospital could find a record of a Dr. O'Neill, the patient would call to find out her first name. Cross said that the staff were instructed to say that O'Neill was a student and that Massof was a resident. The patients were told to use Gosnell's name even if they thought they were patients of "Dr. O'Neill" and "Dr." Steve. By defrauding patients, Gosnell, O'Neill, and Massof could charge for doctors' appointments even when no licensed physician was present.

Gosnell also defrauded insurance companies. For example, although Gosnell was not an approved provider for Keystone East Health Insurance subscribers, this did not stop him and O'Neill from treating Keystone East subscribers and charging the insurer for their services. According to Randy Hutchins and others, Gosnell simply asked Dr. Agnes Simmons, a fellow West Philadelphia doctor, who was a Keystone provider, to pretend that she worked at the Women's Medical Society so that the clinic could bill Keystone under her name.

Maddline Joe, the office manager in charge of submitting insurance forms, claimed, unconvincingly, that Dr. Simmons saw some patients at Gosnell's clinic. But no other worker, including the receptionist, Tina Baldwin, ever saw Dr. Simmons working at the clinic. Randy Hutchins testified that he learned that Gosnell would split insurance payments on these claims with Dr. Simmons.

Gosnell defrauded the Delaware Pro-Choice Medical Fund as well. This organization provides financial assistance to Delaware women seeking abortions. Gosnell tapped into the Delaware fund by

Section III: Gosnell's Illegal Practice

falsely claiming that some of his patients lived in Delaware. Ashley Baldwin explained that she would call the Fund for Gosnell:

> Q. Did you have a lot of Delaware patients come to Philadelphia?
> A. No. He used to lie.
> Q. What do you mean 'he used to lie'?
> A. About the Philly addresses. He would change their address to a Delaware address so he could get paid for them.
> * * *
> He would write the price that he want on there. And I would have to call ... and get an okay and a confirmation number, and then the money would be sent to him.
> Q. But these people didn't have anything to do with Delaware?
> A. No.
> Q. They didn't live in Delaware or have anything to do in Delaware?
> A. No.

A national association of abortion providers declined to admit the Women's Medical Society as a member, finding it to be the worst facility its inspector had ever seen.

Immediately following Karnamaya Mongar's death in November 2009, Gosnell sought membership in the National Abortion Federation (NAF), a professional association of 400 abortion providers nationwide that offers referrals and services to member providers. Membership is contingent on meeting NAF's quality assurance standards and is based on an on-site inspection. It is inexplicable that Gosnell believed he could somehow pass such an inspection or meet NAF standards.

A NAF quality assurance evaluator testified before the Grand Jury. She stated that NAF's mission is to ensure safe, legal, and acceptable abortion care, and to promote health and justice for women. To that end, NAF publishes clinical standards, called Clinical Policy Guidelines that members must follow. These guidelines are drawn from a review of evidenced-based medical literature and patient outcomes.

To be certified by NAF, a provider must submit to an on-site inspection and complete a detailed questionnaire designed to determine whether the provider complies with NAF's standards. After the initial approval and certification, members must complete questionnaires annually. NAF re-inspects members every five to seven years, or more often if there is a complication or a serious event with a patient.

Gosnell submitted an application to become a NAF member in November 2009 — apparently, and astonishingly, the day after Karnamaya Mongar died. The NAF evaluator conducted a site review on December 14 and 15, 2009. Despite the odd fact that Gosnell's decision to seek NAF certification coincided with a patient's death at his clinic, he made no mention of this significant event to the evaluator before she visited. In fact, it was not until their final interview, after she had spent two days with Gosnell at the facility, that he informed her of Mrs. Mongar's death.

In preparation for NAF's visit, Latosha Lewis said that Gosnell and his wife frantically cleaned the facility. The doctor bought new lounge chairs to replace the bloody ones that were there, although by February 18, 2010, they were filthy again. He also re-hired former employee Della Mann, a registered nurse who was a friend of Randy Hutchins and a patient of Eileen O'Neill.

Randy Hutchins referred Ms. Mann to Gosnell because the

Section III: Gosnell's Illegal Practice

doctor had told Hutchins that he wanted to hire a registered nurse "for a short amount of time." Mann had worked at the clinic years earlier. But in fact, Gosnell was not offering Mann a real job—he was paying to use her license for a few days. Gosnell hired Mann, at $31 an hour, to work 6:00 to 9:00 p.m., Mondays and Tuesdays only. He told her that he wanted her to look at charts, evaluate lab work, and initial patient charts as if she—a licensed nurse—had been the person who had taken vital signs and recorded information in the charts.

This short-term job lasted four days and coincided with the NAF site review. Mann said she quit because she was uncomfortable with Gosnell's fraud, which included paying her with a check, then taking the check back and giving her cash. Gosnell accomplished what he intended: He ostensibly had a licensed registered nurse on his staff—and her license number in his files—during the NAF review.

Despite these efforts, the NAF review did not go well. The first thing the evaluator noted when she arrived at 3801 Lancaster Avenue was the lack of an effective security system. Although the door was locked, when she rang the bell, no one answered. Even though she could not gain entry by ringing, she was able to walk right in when a man exited the clinic. Once inside, she found that the facility was packed with so much "stuff, kind of crowded and piled all over the place," that she couldn't find a space to put her small overnight bag. She found the facility's layout confusing, and was concerned that patients could not find their way around it or out of it. She was also concerned that there were plants everywhere, including in the procedure room and rooms designated as "labs." Most alarming was the bed where Gosnell told her out-of-state patients were allowed to spend the night. These patients were unattended and it was difficult to locate the bathroom facilities and the exits. Such a practice does not meet NAF protocols.

The NAF evaluator watched a few first-trimester procedures. She noticed that no one was monitoring or taking vital signs of patients who were sedated during procedures. She asked Gosnell about the pulse oximeter that should have been used for monitoring, but he told her it was broken. Apparently, Karnamaya Mongar's death a month earlier had not caused Gosnell to obtain equipment that worked.

The evaluator did not observe Gosnell's practice of allowing unlicensed workers to sedate patients when he was not at the facility, as she was there only when Gosnell was there. Such a practice would not comply with NAF standards.

The evaluator did note, however, that while she was talking to Gosnell in his office, a patient appeared to have been sedated by one of the staff. Such an action does not comport with NAF standards either. The evaluator cautioned Gosnell that he should make sure he was complying with state requirements because many states —including Pennsylvania—do not allow unlicensed workers to administer IV medications.

The level of medication administered was also troubling to the evaluator. She testified that Gosnell's own description of the effects of his routine second-trimester dose—that the patient would feel no pain at all—was a description of deep sedation. She added: "that ... would really not be a safe situation ... for him to be handling himself." She explained that when deep sedation or general anesthesia is administered, NAF standards not only require that the doctor performing the procedure be present when the anesthesia is administered, they also require that another doctor or

Section III: Gosnell's Illegal Practice

an anesthesiologist administer the sedation and monitor the patient. Instead, Gosnell had Lynda Williams, Sherry West, and his other unlicensed workers routinely administer anesthesia without proper supervision or appropriate monitoring of patients.

The evaluator explained to the Grand Jury, as did several medical experts, that because everyone reacts differently to anesthesia, a doctor has to be prepared for a patient to slip into a level of sedation beyond that intended. In cases in which Gosnell's objective was deep sedation, therefore, he should have been prepared for the patient to react as if under general anesthesia. Significantly, it is not uncommon for patients under general anesthesia to lose the ability to breathe on their own.

Gosnell's clinic—without the drugs, staff, or equipment necessary to monitor, resuscitate, or assist his patients in breathing—was not even close to meeting NAF standards or any other standard of care. The evaluator noted that Pennsylvania requires that anesthesia be administered only by licensed personnel, a regulation that Gosnell failed to follow even during the NAF review.

Aside from these life-threatening practices, the evaluator noted numerous deficiencies in the clinic's recordkeeping, including no notation of RH blood-typing and no record of sedation medications administered or the level of sedation. The clinic's consent procedures also failed to meet NAF standards. Even with the evaluator watching, patients were not being informed of the risks of the medications, the sedation, or the procedure itself.

The evaluator testified that during the "counseling" she witnessed, a patient was told that Pennsylvania requires a 24-hour waiting period between when a patient is counseled and when the abortion can be performed. After stating the requirement, however, the counselor, according to the evaluator, said: "Okay, well. When do you want to come back for the abortion? Do you want to come back at 8 p.m.?" When the patient's mother said, "but I thought we had to wait 24 hours," the staff person responded, "if you want to come back at 8 p.m., you can come back at 8 p.m."

Patient confidentiality is another important standard for NAF, and another that Gosnell flagrantly violated. The evaluator was troubled to find:

> Throughout the office, there were patient charts everywhere. On desks, on this — the area in that upstairs sleeping area by the sleeping room. There were piles and piles and piles of medical records. That was — if that were in an area that was closed off and nobody had access to it, charts being stored there weren't a big deal, but if there were patients in the sleeping room, who had to leave there to go to the restroom, they had full access to all of these people's medical information if they wanted to look through it, it was very, very concerning to me.

When asked if she had ever seen anything like the conditions and practices she observed at Gosnell's clinic in any of the roughly one hundred clinics she has visited in the United States, Canada, and Mexico, the evaluator answered: "No."

Based on her observations, the evaluator determined that there were far too many deficiencies at the clinic and in how it operated to even consider admitting Gosnell to NAF membership. On January 4, 2010, she wrote to Gosnell informing him of NAF's decision and outlining the areas in which his clinic was not in compliance. The evaluator told the Grand Jury that this was the first time in her experience that NAF had outright rejected a provider for membership.

Section III: Gosnell's Illegal Practice

Usually, if a clinic is able to fix deficiencies and come into compliance with the standards, NAF will admit them. Gosnell's clinic, however, was deemed beyond redemption.

We understand that NAF's goal is to assist clinics to comply with its standards, not to sanction them for deficiencies. Nevertheless, we have to question why an evaluator from NAF, whose stated mission is to ensure safe, legal, and acceptable abortion care, and to promote health and justice for women, did not report Gosnell to authorities.

To the jurors, the most appalling thing revealed by the NAF review is not that Gosnell tried to bluff his way through the application process with a borrowed nurse and some new lounge chairs. It is that he made no effort to address the grave deficiencies in his practice that had caused Karnamaya Mongar's death.

Gosnell's contemptuous disregard for the health, safety, and dignity of his patients continued for 40 years.

Gosnell's disregard for his patients' safety was nothing new. The Pennsylvania Department of Health has records as far back as the 1980s documenting Gosnell's dangerous practices. For decades, Gosnell did not staff his facility with licensed or qualified employees. He never properly monitored women under sedation. He botched surgeries and then failed to summon emergency help when it was needed. His entire practice showed nothing but a callous disdain for the lives of his patients. As far back as 1972, he was notorious for his mistreatment of the women who came to him for treatment.

Randy Hutchins testified that Gosnell told him about what has been called the "Mother's Day Massacre." According to a February 25, 2010, article in The Philadelphia Inquirer, Gosnell offered to perform abortions on 15 poor women who were bused to his clinic from Chicago on Mother's Day 1972, in their second trimester of pregnancy. Unbeknownst to the women, Gosnell planned to use an experimental device called a "super coil" developed by a California man named Harvey Karman, who had run an underground abortion service in the 1950s. Hutchins related what Gosnell explained to him:

> At the time that he agreed to do this, there was a device that he and a psychologist were working on that was supposed to be plastic—basically plastic razors that were formed into a ball. All right. They were coated into a gel, so that they would remain closed. These would be inserted into the woman's uterus. And after several hours of body temperature, it would then—the gel would melt and these things would spring open, supposedly cutting up the fetus, and the fetus would be expelled.

The problem was that they never tested it. They didn't test it on any animals. They never did any—any—any other human trials. This was not something that was sanctioned by the FDA. This was just something that he decided—he and this guy decided they were going to use on these women.

Hutchins actually was mistaken in his belief that no other human trials been conducted. According to the Philadelphia Inquirer article, Karman had tested his device on hundreds of Bangladeshi women who had been raped by Pakistani soldiers. Those women suffered a high rate of complications. Nonetheless, Karman brought his "super coil" to Philadelphia, where he found an ally in Gosnell.

Gosnell, according to Hutchins, inserted the super coils into the women's uteruses. The event was filmed and later shown on a New York City educational television program. The Inquirer reported the results of this human experimentation as follows:

Section III: Gosnell's Illegal Practice

The federal Centers for Disease Control and Prevention and the Philadelphia Department of Public Health subsequently did an investigation that detailed serious complications suffered by nine of the 15 women, including one who needed a hysterectomy.

The complications included a punctured uterus, hemorrhage, infections, and retained fetal remains.

The CDC researchers recommended strict controls on any future testing of the device ... Karman spent two years in court battles in Philadelphia. He was convicted of practicing medicine without a license, but a Common Pleas Court judge overturned the conviction in 1974, saying then-District Attorney Arlen Specter had failed to show which women Karman had treated.

Gosnell—who testified that Karman had done an "innocuous" part of the procedures but not fetal extractions—was not charged with anything.

According to Hutchins, Gosnell told him that he left Pennsylvania for an extended period after the super coil incident. First he went to the Bahamas, and then to New York. Hutchins explained Gosnell's reasoning:

> If the State Board of Medicine hadn't brought any charges against you, all right, and you were away long enough, you could come back and your license was still considered to be in good standing.

Gosnell was apparently correct. The Pennsylvania Board of Medicine ignored his role in this grotesquely unsuccessful experiment, which seriously and permanently maimed several women. The Board overlooked Gosnell's unprofessional conduct not only in the 1970s but for the next three decades, as he continued to employ unlicensed workers to practice medicine at his clinic, and as his patients continued to suffer serious injuries or worse during abortion procedures.

SECTION IV:
THE INTENTIONAL KILLING OF VIABLE BABIES

Gosnell left dozens of damaged women in his wake. His reckless treatment left them infected, sterilized, permanently maimed, close to death, and, in at least two cases, dead. Their injuries and deaths resulted directly from Gosnell's utter disregard for their health and safety. However, if their fate was entirely foreseeable, it was not necessarily the product of specific intent to kill. The same cannot be said of untold numbers of babies—not fetuses in the womb, but live babies, born outside their mothers—whose brief lives ended in Gosnell's filthy facility. The doctor, or his employees acting at his direction, deliberately killed them as part of the normal course of business.

> **Gosnell and his staff severed the spinal cords of viable, moving, breathing babies who were born alive.**

Surgical abortions in Pennsylvania, performed up to 24 weeks of gestational age, are legal. Killing living babies outside the womb is not. The neonatologist who testified before the Grand Jury defined "born alive." According to this expert witness, the federal Born-Alive Infants Protection Act defines a human as "somebody who's been completely expelled from the mother and has either a heartbeat, pulsating cord, or is moving." Pennsylvania's Abortion Control Act defines "born alive" similarly, but adds breathing and brain wave activity as indicators of life. 18 Pa.C.S. §3203.

Gosnell's staff testified about scores of gruesome killings of such born-alive infants carried out mainly by Gosnell, but also by employees Steve Massof, Lynda Williams, and Adrienne Moton. These killings became so routine that no one could put an exact number on them. They were considered "standard procedure." Yet some of the slaughtered were so fully formed, so much like babies that should be dressed and taken home, that even clinic employees who were accustomed to the practice were shocked.

Baby Boy A

One such baby was a boy born in July 2008 to 17-year-old we will call "Sue." Sue first met Gosnell at the Atlantic Women's Medical Services, an abortion clinic in Wilmington, Delaware, where Gosnell worked one day a week. The girl was accompanied by her great aunt, who had agreed to pay for the procedure, and who testified before the Grand Jury.

After an ultrasound was performed on Sue, Gosnell told the aunt that the girl's pregnancy was further along than she had originally told him, and that, therefore, the procedure would cost more than the $1,500 that had been agreed upon; it would now cost $2,500. (Gosnell normally charged $1,625 for 23-24 week abortions.) The aunt paid Gosnell in cash at the Delaware clinic. He inserted laminaria, gave Sue pills to begin labor, and instructed her to be at the Women's Medical Center in Philadelphia at 9:00 the next morning.

Sue arrived with her aunt at 9:00 a.m. and did not leave the clinic until almost 11:00 that night. An ultrasound conducted by Kareema Cross recorded a gestational age of 29.4 weeks. Cross testified that the girl appeared to be seven or eight months pregnant. Cross said that, during 13-plus hours, the girl was given a large amount of Cytotec to induce labor and delivery. Sue complained of pain and was heavily

Section IV: The Intentional Killing of Viable Babies

sedated. According to Cross, the girl was left to labor for hours and hours. Eventually, she gave birth to a large baby boy. Cross estimated that the baby was 18 to 19 inches long. She said he was nearly the size of her own six pound, six ounce, newborn daughter.

After the baby was expelled, Cross noticed that he was breathing, though not for long. After about 10 to 20 seconds, while the mother was asleep, "the doctor just slit the neck," said Cross. Gosnell put the boy's body in a shoebox. Cross described the baby as so big that his feet and arms hung out over the sides of the container. Cross said that she saw the baby move after his neck was cut, and after the doctor placed it in the shoebox. Gosnell told her, "it's the baby's reflexes. It's not really moving."

The neonatologist testified that what Gosnell told his people was absolutely false. If a baby moves, it is alive. Equally troubling, it feels a "tremendous amount of pain" when its spinal cord is severed. So, the fact that Baby Boy A. continued to move after his spinal cord was cut with scissors means that he did not die instantly. Maybe the cord was not completely severed. In any case, his few moments of life were spent in excruciating pain.

Cross was not the only one startled by the size and maturity of Baby Boy A. Adrienne Moton and Ashley Baldwin, along with Cross, took photographs because they knew this was a baby that could and should have lived. Cross explained:

> Q. Why did you all take a photograph of this baby?
> A. Because it was big and it was wrong and we knew it. We knew something was wrong.
> ***
> I'm not sure who took the picture first, but when we seen this baby, it was—it was a shock to us because I never seen a

baby that big that he had done. So it was—I knew something was wrong because everything, like you can see everything, the hair, eyes, everything. And I never seen for any other procedure that he did, I never seen any like that.

The neonatologist viewed a photograph of Baby Boy A. Based on the baby's size, hairline, muscle mass, subcutaneous tissue, well-developed scrotum, and other characteristics, the doctor opined that the boy was at least 32 weeks, if not more, in gestational age.

Gosnell simply noted the baby boy's size by joking, as he often did after delivering a large baby. According to Cross, the doctor said: "This baby is big enough to walk around with me or walk me to the bus stop."

The doctor released Sue to go home 13 or 14 hours after she arrived. Her aunt described her condition: "She was moaning. She was standing up. She was like holding her stomach, doubled over." She remained in pain for days and could barely eat. When she developed a fever, her aunt called Gosnell. He instructed the aunt to take her temperature and asked if she was taking pain medicine he had given her—which she was. But he did not have her come in to be checked out. And he did not suggest that she go to a hospital. When Sue started throwing up a few days later, her grandmother contacted a different doctor, who told her to get to a hospital right away.

Sue was admitted to Crozier-Chester Hospital. Doctors there found that she had a severe infection and blood clots that had travelled to her lungs. According to Kareema Cross, who spoke to the aunt, Sue almost died. The teen stayed at the hospital for a week and a half. She became extremely thin and took months to recover, according to her aunt.

Section IV: The Intentional Killing of Viable Babies

Other babies killed by Gosnell and his staff

"Baby Boy A" was among the more memorable large babies that Gosnell killed, perhaps because of the photographs, or because his teenage mother almost died too. He was not, however, the only one. Ashley Baldwin remembered Gosnell severing the neck of a baby that cried after being born. The baby had "precipitated" when the doctor was not in the clinic. Lynda Williams placed the baby in a basin on the counter where the instruments were washed and called the doctor to come.

Ashley heard the infant cry. She saw the baby move while it was on the counter. She estimated the infant was at least 12 inches long. When Gosnell arrived at the clinic, she recalled, "he snipped the neck, and said there is nothing to worry about, and he suctioned it."

If Gosnell was absent, his employees would kill viable babies. Ashley Baldwin saw Steve Massof slit the necks of babies that moved or breathed "five or ten" times. Massof, repeating what he had been taught by Gosnell, told her that that it was standard procedure to cut the spine in all cases. Ashley testified:

> Q. These larger babies, when Dr. Steve was there, did he ever— was he ever there when any of the larger babies precipitated?
> A. Yes
> Q. Babies that would move?
> A. Yes.
> Q. So, Dr. Steve—what would Dr. Steve do with babies that moved?
> A. The same thing.
> Q. The same thing. And how many time did you see Dr. Steve?
> A. A lot. He told me that—don't worry about it. They are not living. It is just a reaction.

BLACKOUT: The Official GOSNELL Grand Jury Report

Kareema Cross testified that, between 2005 and 2008, she saw Steve Massof sever the spinal cords of at least ten babies who were breathing and about five that were moving.

When Massof left the clinic in 2008, Lynda Williams took over the job of cutting baby's necks when Gosnell was not there. Cross saw Williams slit the neck of a baby ("Baby C") who had been moving and breathing for approximately twenty minutes. Gosnell had delivered the baby and put it on a counter while he suctioned the placenta from the mother. Williams called Cross over to look at the baby because it was breathing and moving its arms when Williams pulled on them. After playing with the baby, Williams slit its neck.

When asked why Williams had killed the baby, Cross answered:

> Because the baby, I guess, because the baby was moving and breathing. And she see Dr. Gosnell do it so many times, I guess she felt, you know, she can do it. It's okay.

Adrienne Moton also killed at least one baby by cutting its spinal cord. Cross testified that a woman had delivered a large baby into the toilet before Gosnell arrived at work for the night. Cross said that the baby was moving and looked like it was swimming. Moton reached into the toilet, got the baby out and cut its neck. Cross said the baby was between 10 and 15 inches long and had a head the size of a "big pancake." Gosnell later measured one of the baby's feet and said that it was 24.5 weeks.

Section IV: The Intentional Killing of Viable Babies

Gosnell's illegal and unorthodox practices resulted in the birth and then killing of many viable, live babies.

Killing really had to be part of Gosnell's plan. His method for performing late-term abortions was to induce labor and delivery of intact fetuses, and he specialized in patients who were well beyond 24 weeks. Thus, the birth of live, viable babies was a natural and predictable consequence. The subsequent slitting of spinal cords, without any consideration for the babies' viability, was an integral part of what Gosnell's employees called his "standard procedure."

Steve Massof described this "standard procedure." It required the clinic's unequipped staff to manage a clinic full of sedated patients who were thrown into full labor, and then to "deal" with whatever precipitated, including live babies—all while the doctor was at home, or jogging, or working at a clinic in Wilmington. In particular, Massof described what Gosnell expected him to do when babies precipitated in the afternoon and evening before the doctor arrived:

> A: As I mentioned earlier, Dr. Gosnell would dilate the cervix to make room for passage of the products. And with the Cytotec, softening the cervix, the outlet of the uterus, well, mother nature would take its course. Every woman is different.
> Q: What would happen?
> A: Well, the fetus would precipitate.
> Q: What do you mean?
> A: Oh, come right out, right out. Just you know, I would be called, somebody would call me and at that point what I would have to do is, I'd have to go and tend to that patient.
> Q: How would you do that? What would you do?
> A: As—well, my first—my first reaction would be is at that point it depended sometimes it happened in the waiting room, sometimes it happened in the bathroom because, you know, a woman would be pushing in the bathroom. Sometimes, you know, it happened everywhere in the clinic.

So what I would do is, I'd make sure that when—if the fetus precipitated, the cord was cut. Also, a standard procedure, the cervical spine was cut, as well as make sure that there wasn't bleeding or, in other words, the placenta came down and that's the way—we insured less blood would be lost.

Q: How often did this happen?

A: More times than I really care to remember. I would have to say every week it would happen to at least 50 percent of the patients.

Q: Fifty percent of the time?

A: Yeah, easy, easy. That—you know, and that is how, you know, and that's what would happen.

Q: You said it was standard procedure to cut the—first to cut the umbilical cord?

A: Yes.

Q: That's from the mother or how is that attached?

A: Well that is from the mother to the fetus.

Q: And where would it be? Would it still be—the placenta would still be in the mother's uterus?

A: Yes.

Q: Okay.

A: Yes. And so I would cut the attachment and you know, then the cervical portion of the spine at that point. Those were the larger patients.

Q: So you said that was standard procedure. What do you mean when you say standard procedure?

A: Well, that's—that was his standard procedure.

Q: When you say his, do you mean Gosnell?

A: Yes.

Q: Did he show you how to do that?

A: Yes, he did.

Q: When did he show you how to do that?

A: He showed me how to do that maybe 2004, sometime within a year I started working there, that is what he did during his [second-trimester] procedures.

Section IV: The Intentional Killing of Viable Babies

Tina Baldwin corroborated that this was Gosnell's standard procedure. She explained that after a fetus was expelled, Gosnell "used to go ahead and do the suction in the back of the neck." She saw this "hundreds" of times. Gosnell told her that this was "part of the demise."

Gosnell's technique of aborting pregnancies by inducing labor and delivery, while unnecessarily painful for the women, did not itself constitute a crime. What made his procedure criminal was that he routinely performed these abortions past the 24-week limit prescribed by law. Not only was this a crime in itself, it also meant that he was regularly delivering babies who had a reasonable chance of survival.

Except Gosnell would not give them that chance. Pennsylvania law requires physicians to provide customary care for living babies outside the womb. Gosnell chose instead to slit their necks and store their bodies in various household containers, as if they were trash.

Although the Grand Jury learned that there is some difference of opinion as to the earliest point of viability, the experts who appeared before the Grand Jury all agreed that, by 24 weeks, organs are sufficiently developed that prognosis for survival is good. These babies can sometimes breathe on their own, though many require assistance. When a woman delivers at 24 weeks or later in a responsible medical setting, such assistance is provided, and resuscitation of the baby is routine. Indeed, a doctor's failure to provide assistance constitutes infanticide under Pennsylvania law.

Gosnell's intent to never resuscitate was obvious from his failure to employ even minimally qualified personnel or to have the equipment necessary to save the lives of newborn infants. The policy he instituted and carried out was not to try to revive live, viable babies. It was to kill them.

Gosnell severed spinal cords and suctioned and crushed skulls after the babies were fully delivered.

At one point in his Grand Jury testimony, Steve Massof tried to suggest that the clinic's practice of cutting babies' spinal cords was somehow part of a late-term procedure called intact dilation and extraction (IDX), commonly referred to as "partial-birth abortion" and banned under federal law since 2007. In an intact dilation and extraction, which was used most often to abort pregnancies beyond 17 weeks, the fetus was removed from the uterus as a whole. In order for the head to pass through the cervix without damage to the mother, the doctor would collapse the fetal skull by making an incision at the base of the neck and suctioning the contents. This procedure was done while the baby was still inside the mother.

This was not the procedure Gosnell used. Under further questioning, Massof acknowledged that Gosnell and he almost always cut the spinal cords, and sometimes suctioned skulls as well, after the babies were fully expelled by their mothers, when there was clearly no need or medical reason to collapse the skull.

Tina Baldwin's testimony also made it clear that Gosnell was not cutting spinal cords, crushing babies' skulls, or suctioning in order to allow the head to pass through the cervix. Even while claiming that Gosnell sometimes suctioned a fetus's skull in order to get it through the birth canal, her description of his technique belied her claim: She said that he would "crack" the neck after

Section IV: The Intentional Killing of Viable Babies

the head was out — when only the baby's torso was still inside the mother — and then suction the brain matter out.

Tina Baldwin tried to explain:

> Q: He was delivering, for lack of a better word —
> A: Yes.
> Q: — a fetus?
> A: Yeah.
> Q: And then he was taking care of the problem after the fact?
> A: Yes.
> Q: Did you see him do this in instances where the fetus had been completely expelled from the mother's body before he crushed the head?
> A: And then he crushed it.
> Q: and then he crushed it. I mean I guess you just told the members of the jury about episodes where he would leave the shoulders or —
> A: Uh-huh.
> Q: — the shoulders would be out?
> A: The shoulders would be out, yeah
> Q: And he would go work on the neck, you said he would crush the neck and suction the head?
> A: Uh-huh.
> Q: Did you ever see instances where the fetus was completely expelled from its mother's body?
> A: Oh, yeah, yeah. That's what we call precipitation.
> Q: What do you mean by that? Tell the members of the jury, what would happen.
> A: That's when a patient would precipitate. Usually by the Cytotec that was given to the patient and it just made the uterus so flimsy to where the baby just falls and we had a lot of patients that was second-trimester, it would just fall wherever she was at. And it was picked up and it was put in a dish and it just traveled with the mother. And then the person put the mother up on the table, the baby was put inside the — in the dish on the table and the doctor was called to come in.
> Q: And then what would the doctor do when he came in?
> A: Let me think back then. Usually he would check and see, check on the fetus and then I think that's when he used to go ahead and do the suction in the back of the neck.

> Q: Even though the fetuses had already been removed from their mother?
> A: Yeah, they had already been removed. He would just go ahead and finish it.
> Q: Would he explain to you why he did that?
> A: No.
> Q: Or why that was his practice?
> A: No.
> Q: Did you ever question it?
> A: No.
> Q: Okay, how many times would you say you've seen this?
> A: Hundreds. I've seen hundreds …

Kareema Cross testified that when she first started working at the clinic, in 2005, Gosnell slit the neck of every baby. But he subsequently told the workers that the law changed so that he could not do that anymore. (The law, in fact, never allowed him to cut necks of viable babies after they were fully expelled.) Cross said that Gosnell then tried a few times to use a new procedure: He tried to inject a drug called digoxin into the fetus's heart while it was in the womb. This was supposed to cause fetal demise in utero. But because Gosnell was not skillful enough to successfully administer digoxin, late-term babies continued to be born alive, and he continued to kill them by slitting their necks.

Cross testified:

> So he tried to do the needle in the stomach and that's what was supposed to have killed the baby before the baby came out, but if it didn't, he'll say, oh, well, the law says that I can do it. I can still slit the baby's neck because it didn't work. The needle didn't work.

Section IV: The Intentional Killing of Viable Babies

And according to his staff, the needle never worked. So Gosnell stopped trying and reverted to his old system of killing babies after they were born.

Gosnell's staff testified that he constantly tried to explain to them why what he was doing was legal—even though it clearly was not legal. Severing the spinal cord of viable, live babies after they have been delivered is simply murder. To then crush and suction their skulls defies medical explanation. It can only be understood as an attempt to conceal the true and only purpose of the neat scissor incision at the back of the neck: to kill the babies.

The clinic's employees used the term "snip" to describe the severing of the spinal cord, but this is misleading. Our neonatal expert testified that, because of the bony vertebrae surrounding the spinal cord, it would actually take quite a bit of pressure to cut all the way through the spinal cord and the bone—even at 23 or 24 weeks gestation. At 29 weeks, on babies such as Baby Boy A, the expert said, "it would be really hard." The baby, we were told, would feel "tremendous pain."

When we asked our medical experts if there could be any legitimate, medical purpose behind Gosnell's practice, one said: "it would be the same as putting a pillow over the baby's face, that the intention would be to kill the baby." Another likened the practice of severing babies' spinal cords to pithing frogs in biology class.

BLACKOUT: The Official GOSNELL Grand Jury Report

> **Gosnell and his staff regularly cut necks of viable babies after observing signs of life.**

Although no one could place an exact number on the instances, Gosnell's staff testified that killing large, late-term babies who had been observed breathing and moving was a regular occurrence. Massof said that Gosnell cut the spinal cord "100 percent of the time" in second-trimester (and, presumably, third-trimester) procedures, and that he did so after the baby was delivered.

Massof testified that he saw signs of life in some of these babies. He recalled seeing a heartbeat in one baby and observed a "respiratory excursion" (meaning a breath) in another. On other occasions, he observed "pulsation." Gosnell dismissed these observations as "spontaneous movement." "That was his answer for if we ever saw anything that was out of the ordinary, it was always a spontaneous movement."

Latosha Lewis testified that she saw babies precipitate at 23 to 28 weeks. In those cases, Massof or Gosnell:

> ...would cut the back of the neck and insert a curette, which is a plastic tubing ... that is used to do a suction. You would insert it in the back of the neck of the baby, so that the brain would come out.

Sometimes, according to Lewis, "he [Gosnell] would just snip the neck." Lewis saw babies move before Gosnell did this:

> Q. How many times did you see precipitated babies that had been fully expelled from its mother moving before he snipped the neck?
> A. A lot.

* * *

Section IV: The Intentional Killing of Viable Babies

> Q. Can you give us a percentage of the time?
> A. Probably 25 percent of the time.

No steps were ever taken to attend to these babies; "we never even checked to see if [there] was a heartbeat." Lewis, who had herself given birth twice, recognized that the larger precipitated babies were viable:

> ... The bigger cases, you would see more movement or the baby would look a little bit more realer to you.
> Q. What do you mean?
> A. Like the skin would be a lot different. The color of the skin would be a lot different.

The Grand Jurors learned from the neonatology expert that the skin of viable babies does, in fact, appear different from the typically translucent skin of a pre-24-week fetus.

Kareema Cross said she saw Gosnell slit the neck of babies born alive "more than 15 times" — "over 10 times," when she had seen a baby breathing, and about "five times" when she had seen a baby move. She could tell these babies were breathing because "I just seen a baby's chest go up and down and it would go real fast, real fast."

Ashley Baldwin also saw Gosnell slice the neck of moving and breathing babies. When asked how many times Ashley had observed babies being delivered that were moving or breathing or crying and the doctor cut the neck, she answered: "Most of the second tris that were over 20 weeks." She said this happened probably dozens of times, maybe more. She described at least 10 babies as big enough to buy clothes for, to dress, and to take care of. She told the Grand Jury what happened to them:

> Q. And what happened to those ten babies that came out from their mother, that were big enough that you could put clothes on and take home and take care of, that moved around, what did you see happen to them?
> A. He killed them.
> Q. Who killed them?
> A. Doc.
> Q. How did he kill them?
> A. He cut the back of the neck.

Ashley said Gosnell told her this was "normal."

Tina Baldwin told the jurors that Gosnell once joked about a baby that was writhing as he cut its neck: "that's what you call a chicken with its head cut off."

Although Massof was not as cavalier about what he did, he admitted that there were about 100 instances in which he severed the spinal cord after seeing a breath or some sign of life:

> Q. ... of those 100 how many were larger than 24 weeks?
> A. That I couldn't tell you for sure. I would have to think that they would all be because they were all able—after a certain period in weeks, you know, there's—they would have to be capable. I mean premature births are quite common.

When investigators raided the clinic in February 2010, they sent the fetuses they discovered to the Philadelphia medical examiner's office. The medical examiner concluded that two of them—aborted at 26 and 28 weeks—were viable, and another, aborted at 22 weeks, was possibly viable. The 28-week fetus, a male (Baby Boy B) had a surgical incision on the back of the neck, which penetrated the first and second vertebrae. The 22-week fetus, female, had a similar incision.

Section IV: The Intentional Killing of Viable Babies

We believe, given the manner in which Gosnell operated, that he killed the vast majority of babies that he aborted after 24 weeks. We cannot, however, recommend murder charges for all of these cases. In order to constitute murder, the act must involve a baby who was born alive. Because files were falsified or removed from the facility and possibly destroyed, we cannot substantiate all of the individual cases in which charges might otherwise have resulted.

While the evidence before the Grand Jury supports only a limited number of murder charges, it is without challenge that Kermit Gosnell, under the pretext of providing medical care, routinely killed viable babies and irreparably damaged women. At least two of his patients, he also killed.

SECTION V:
THE DEATH OF KARNAMAYA MONGAR

Karnamaya Mongar died because Gosnell's unlicensed employees excessively drugged her.

On November 19, 2009, 41-year-old Karnamaya Mongar suffered a fatal drug overdose during an abortion procedure at the Women's Medical Society in West Philadelphia. Along with her husband, Ash, the mother of three and grandmother of one had arrived in the United States only four months before, after spending nearly 20 years in a refugee camp in Nepal. She and her family had been among the thousands expelled from their homeland of Bhutan following pro-democracy protests. They came to the United States on July 19, 2009, as part of a humanitarian resettlement program. Her husband had just found a job in a chicken factory in Virginia where they lived. Mrs. Mongar spoke no English.

When Mrs. Mongar was more than 18 weeks pregnant, she asked a family friend, Damber Ghalley, to take her to a clinic in Virginia to terminate her pregnancy. But the Virginia clinic, and another in Washington, D.C., would not do the second-trimester procedure. She was referred to the Women's Medical Society because Gosnell had a reputation for performing abortions regardless of gestational age.

Mr. Ghalley drove Mrs. Mongar and her daughter to the Women's Medical Society on November 18, 2009, and waited for them in the car. That afternoon, Latosha Lewis conducted the clinic's version of a "pre-examination." She performed an ultrasound, which showed that Mrs. Mongar was 19 weeks pregnant, and drew blood, purportedly for lab work. No one counseled the patient, as is required by Pennsylvania's Abortion Control Act, or recorded her weight. (The next day it was recorded as 110 pounds.) Gosnell did not even meet her, although he had pre-signed a form entitled "24 Hour Counseling Certificate" that falsely certified he had counseled her—a fraud that was his customary practice.

Mrs. Mongar's initials, perhaps written by someone else, appear on a form entitled "Consent to Office Procedure Administration of Anesthesia and Rendering of Other Medical Services." This form purported to authorize Gosnell or "whomever he may designate as his assistant" to perform a therapeutic abortion. Unspecified anesthesia was to be administered "by or under the direction of one of the staff members." The form included a waiver of "any claim that my consent is not informed consent." This consent form and waiver were supposedly initialed by the non-English-speaking patient. Her daughter, who also spoke almost no English, was asked to sign as a witness.

After the pre-exam and the signing of forms, Randy Hutchins, the part-time physician's assistant who worked without State Board of Medicine approval, inserted laminaria to dilate Mrs. Mongar's cervix and administered Cytotec. Hutchins instructed Mrs. Mongar to return the next day to complete the abortion procedure.

Mrs. Mongar arrived at the clinic on November 19 around 2:30 p.m., accompanied by her daughter and her mother-in-law. (Damber Ghalley, who drove them, again waited in the car.) At the front desk, Tina Baldwin gave the patient her initial medication—a 200 mg. pill of Cytotec (misoprostol) to soften the cervix and to cause contractions; and

Section V: The Death of Karnamaya Mongar

a 45 mg. pill of Restoril (temazapan), a drug that causes drowsiness. Mrs. Mongar was then instructed to wait in the recovery area until the doctor arrived to perform the abortion.

Lynda Williams and Sherry West, by all accounts the least competent and most careless of Gosnell's unlicensed and unqualified crew, were supposed to medicate and attend to Mrs. Mongar in the "recovery room," where she awaited her procedure. Gosnell assigned Williams this duty even though Kareema Cross had warned him, at least a year earlier, that Williams did not know what she was doing and that she routinely overmedicated patients. Randy Hutchins also spoke to Gosnell about Williams anesthetizing patients in Gosnell's absence. Gosnell assured him that "Williams was a trained professional and that it was not a problem."

Mrs. Mongar's daughter, Yashoda Gurung, clearly believed Williams was a trained medical professional—she referred to the unlicensed and unskilled worker as a "doctor" when she testified. Ms. Gurung told the Grand Jury, through an interpreter, that she was permitted to wait with her mother in the recovery room for several hours. Mrs. Gurung testified that, between 3:30 and 8:00 p.m., her mother was given five or six doses of oral medicine—pills that were placed between her mother's lip and cheek, which is consistent with how the clinic administered Cytotec orally.

Mrs. Gurung also saw her mother receive additional medication by injection through an IV line they inserted in Mrs. Mongar's hand. This was consistent with Gosnell's standard practice, which was to keep the second-trimester patients asleep while the Cytotec induced cramping and labor, in the hope that the women would deliver their babies without a surgical procedure. Also consistent with standard practice at the clinic, no equipment was available to ensure proper monitoring of Mrs. Mongar's vital signs.

Mrs. Gurung did not know what drugs were being given throughout the afternoon and evening, but typically the doctor's employees gave repeated injections of the concoction of sedative drugs that Gosnell referred to as a "twilight" dose. Each of these "twilight" doses, repeated a number of times at the discretion of the unlicensed workers, consisted of 75 milligrams of Demerol (meperidine); 12.5 milligrams of promethazine (Phenergan); and 7.5 milligrams of diazepam (Valium).

Lynda Williams admitted to detectives that she had administered IV sedation to Mrs. Mongar in the recovery room when the doctor was not on site. But she claimed that the amount she gave was significantly less than what others said was standard — Williams said she gave only 10 mg. of Demerol and 12.5 mg. of promethazine, a dosage she called a "local." (The chart describing the clinic's anesthesia options, however, describes the "local" dose as 10 mg. of a different drug, nalbuphine, and 12.5 mg. of promethazine. *See* Appendix A.)

A little before 8:00 p.m., West and Williams told Mrs. Gurung that she would have to leave the recovery room. Gosnell was not yet at the clinic, but they told her that he would be arriving at about 8:00 p.m. Mrs. Gurung tried to wake her mother before she left the recovery room, but was unsuccessful. West and Williams told her not to rouse her mother because the medicine was supposed to keep her asleep. Mrs. Gurung was sent to another waiting room, away from her mother. She heard nothing else about her mother's condition until after an ambulance arrived after 11:00 p.m. to take her lifeless mother to the hospital.

Section V: The Death of Karnamaya Mongar

> **Repeated injections of strong narcotics, administered in accordance with Gosnell's standard procedures, killed Mrs. Mongar.**

Sherry West and Lynda Williams provided several contradictory and unreliable versions of what took place in the three hours between when they sent Mrs. Mongar's daughter away from her mother and when the ambulance was called. (Both women chose not to testify before the Grand Jury but made statements to the federal authorities.) What is clear, however, is that they administered a combination of dangerous, sedative drugs, and they did so under Gosnell's standard instructions and with his carte blanche approval—but without the doctor's personal supervision or presence in the facility. Indeed, Gosnell had never met the 4' 11", 110 lb., Asian woman before allowing his unlicensed staff to administer the narcotics that put Mrs. Mongar into a deep sleep.

It is also clear that more than three hours passed from the time Mrs. Gurung was unable to rouse her mother and was told to leave the recovery room until the ambulance arrived at the clinic. Ashley Baldwin testified that just before Mrs. Mongar was taken into the procedure room, she was awake again and groaning in pain. Ashley called Williams, and Williams escorted Mrs. Mongar into the procedure room, put her on the table, and placed her feet in stirrups.

Ashley said she expected that Mrs. Mongar would continue to be medicated until she precipitated. According to her testimony, she could tell that Williams did in fact sedate Mrs. Mongar after placing her onto the procedure table. The patient, who had been groaning in pain and moving around, suddenly became completely still and silent. Yet Mrs. Mongar was left alone. Williams, according to

BLACKOUT: The Official GOSNELL Grand Jury Report

Ashley, sat outside the procedure room, even though no machines were monitoring the heavily sedated patient.

Williams acknowledged that, after she took Mrs. Mongar to the procedure room, she gave the patient more sedating medication — this time the clinic's "custom" dose. The "custom" dose, as described on the clinic's anesthesia chart, consists of 75 mg. of Demerol, 12.5 mg. of promethazine, and 10 mg. of diazepam. (See Appendix A.)

West told the FBI that, before Williams anesthetized Mrs. Mongar in the procedure room, she and Williams telephoned Gosnell, who had yet not arrived at the clinic. According to Williams's statement, Gosnell instructed her to "med her up," meaning to medicate the patient and get her ready for the procedure. Williams said that Gosnell came down (she claimed that he was upstairs when she called him) to do the procedure about 10 to 15 minutes later.

Dr. Andrew Herlich, the Chairman of the Anesthesia Department at the University of Pittsburgh Medical Center, testified that even a single "custom" dose was a "very, very heavy dose" that would constitute deep sedation or even general anesthesia. He explained that the promethazine, although helpful in treating nausea, can have a multiplier effect on Demerol. Together with 10 mg. of diazepam, the drugs constituted a "very potent sedative."

Dr. Timothy Rohrig, the Director of the Sedgwick County (Kansas) Regional Forensic Science Center, testified as an expert in forensic toxicology. Dr Rohrig's testimony substantiated that Mrs. Mongar received either multiple (more than two) doses of 75 mg. Demerol or one extremely large dose. Still, Dr. Herlich was incredulous when asked, hypothetically, about the effects of two "custom" doses (each containing 75 mg. Demerol, along with smaller

Section V: The Death of Karnamaya Mongar

doses of promethazine and diazepam). The anesthesiologist could not conceive why a doctor would ever give two doses. Dr. Herlich opined that if average-sized adults, with no particular sensitivities to the drugs, were given two "custom" doses within four hours, "most would stop breathing." Mrs. Mongar was 4'11" and 110 pounds — significantly smaller than average. And she did in fact stop breathing.

Assistant Medical Examiner Dr. Gary Collins determined that Mrs. Mongar died as a result of an overdose of Demerol. He also confirmed Dr. Herlich's testimony that the combination of diazepam and Demerol "work[ed] together to make her respiration or respiratory depression even worse."

The medical examiner's toxicology report showed that, approximately 18 hours after the paramedics were summoned (after which no further Demerol was given), Mrs. Mongar still had a Demerol concentration of over 700 mg/L (micrograms per liter) in her blood. When the toxicology expert attempted to draw a chart to illustrate the corresponding concentration level at the time the medication was administered, he literally pointed off the chart, saying: "The peak concentration is going to be off the scale way up here."

Dr. Herlich was appalled not only by the dangerous mixtures of drugs administered, but also by the clinic's procedures. He explained that it is absolutely essential for a doctor who is ordering anesthesia to meet with the patient beforehand. Different patients, he noted, react differently to the drugs, depending on factors such as height, weight, age, medical history, pregnancy, and race. (Mrs. Mongar's small stature, her ethnicity, and her pregnancy were all factors indicating that she could be more sensitive to anesthesia than average adults.) He stated that it was "incredible to" him that a doctor would have staff administer sedation when he was not on-site and had not seen and consulted with the patients.

Dr. Herlich also emphasized that anytime sedation is injected intravenously—and especially when it is deep sedation, as was administered to Mrs. Mongar—the patient needs to be monitored. The standards of professional care require, at a minimum, that an anesthesiologist monitor blood pressure, heart rate, heart rhythm, oxygen in the blood, and breathing. No physician should proceed with a second-trimester abortion, Dr. Herlich said, without all of the appropriate monitors—including an electrocardiogram to monitor heart rhythm and a pulse oximeter to monitor the oxygen saturation of a patient's blood. Performing such procedures without monitors, the anesthesiologist testified, "is offensive to me as a physician."

Dr. Herlich explained that drugs injected intravenously, as Lynda Williams did to Mrs. Mongar, can reach the heart in 9 seconds and the brain in 16 to 18 seconds. It is crucial, therefore, not only to monitor constantly, but also to administer the medications slowly, a little at a time, and to watch carefully to see how the patient reacts. It was beyond reckless for Gosnell to entrust this delicate and dangerous medical procedure to Williams or any of his other unlicensed, untrained, and unsupervised employees—particularly with no monitoring equipment and no doctor on-site to step in if there was trouble.

The reckless practices that killed Mrs. Mongar were even more irresponsible and dangerous because of the drugs involved. Dr. Herlich testified that Demerol has been out of favor for 10 to 15 years because it has serious side effects and because there are better, safer drugs to use during procedures. Demerol is made more dangerous

Section V: The Death of Karnamaya Mongar

by mixing it with diazepam, he said, and its potency is multiplied by promethazine. One of the safer drug options the anesthesiologist mentioned is Nalbuphine, a drug that Gosnell sometimes used in his so-called "local" concoctions. But Eileen O'Neill testified that Gosnell would substitute Demerol because it was "very cheap versus the Nalbuphine." Massof also told the Grand Jury that Demerol "was easier to obtain at a better price."

The expert testimony substantiated that it was hazardous to have the untrained employees administering even the promethazine. Promethazine, Dr. Herlich testified, has a "black box warning" attached to it, meaning that it has "a side effect that is so terrible that you better be cautious about using it." The side effect is that if the drug escapes the vein while being administered intravenously, it can cause tissue necrosis, a condition that looks like a burn or a crater.

In light of the testimony of Dr. Herlich and other experts, it is no surprise that the combination of callously reckless and illegal procedures, unlicensed and unsupervised employees, and outrageously excessive sedation at Gosnell's clinic proved lethal to Mrs. Mongar.

Gosnell and his staff made inadequate efforts to resuscitate Mrs. Mongar.

Sherry West told detectives that, some time after Williams had sedated Mrs. Mongar, Williams came out of the procedure room, yelling that "she needed help." Liz Hampton testified that she was in the room next to the procedure room when Williams emerged and said that she was having a problem. Although Hampton could not remember if Gosnell was in the procedure room when Williams came out, West said that when she subsequently entered the procedure room, Gosnell was there performing what she thought was CPR on Mrs. Mongar. Eileen O'Neill eventually came in to assist Gosnell, according to West.

O'Neill testified that Lynda Williams summoned her from her second-floor office. The unlicensed "doctor" told the Grand Jury that she thought Mrs. Mongar was already dead by the time she got to the procedure room. Nevertheless, she took over administering CPR to the lifeless body because, she said, Gosnell was not doing the CPR correctly. Gosnell, meanwhile, left to retrieve the clinic's only "crash cart" from the third floor. A crash cart is usually a set of drawers or shelves that contains the tools and drugs needed to treat a person in or near cardiac arrest.

After returning several minutes later with the medicine case, however, Gosnell did not use any of the drugs in it to try to save Mrs. Mongar's life. O'Neill said that she tried to use the defibrillator "paddles" to revive Mrs. Mongar, but that they did not work. Still no one called 911.

Even though an overdose was immediately suspected as the cause of Mrs. Mongar's cardiac arrest, O'Neill testified that Gosnell instructed her not to administer Narcan, a drug that could have reversed the effects of the Demerol. She said that Gosnell told her it would not work on Demerol—which is not true according to the toxicology expert who appeared before the Grand Jury. O'Neill testified that Gosnell took the time to look through the case of medicines and that he was "thrilled" to find it was up-to-date. This is puzzling, since he seemed to have no intent of actually using the drugs to try to save Mrs. Mongar.

Section V: The Death of Karnamaya Mongar

Gosnell and his staff attempted to cover up the cause of Mrs. Mongar's death before paramedics arrived.

Gosnell's odd behavior—retrieving the clinic's case of emergency medicines from the third floor, appearing thrilled that the case supposedly was up to date, and then making no effort to use the supplies to resuscitate his patient—can only be explained as a cover-up: He simply wanted to have a "crash cart" on hand when the paramedics were finally summoned. Gosnell clearly knew it was a violation of the law—as well as of the standards of the medical profession—to sedate a patient without having resuscitation drugs and equipment ready for use.

In fact, when the ambulance was finally called, the paramedics noted that the patient had no IV access for administering life-saving drugs. Someone had evidently taken out the IV access that had been used that afternoon and evening to administer sedatives. No one told the paramedics that Mrs. Mongar had been given heavy doses of Demerol before her heart stopped. There is no other explanation than that Gosnell was trying to hide from the paramedics the cause of Mrs. Mongar's cardiac arrest. The effect of this deception was to further delay potentially effective efforts to save the patient's life.

It is also odd that Gosnell placed Karnamaya Mongar's feet in the stirrups of the procedure table before the paramedics arrived. Eileen O'Neill and Ashley Baldwin both testified that they remembered clearly that the patient's legs were dangling off the table when they saw her lifeless body before the paramedics were called. Yet, when the paramedics arrived, her feet were in the stirrups, as if she had just undergone the abortion procedure.

BLACKOUT: The Official GOSNELL Grand Jury Report

Ashley Baldwin also testified that, after she called 911, she went back into the procedure room where Gosnell was with Mrs. Mongar. O'Neill was back upstairs by then, and Ashley never even knew she had been in the room for nearly 10 minutes performing CPR and discussing the crash cart with Gosnell. It was only then, a good 10 minutes after O'Neill thought Mrs. Mongar was dead, that Gosnell asked Ashley to plug in the pulse oximeter—the machine that, had it worked, should have been used to monitor Mrs. Mongar's blood oxygen level during the procedure.

This action by Gosnell was, again, entirely for appearances—an effort to prevent the paramedics from noticing that the monitor was unplugged. Ashley said that Gosnell knew the machine was broken and had been for months. He had said he would get it fixed, but he never did. She said it shocked her when she tried to plug it in the night Mrs. Mongar died.

Emergency personnel, who were called far too late, found Mrs. Mongar without a pulse when they arrived.

It was after 11 p.m.—long after O'Neill, at least, had decided Mrs. Mongar was dead—that Lynda Williams finally asked Ashley Baldwin to call 911. Emergency personnel responded to the "code blue," indicating cardiac arrest, within two minutes of receiving the call, arriving at the clinic at 11:13. They found Mrs. Mongar in the procedure room, lifeless. She had no pulse and was not breathing. Paramedics reported that Gosnell was just standing there, not doing anything.

The paramedics immediately intubated Mrs. Mongar to give her oxygen, and started an intravenous line to administer emergency

Section V: The Death of Karnamaya Mongar

medications to stimulate her heart. They hooked up the patient to a heart monitor, confirmed that her heart was not beating, and began CPR. They were surprised that, in a medical clinic, basic steps had not already been taken before their arrival. After twice administering medication—epinephrine and atropine—to stimulate Mrs. Mongar's heart, the paramedics also used a defibrillator that they had brought to the scene, and were able to restore weak heart activity.

Mrs. Mongar's slim chances of survival were seriously hampered because it was exceedingly difficult for responders to get her to the waiting ambulance. The emergency exit was locked. Gosnell sent Ashley to the front desk to look for the key, but she could not find it. Ashley told us that a firefighter needed to cut the lock, but "It took him awhile ... because the locks is old." She testified that it took "twenty minutes, probably trying to get the locks unlocked." Mrs. Gurung and her mother-in-law ran outside, crying. Mr. Ghalley and Mrs. Gurung, frightened, watched the firefighters struggling to get the door open, while Karnamaya Mongar lay motionless. After cutting the locks, responders had to waste precious more minutes trying to maneuver through the narrow cramped hallways that could not accommodate a stretcher.

Once the EMTs finally succeeded in getting Mrs. Mongar into the ambulance, they continued to administer medication and use the defibrillator. Sherry West went to the hospital with Mr. Ghalley and the family, in Ghalley's car. According to the family, West gave directions, but there was no real conversation. West told them that Mrs. Mongar was unconscious, but not to worry.

When the ambulance arrived at the Hospital of the University of Pennsylvania shortly after midnight, Mrs. Mongar was in extremely critical condition. She had no heartbeat, no blood pressure, and was not breathing. After 45 minutes to an hour of aggressive resuscitation efforts, doctors were able to restore a weak heartbeat.

Mrs. Mongar was sent to the Intensive Care Unit in extremely critical and unstable condition. She never regained consciousness and had no neurological function. One doctor explained to us that, while many of the body's organs can be resuscitated 15 or 30 minutes after the heart stops pumping, the brain will shut down after about 10 minutes (the amount of time that Gosnell wasted retrieving the crash cart that he did not use and talking with O'Neill before calling 911). The doctor testified that, even though medical personnel were able to restore a weak heartbeat at the hospital, Mrs. Mongar was, by most people's definition, "dead" at the abortion clinic.

Mrs. Mongar remained on life support until family members could make the trip from Virginia to say good-bye. As a result of the cardiac arrest, she had stopped breathing and suffered acute anoxic encephalopathy—brain damage due to a lack of oxygen. She was pronounced dead at 6:15 p.m. on November 20, 2009. The medical examiner concluded that the acute anoxic encephalopathy resulted from the cardiac arrest, which itself had been caused "because somebody gave her a Demerol overdose."

While the family was waiting at the hospital, Gosnell came to the hospital to pick up West. Mr. Ghalley, waiting outside, saw him and asked Gosnell to explain what had happened. Gosnell repeatedly told Ghalley that he hadn't done any thing wrong, that he hadn't made a mistake. Gosnell, according to Ghalley, said the victim's heart stopped beating, but "don't blame me."

Section V: The Death of Karnamaya Mongar

Gosnell and his staff tried to cover up what drugs were administered, who administered them, when, and how.

The evidence indicates that Sherry West made false entries on Mrs. Mongar's file before handing it over to the Hospital of the University of Pennsylvania. Ashley Baldwin testified that the paramedics asked for Mrs. Mongar's file so they could take it with them to the hospital. Instead of giving it to them, Ashley said, West grabbed the chart and took it herself to the hospital. By the time the file was turned in to the hospital doctors, it had notations about medications that Ashley said had not previously been there (See Appendix D). The notations were totally inconsistent with all of the other evidence — from Lynda Williams, from Mrs. Gurung, and even from Gosnell — and grossly understated the amount of medication that was given.

Williams, West, and Gosnell all contradicted themselves and each other about how much medication Mrs. Mongar received, who gave it to her, when, and even how. The file notations indicated that Mrs. Mongar received 10 mg. Demerol, 0.6 cc (cubic centimeters) promethazine, and 1 cc. diazepam at 8:14 p.m., followed by another dose of 10 mg. Demerol, 0.6 cc promethazine, and 2 cc diazepam at 10:45 p.m. An entry made by West in the clinic logbook, however, indicated that Mrs. Mongar was given a much larger dose: 75 mg. Demerol, 12.5 mg. promethazine, and 10 mg. diazepam.

Lynda Williams was interviewed by law enforcement on the night of the February 2010 raid. At first, she told her interviewers that she did not put IVs in patients, that Gosnell administered the medication, and that she thought he gave a "heavy" dose (50 mg. Demerol, 12.5 mg. promethazine, and 5mg. diazepam). When pressed to tell the truth, Williams changed her story, admitting that she had administered the anesthesia. She insisted, however, that she had called Gosnell before administering 10 mg. Demerol and 12.5 mg. promethazine at 6:00 p.m., and an additional "custom" dose (75 mg. Demerol, 12.5 mg. promethazine, and 10 mg. diazepam) when the "local anesthesia" wore off. She said that she injected these medications into the patient's arm.

Dr. Herlich, the University of Pittsburgh Medical Center anesthesiologist, testified that the first dose of Demerol described by Williams made no sense—that there is no such thing as a 10 mg. dose of Demerol. He further explained that a 10 mg. dose of Demerol, if it existed, "would be barely noticeable in terms of pain control" in the average adult. The dosage Williams claimed had been administered would not, in any case, have had the effect witnessed by Mrs. Mongar's daughter. She said that her mother had been in a lot of pain in the recovery room before the procedure, but that the medicine administered intravenously by Williams and West put her mother "to sleep."

It is notable that Williams's story was different from the one given by Gosnell when he was interviewed by Detective James Wood, the FBI, and the DEA on the night of the raid. According to Detective Woods's notes, Gosnell first told his interviewers that medication was given by "one of his nurses or by a medical assistant, he wasn't sure who ..."—even though no nurses were employed in the clinic. He then said that during the "evening," before the procedure, "one of the nursing staff" administered an unspecified dose of Demerol and diazepam (not promethazine) intramuscularly (meaning an injection into a muscle rather than a vein—which would be intravenous). He

Section V: The Death of Karnamaya Mongar

said that he then administered a dose of Demerol intravenously when he did the abortion procedure.

He also told the DEA that he had performed a "successful and uneventful ... suction and curette procedure"—even though Mrs. Mongar's 19-week-old fetus was found in the clinic's freezer completely intact.

Gosnell's statements to law enforcement contradicted what he had earlier reported to the Department of Health shortly after Mrs. Mongar's death. On November 26, 2009, Gosnell wrote a letter to health department officials advising them of his patient's death.

At that time, he reported that Mrs. Mongar had been given two doses of sedation intravenously, each containing 50 mg. of Demerol and 5 mg. of diazepam. He did not say who had administered this mix of drugs, which he called "customary." All the evidence is to the contrary: This combination of drugs was nowhere listed on the clinic's medication chart, and every other staff member stated that the final dose given to every second-trimester patient was 75 mg. Demerol, 12.5 mg. promethazine, and 10 mg. diazepam.

Kareema Cross explained to the Grand Jury why it was significant that Williams, as opposed to the doctor, had given Mrs. Mongar the lethal drugs. Cross said that Williams had confided in her that Gosnell was willing to say that he had administered the drugs. Cross testified that "Dr. Gosnell told her that she's not going to be in trouble. He's going to say that he gave the patient the medication." Asked why this mattered, Cross said:

BLACKOUT: The Official GOSNELL Grand Jury Report

A. Because she's not certified, none of us are certified to do it.

* * *

Q. But if he gave the medicine, was it your understanding that no one would get in any trouble because he's a doctor?
A. Right.
Q. And it would just be malpractice; is that right?
A. Yes
Q. And not criminal; is that right?
A. Yes.
Q. Is that how it was told to you?
A. Yes.
Q. Is that how Lynda [Williams] explained it to you?
A. Yes.

In fact, according to Cross, Gosnell rarely gave medication; he almost always left this task to his untrained and uncertified workers.

The toxicology expert's testimony flatly contradicted these self-serving statements. Dr. Rohrig, the toxicology expert, explained to the Grand Jury that all of Gosnell's, Williams's, and West's shifting accounts of the drugs given to Mrs. Mongar were inconsistent with the levels of medications found in Mrs. Mongar's blood post mortem. Those levels were consistent, however, with what Kareema Cross said was the clinic's standard practice—to give multiple doses of 75 mg. Demerol, along with promethazine and diazepam, throughout the afternoon and evening before the procedure.

The expert explained that Demerol has a "half-life" of about three hours, meaning that it takes about that long for the concentration of the drug in the body to be reduced by half. It then takes another three hours for the remaining concentration to be reduced by 50 percent, and this pattern continues until all of the drug has dissipated. Demerol is thus "fairly quickly removed from the body." At least

Section V: The Death of Karnamaya Mongar

18 hours after the drugs were administered, Mrs. Mongar still had a Demerol concentration of 750 micrograms per liter in her blood.

While Dr. Rohrig was unable to determine precisely how much Demerol Mrs. Mongar had been given, he testified that, based on the high concentration still in her blood, it was far more than Gosnell, Williams, and West claimed. The expert explained that if Mrs. Mongar had been given 100 mg. of Demerol (as Gosnell told the Department of Health), the peak drug concentration would have been about 300 micrograms per liter. Mrs. Mongar's level—over 700 micrograms a day later—was totally inconsistent with Gosnell's, Williams's, and West's stories. "You just can't have that high concentration 18 hours later ... That's enough [time] to cause the normal therapeutic doses to go to zero." Mrs. Mongar had to have been given multiple 75-mg. doses of Demerol, or the doses she was given had to have contained well over 75 mg. of Demerol.

What Gosnell and others reported to the hospital, to the Health Department, and to law enforcement about the amount of medication they gave to Mrs. Mongar was demonstrably false.

Predictably, Gosnell and his staff also tried to avoid responsibility by blaming the victim. The day after Mrs. Mongar died, West said to Ashley Baldwin that one of the family members had told her that Mrs. Mongar "took some pills, because she was trying to get rid of it at home." Similarly, Liz Hampton in her testimony before the Grand Jury claimed that she had had a discussion with Mrs. Mongar's "husband and two daughters" upstairs at the clinic. Hampton insisted, under oath, that they had said to her: "we told her not to take the drugs." But the only family members to enter the clinic were Mrs. Mongar's daughter and the daughter's mother-in-law, and neither of them spoke English. Mrs. Mongar's husband was in Virginia and Mr. Ghalley was waiting outside in the car. Mrs. Mongar's daughter flatly denied that anyone in her group ever said any such thing. Her mother, she testified with the help of a translator, had taken nothing other than the medication given to her at the clinic the night before.

Ashley Baldwin testified that she did not believe West and Hampton's claims, because it seemed odd to be hearing about them only after the patient had to be transported to the hospital. In any event, expert testimony established that Mrs. Mongar died from an overdose of Demerol, the drug administered in Gosnell's clinic, and not some mystery pill.

SECTION VI:
HOW DID THIS GO ON SO LONG?

The callous killing of babies outside the womb, the routinely performed third-trimester abortions, the deaths of at least two patients, and the grievous health risks inflicted on countless other women by Gosnell and his unlicensed staff are not the only shocking things that this Grand Jury investigation uncovered. What surprised the jurors even more is the official neglect that allowed these crimes and conditions to persist for years in a Philadelphia medical facility.

THE STATE DEPARTMENT OF HEALTH NEGLECTED ITS DUTY TO ENSURE THE HEALTH AND SAFETY OF PATIENTS IN PENNSYLVANIA'S ABORTION CLINICS.

We discovered that Pennsylvania's Department of Health has deliberately chosen not to enforce laws that should afford patients at abortion clinics the same safeguards and assurances of quality health care as patients of other medical service providers. Even nail salons in Pennsylvania are monitored more closely for client safety.

The State Legislature has charged the Department of Health (DOH) with responsibility for writing and enforcing regulations to protect health and safety in abortion clinics as well as in hospitals and other health care facilities. Yet a significant difference exists between how DOH monitors abortion clinics and how it monitors facilities where other medical procedures are performed.

Indeed, the department has shown an utter disregard both for the safety of women who seek treatment at abortion clinics and for the health of fetuses after they have become viable. State health officials have also shown a disregard for the laws the department is supposed to enforce. Most appalling of all, the Department of Health's neglect of abortion patients' safety and of Pennsylvania laws is clearly not inadvertent: It is by design.

Many organizations that perform safe abortion procedures do their own monitoring and adhere to strict, self-imposed standards of quality. But the excellent safety records and the quality of care that these independently monitored clinics deliver to patients are no thanks to the Pennsylvania Department of Health. And not all women seeking abortion find their way to these high-quality facilities; some end up in a filthy, dangerous clinic such as Gosnell's. There the patients have to depend on DOH oversight to protect them — as do babies born alive, and helpless but viable fetuses after 24 weeks of gestation. Yet no protection is forthcoming.

State health officials knew that Gosnell and his clinic were offering unacceptable medical care to women and girls, yet DOH failed to take any action to stop the atrocities documented by this Grand Jury. These officials were far more protective of themselves when they testified before the Grand Jury. Even DOH lawyers, including the chief counsel, brought private attorneys with them — presumably at government expense.

Gosnell's clinic — with its untrained staff, its unsanitary conditions and practices, its perilously lax anesthesia protocols, its willingness to perform late-term abortions for exorbitant amounts of cash, and its routine procedure of killing babies after they were delivered by their unconscious mothers — offers a telling example of how horrendous a Pennsylvania facility can be and still operate with DOH "approval."

Section VI: How Did This Go On So Long?

The Department of Health conducted sporadic, inadequate inspections for 13 years, and then none at all between 1993 and 2010.

Witnesses from DOH acknowledged before the Grand Jury that it is their department's responsibility to oversee clinics such as Gosnell's. Pennsylvania's Abortion Control Act charges DOH with regulating and overseeing the performance of abortions and the facilities where abortions are performed "so as to protect the health and safety of women having abortions and of premature babies aborted alive." 18 Pa.C.S. §3207(a). Abortion facilities require the department's approval to begin operating.

The Department of Health first granted approval for the Women's Medical Center to provide abortions at 3801 Lancaster Avenue on December 20, 1979. The approval followed an on-site review and was good for 12 months. The DOH "site review" at the time identified a certified obstetrician/gynecologist, Joni Magee, as the medical director, with Gosnell listed as a staff physician. The report noted that a registered nurse worked two days a week, four hours a day, and that lab work was sent out to an outside laboratory.

Other topics covered in the 1979 site review included: counseling for women to be sure they had considered alternatives to abortion and were sure about their decision; the physical facility (whether there was adequate space, and whether wheelchairs and stretchers could maneuver through doorways and to the outside); cleaning procedures; emergency preparedness (including the availability of resuscitation equipment and arrangements with an ambulance service and hospital for emergency treatment); and procedures for before, during, and after the operation. It is unclear from the site review who provided most of the information, but much of it appears to come from staff interviews. One significant finding in the 1979 evaluation was that there was adequate access for a stretcher, something that proved not to be the case when EMTs needed to transport Karnamaya Mongar from the facility in November 2009.

Even though the first DOH Certificate of Approval for Gosnell's clinic expired on December 20, 1980, the next documented site review was not conducted until August 1989. (There is a notation on the 1989 report that a review was conducted in February 1986, but DOH could not provide any documentation of it in response to the Grand Jury's subpoena.) The 1989 evaluation was conducted by Elizabeth Stein and Susan Mitchell. Over 20 years later, Mitchell was part of the team that inspected Gosnell's clinic in February 2010 when law enforcement officials invited DOH to participate in their search.

By 1989, Gosnell, who is not board-certified as either an obstetrician or a gynecologist, was the only doctor at the facility. The DOH site reviewers also noted that there were no nurses working at the clinic. Blood work was no longer sent out to an independent lab, but was done, supposedly, by "medical assistants." And in 7 of the 30 patient files reviewed, there was no lab work recorded. The evaluators noted several violations of Pennsylvania abortion regulations, including: no board-certified doctor on staff or contracted as a consultant; no nurses overseeing the recovery of patients; no transfer agreement with a hospital for emergency care; and no lab work recorded in several files. Even so, based on mere promises to improve documentation and filing, and to hire nurses, the DOH site reviewers recommended approval of Gosnell's clinic for another 12 months.

Section VI: How Did This Go On So Long?

Two and a half years later, in March 1992, when DOH representatives next inspected the clinic, there were still no nurses to monitor patient recovery. Evaluators Janice Staloski and Sara Telencio noted that Gosnell was still the only doctor (a Dr. Martin Weisberg was listed as a consultant); that the facility employed no nurses; and that medical assistants were doing lab work. They did indicate there was adequate access for stretchers and wheelchairs, though it is not clear how they reached this conclusion: The facility is multi-leveled and has no elevator.

There is nothing to suggest that these evaluators reviewed any patient files. Gosnell reported performing 62 second-trimester abortions in the previous year, yet the DOH inspectors left blank the section in their report on anesthesia, including who is permitted to give it, what their qualifications are, and the type of anesthesia they are permitted to administer. Also left blank was a section titled "Post-Operative Care," which addresses the legal requirement that the recovery room be monitored at all times by a registered nurse or a licensed practical nurse under the supervision of a physician — the same regulation that the clinic was cited for violating three years earlier. Nevertheless, the evaluators inexplicably concluded on March 12, 1992, that there were "no deficiencies," and DOH approved Gosnell's clinic to continue to perform abortions.

The next inspection was conducted on April 8, 1993, by DOH evaluators Susan Mitchell and Georgette Freed-Wolf. This was also the last site review — until February 2010, when an inspection occurred because law enforcement executed search warrants for illegal drug activity. In the 1993 review, Gosnell was the only doctor listed on staff, but "Dr. Weisberg" was still described as a consultant.

BLACKOUT: The Official GOSNELL Grand Jury Report

Four years after Gosnell had promised to hire nurses to oversee the recovery room, there was still none. Lab work was still being performed by unspecified "medical assistants," whose qualifications the evaluators apparently did not question, since that section of the review was left blank. For the third time, inspectors found the access for stretchers and wheelchairs adequate, even though the facility's layout had become even more convoluted and the building still did not have an elevator.

The 1993 site review did not include any first-hand observations about the cleanliness of the facility or the condition of the emergency equipment required for resuscitation. Instead of making their own inspection, the evaluators appeared to have relied on representations by staff about procedures for cleaning and checking equipment. They did, however, find drugs past their expiration dates. In reviewing 12 patient files, the surveyors found that 4 involved second-trimester abortions. In three of these four files, there were no pathology reports on the tissue, as required by the Abortion Control Act. In one file, there was no evidence that the tissue was sent to a pathologist at all. In 3 of the 12 files, the evaluators found that required lab work was missing.

On July 23, 1993, without a follow-up inspection, Susan Mitchell recorded that the deficiencies had been corrected. DOH sent Gosnell another Certificate of Approval. The certificate stated that it was "Effective From The 1st Day Of April 1993 Until March 31, 1994 In Accordance With Law."

Gosnell's clinic had, on May 1, 1993, submitted an "Abortion Facility Registration Form" to DOH. Whoever filled it out (it is not signed), filled in the name of the facility — Women's Medical Society —

Section VI: How Did This Go On So Long?

and its mailing address, and checked off boxes indicating that the Women's Medical Society had no parent, subsidiaries, or affiliated organizations and whether or not it had received state funds in the preceding 12 months.

During the next 16 plus years—as Gosnell collected fetuses' feet in jars in his office and allowed medical waste to pile up in the basement; as he replaced his few licensed medical assistants with untrained workers and a high school student; as his outdated equipment rusted and broke and he routinely reused instruments designed for single-use; as he allowed unqualified staff to administer anesthesia and to deal with babies born before he arrived at work for the day; and as he caused the deaths of at least two patients while continuing to perform illegal third-trimester abortions and to kill babies outside their mothers' wombs—DOH never conducted another on-site inspection at the Lancaster Avenue facility.

The state Department of Health failed to investigate Gosnell's clinic even in response to complaints.

According to DOH witnesses, sometime after 1993, DOH instituted a policy of inspecting abortion clinics only when there was a complaint. In fact, as this Grand Jury's investigation makes clear, the department did not even do that.

Janice Staloski, one of the evaluators of Gosnell's clinic in 1992, 10 years later was the Director of DOH's Division of Home Health—the unit that is inexplicably responsible for overseeing the quality of care in abortion clinics. In January 2002, an attorney representing Semika Shaw, a 22-year-old woman who had died following an abortion at Gosnell's clinic, wrote to Staloski requesting copies of inspection reports for any on-site inspections of the clinic conducted by DOH. Staloski wrote to the attorney that no inspections had been conducted since 1993 because DOH had received no complaints about the clinic in that time.

Except that it had. In 1996, another attorney, representing a different patient of Gosnell's, informed Staloski's predecessor as director of the Home Health Division that his client had suffered a perforated uterus, requiring a radical hysterectomy, as a result of Gosnell's negligence. The Home Health director discussed this patient with DOH Senior Counsel Kenneth Brody, and the complaint report was documented in records turned over to the Grand Jury. It was surely available to Staloski when she inaccurately told the attorney in January 2002 that DOH had received no complaints regarding Gosnell's clinic.

Not documented in the records turned over to the Grand Jury was a second complaint registered between 1996 and 1997. This one was hand-delivered to the secretary of health's administrative assistant by Dr. Donald Schwarz, now Philadelphia's health commissioner. Dr. Schwarz, a pediatrician, is the former head of adolescent services at Children's Hospital of Philadelphia and was the directing physician of a private practice in West Philadelphia. For 17 years, he treated teenage girls from the West Philadelphia community. Occasionally, he referred patients who wanted to terminate their pregnancies to abortion providers.

Gosnell's clinic was originally included as a provider in the referral information that Dr. Schwarz gave to his patients. He and his physician partners noticed, however, that patients who had abortions at Woman's Medical Society were returning to their

Section VI: How Did This Go On So Long?

private practice, soon after, infected with trichomoniasis, a sexually transmitted parasite, that they did not have before the abortions.

When this happened repeatedly, Dr. Schwarz sent a social worker to talk to people at Gosnell's facility. Based on the social worker's visit to Women's Medical Society, Dr. Schwarz stopped referring patients to the clinic. He also hand-delivered a formal letter of complaint to the office of the Pennsylvania Secretary of Health.

Dr. Schwarz told the Grand Jury that he does not know what happened to his complaint. He never heard back from DOH. And the department did not include it in response to the Grand Jury's subpoena requesting all complaints relating to Gosnell's' clinic. We know that no inspection resulted.

We are very troubled that state health officials ignored this respected physician's report that girls were becoming infected with sexually transmitted diseases at Gosnell's clinic when they had abortions there. If Dr. Schwarz's complaint did not trigger an inspection, we are convinced that none would.

We also do not understand how a report of this magnitude was not at least added to Gosnell's file at the state department of health. It suggests to us that there may have been many more complaints that were never turned over to the Grand Jury.

We heard testimony from DOH officials who should have been aware of Dr. Schwarz's complaint—Kenneth Brody and Janice Staloski, at the least. Yet they made no mention of it to the Grand Jury. Did they remember the complaint and choose to exclude it from their testimony? Is ignoring complaints of this seriousness so routine at DOH that they honestly do not remember it? Or did the secretary of health never even forward it on for action? Of these possible explanations, we are not sure which is the most troubling.

In addition to these two complaints filed in 1996 and 1997, Staloski herself received two inquiries from attorneys' offices about Gosnell's clinic in the first two months of 2002. One was from the Shaw family's attorney. The other was from a paralegal for yet a third attorney who phoned her on February 6, 2002, asking for information concerning the clinic. Surely these two inquiries in 2002 should have alerted Staloski that there were complaints from at least two people about the clinic, complaints serious enough to warrant civil attorneys' involvement. Yet she ordered no investigation of the clinic, even though it had not been site-reviewed in nine years.

In 2007, Dr. Frederick Hellman, the Medical Examiner for Delaware County, reported to DOH the stillbirth of a 30-week-old baby girl. A medical examiner investigator, Irene LaFlore, made the phone calls. She spoke to several DOH employees, including Brody, the senior counsel. The investigator reported to the DOH officials that the medical examiner had conducted an autopsy on the stillborn baby delivered by a 14-year-old girl at Crozier-Chester Medical Center. She explained that the baby's delivery had been induced in the course of an abortion performed by Gosnell, and that the medical examiner was concerned because performing an abortion at 30 weeks was a clear violation of the Abortion Control Act.

According to the investigator's notes, Brody suggested that the medical examiner inform the District Attorney's Office in Delaware County—for possible referral to Philadelphia, where the procedure occurred—because it was a crime to perform an abortion beyond 24 weeks. Brody said that neither DOH nor the state medical board

Section VI: How Did This Go On So Long?

had any authority over the matter. The senior counsel did ask the investigator to keep him informed. The investigator's notes suggest Brody told her that, once the district attorney acted, then the medical board could get involved.

Brody was correct to refer Dr. Hellman to the district attorney to prosecute the abortion of the 30-week pregnancy as a crime. That, however, did not absolve DOH of its responsibility. The information provided by Dr. Hellman's investigator should have been received as a complaint to DOH. The department should have initiated an investigation. DOH could have revoked the clinic's license without waiting for a criminal prosecution that might never (and did not) happen. Yet no one from the department went to investigate Gosnell's clinic.

> **Since February 2010, Department of Health officials have reinstituted regular inspections of abortion clinics—finding authority in the same statute they used earlier to justify not inspecting.**

Staloski blamed the decision to abandon supposedly annual inspections of abortion clinics on DOH lawyers, who, she said, changed their legal opinions and advice to suit the policy preferences of different governors. Under Governor Robert Casey, she said, the department inspected abortion facilities annually. Yet, when Governor Tom Ridge came in, the attorneys interpreted the same regulations that had permitted annual inspections for years to no longer authorize those inspections. Then, only complaint-driven inspections supposedly were authorized. Staloski said that DOH's policy during Governor Ridge's administration was motivated by a desire not to be "putting a barrier up to women" seeking abortions.

BLACKOUT: The Official GOSNELL Grand Jury Report

Brody confirmed some of what Staloski told the Grand Jury. He described a meeting of high-level government officials in 1999 at which a decision was made not to accept a recommendation to reinstitute regular inspections of abortion clinics. The reasoning, as Brody recalled, was: "there was a concern that if they did routine inspections, that they may find a lot of these facilities didn't meet [the standards for getting patients out by stretcher or wheelchair in an emergency], and then there would be less abortion facilities, less access to women to have an abortion."

Brody testified that he did not consider the "access issue" a legal one. The Abortion Control Act, he told the Grand Jurors, charges DOH with protecting the health and safety of women having abortions and premature infants aborted alive. To carry out this responsibility, he said, DOH should regularly inspect the facilities.

Nevertheless, the position of DOH remained the same after Edward Rendell became governor. Using the legally faulty excuse that the department lacked the authority to inspect abortion clinics, Staloski left them unmonitored, presumably with the knowledge and blessing of her bosses, Deputy Secretary Stacy Mitchell and a succession of Secretaries of Health. The department continued its do-nothing policy until 2010, when media attention surrounding the raid of the Gosnell clinic exposed the results of years of hands-off "oversight." Now, once again, the regulations, which have never been modified, apparently allow for regular inspections. This is, and always was, the correct position. The state legislature gave DOH the duty to enforce its regulations; the authority and power to do so are implicit in that duty. The department abandoned this responsibility without explanation, and without notice to the public or the legislature.

Section VI: How Did This Go On So Long?

Whatever its motivation, DOH's deliberate policy decision not to conduct regular inspections of abortion clinics did not serve the women of this Commonwealth. Nor did it protect late-term fetuses or viable babies born alive. The Grand Jury heard testimony from legitimate abortion providers and from abortion-rights advocates, and not one indicated that annual inspections would be unduly burdensome. The doctors we heard from, and the organizations that refer women to abortion providers, told us that the reputable providers comply with all of the state regulations and more. Annual inspections are not an issue with them. Many clinics in Pennsylvania are already inspected by NAF, whose standards are, in many ways, more protective of women's safety than are the state's regulations.

Without regular inspections, providers like Gosnell continue to operate; unlawful and dangerous third-trimester abortions go undetected; and many women, especially poor women, suffer. These are all consequences of DOH's abdication of its responsibility.

Moreover, even if Staloski was instructed not to conduct regular, annual inspections, that does not explain why she failed to order inspections when complaints were received. It is clear to us that she was made aware, numerous times, that serious incidents had occurred at Gosnell's clinic. These incidents, which evidenced alarming as well as illegal long-standing patterns of behavior, warranted investigation. Yet, in all the years she worked at the department, Staloski never ordered even one inspection.

Not even Karnamaya Mongar's death triggered an inspection or investigation.

BLACKOUT: The Official GOSNELL Grand Jury Report

On November 24, 2009, Gosnell sent a fax to the department, followed by a letter addressed to Staloski, notifying DOH that Karnamaya Mongar had died following an abortion at his clinic. (Gosnell's letter inaccurately stated that the second day of her procedure was November 18.) Darlene Augustine, a registered nurse and health quality administrator in the department's Division of Home Health, received the fax.

Augustine, who supervises surveyors who respond to and investigate complaints at health care facilities, testified that she immediately notified her boss, Cynthia Boyne. (Boyne had become director of DOH's Division of Home Health in 2007, when Staloski was promoted to head the Bureau of Community Licensure and Certification.) Augustine said that she told Boyne on November 25 that DOH should immediately go out to the clinic and initiate an investigation. Augustine acknowledged that she generally had the authority to send surveyors out to investigate—and she often did so within an hour of receiving a notice of a serious event such as a death. She testified, however, that she felt she needed Director Boyne's approval because Gosnell's notice involved an abortion clinic.

Boyne did not give her approval. Instead, she went to the bureau director, Staloski, to discuss the matter. Augustine explained that abortion clinics were treated differently from other medical facilities because Staloski had for years overseen the department's handling of complaints and inspections—or lack of inspections—relating to abortion clinics. Staloski, according to Augustine, was "the ultimate decision-maker" with respect to whether DOH would conduct an inspection or investigation. Augustine testified that neither Boyne

Section VI: How Did This Go On So Long?

nor Staloski ever gave her approval to conduct the investigation she thought was appropriate.

Boyne blamed Staloski. She said that her boss told her that DOH did not have the authority to investigate Mrs. Mongar's death. Staloski apparently reached this decision on her own, without ever consulting Brody, the legal counsel. Staloski, according to Boyne, was only interested in making sure that Gosnell filed an on-line report in accordance with a 2002 law, the Medical Care Availability and Reduction of Error (MCARE) Act. That law requires health care facilities to report serious events, including deaths to DOH. 40 P.S. §313.

Staloski's plan, Boyne said, was to then charge Gosnell with failing to file the report in a timely and proper manner. This is absurd, and Boyne should not have accepted such a ridiculous idea. Gosnell had reported Mrs. Mongar's death to DOH on November 24, 2009. While this was three or fours days late, and the notification came by fax and letter rather than computer, it is preposterous to think that Staloski, who had ignored two deaths and other serious injuries at the clinic, would take action against a doctor for filing a report three days late. Staloski was absolutely wrong about DOH's lack of authority to investigate Mrs. Mongar's death.

Appallingly, the chief counsel for the department of health, Christine Dutton, defended Staloski's inaction following Mrs. Mongar's death. Dutton testified that she had reviewed the emails and documents showing that Staloski and her staff were communicating with Gosnell's office to get him to file the MCARE form. Based on these very minimal efforts, Dutton insisted: "we were responsive." Pushed as to whether the death of a woman following an abortion should have prompted more action—perhaps an investigation or a report to law enforcement—Dutton argued there was no reason to think the death was suspicious. "People die," she said.

Not only was a probe into Mrs. Mongar's death authorized and appropriate under the Abortion Control Act, it was required under the MCARE Law 40 P.S. §306. Yet DOH did not investigate. Staloski told the Grand Jury that she remembered reviewing with Boyne the letter in which Gosnell notified DOH of Mrs. Mongar's death. Staloski said that it was really Boyne's responsibility to order an investigation, but acknowledged that she, as the bureau director, also failed to do so. Instead of conducting an investigation, Staloski and Boyne concerned themselves with badgering Gosnell to re-notify them of Mrs. Mongar's death.

Bureau Director Staloski, in fact, readily acknowledged many deficiencies in DOH's, and her own, oversight of abortion facilities. But her dismissive demeanor indicated to us that she did not really understand—or care about—the devastating impact that the department's neglect had had on the women whom Gosnell treated in his filthy, dangerous clinic.

Staloski excused the DOH practices that enabled Gosnell to operate in the manner that killed Ms. Shaw, Mrs. Mongar, and untold numbers of babies. She simply said the abortion regulations—*written by DOH*—do not require DOH to inspect abortion clinics.

When DOH inspectors finally entered Gosnell's clinic in February 2010, not at Staloski's direction but at the urging of law enforcement, Staloski seemed more annoyed than appalled or embarrassed. On the morning after the raid, she received a copy of an email that Boyne wrote to Brody the night of the raid. Boyne reported

Section VI: How Did This Go On So Long?

to the department's senior counsel that, at 12:45 a.m., she had told the Department of Health staff members at the clinic to "wrap it up and secure lodging in the interest of their safety." Boyne told Brody that the "staff walked into a very difficult setup." She complained that a representative of the District Attorney's Office was "badgering" DOH staff to shut down the facility immediately. Boyne was seeking Brody's legal guidance.

Staloski's response to Boyne's email was: "I'd say we were used." Boyne's reply: "Bingo."

Staloksi, the woman most directly responsible for the department's oversight of abortion facilities, told the Grand Jury: "I haven't been in any facilities in probably—in an abortion facility in many, many years." The citizens of Pennsylvania deserve far better from those charged with protecting public health and safety.

Department of Health evaluators found multiple grounds to shut down the Women's Medical Society once they finally entered the facility.

It was not until February 18, 2010, when DOH representatives were escorted in by law enforcement agents, that they finally inspected the clinic that they had not bothered to visit in 13 years. This time, neglecting the horrors at 3801 Lancaster Avenue was no longer an option. Over the next few days, the DOH evaluators identified a multitude of violations of the Abortion Control Act and abortion regulations, many of which were apparent with even a cursory glance around the facility.

The abortion regulations promulgated by DOH (28 Pa. Code §29.33(1)) require that abortion providers have the following ready for use to resuscitate patients whenever anesthesia is used:

(i) Suction source.
(ii) Oxygen source.
(iii) Assorted size oral airways and endotracheal tubes.
(iv) Laryngoscope.
(v) Bag and mask and bag and endotracheal tube attachments for assisted ventilation.
(vi) Intravenous fluids including blood volume expanders.
(vii) Intravenous catheters and cut-down instrument tray.
(viii) Emergency drugs for shock and metabolic imbalance.
(ix) An individual to monitor respiratory rate, blood pressure, and heart rate.

When patients are sedated to the point of being deeply asleep, as they were when Gosnell performed second-trimester abortions, additional equipment is required. Even when the sedation is less deep—a level referred to as conscious sedation, in which the patient can still respond to verbal instructions—Pennsylvania regulations require that additional equipment be readily available, including a "monitor defibrillator with electrocardiogram visual display of heart rate and rhythm" (ECG) and a pulse oximeter.

Women's Medical Society effectively had none of this. A document filed by DOH on March 12, 2010, referred to as an "Order to Show Cause," laid out several grounds for shutting the clinic. It stated that the only items on the list that were in the facility in any form were suction and oxygen sources and an unusable monitor defibrillator and ECG. Yet there was only one suction source for each procedure room, meaning that the same suction source used to perform the abortion would have to be used to resuscitate patients. The DOH document noted, moreover, that neither suction machine had an inspection sticker to indicate that it was functioning properly. The suction tubing on both machines was corroded, according to the report.

Section VI: How Did This Go On So Long?

As for the supposed oxygen sources, DOH noted:

> One oxygen source was an E cylinder oxygen tank that lacked a label to indicate whether the tank was full or empty. The oxygen mask and tubing hanging from the tank were covered in a thick gray layer of a substance that appeared to be dust. ... The other oxygen source at the ... facility was an oxygen concentrator covered with a thin layer of dust. The oxygen concentrator bore no inspection sticker and no evidence of inspection to assure proper functioning. There was no oxygen mask or tubing with the oxygen concentrator.

The DOH document stated that the monitor defibrillator and ECG not only had no inspection sticker, but was unusable because there were no electrodes to attach to the machine. Latosha Lewis testified that the machine had been broken for at least six years.

As the DOH Order to Show Cause noted in "Count I," each time Gosnell performed a procedure without the required equipment and drugs for resuscitation, he violated the abortion regulations §29.33(1). He also violated §29.33(4) by failing to have a doctor certified by the American Board (or Osteopathic Board) of Obstetrics and Gynecology either on staff or available as a consultant. (Count II.) The Department of Health also cited the clinic for failing to conduct or to record required lab tests in violation of §29.33(6). (Counts III and IV.)

After entering Gosnell's facility with law enforcement agents, DOH representatives reviewed the files of some of its patients (some of whom were present and had procedures on February 18, 2010, when the search was conducted; and some of whom had had procedures in the previous few months). Nine of the patients had had second-trimester abortions. Under Pennsylvania's abortion regulations, abortion providers are required to send any tissue from second-trimester procedures to a pathologist to determine whether there is evidence of viability. Gosnell had failed to do this for any of the nine patients, thus violating §29.33(8) nine times. (Count V.)

The Department of Health also charged Gosnell's clinic with failing to have written procedures and policies for the administration of anesthesia and for failing to maintain a list of employees permitted to administer it. These failures constituted violations of §29.33(12). (Count VI.) Other violations detailed by DOH in March 2010 were the failure to have patients in recovery monitored by a registered nurse or a licensed practical nurse, or to have such nurses enter the doctor's orders in the patients' medical records as required by §29.33(13). (Counts VII and VIII.)

The DOH document stated (in Count IX) that the clinic violated §29.33(14) of the abortion regulations by failing to have corridor doors and passages adequate in size and arrangement to allow a stretcher-borne patient to be moved from each procedure room and recovery room to a street-level exit. DOH noted that ambulance crews on February 18, 2010, had wanted to evacuate two patients from Gosnell's clinic on stretchers, but instead had to help them walk through the corridors. The situation was made even worse because the closest exit door to the street was padlocked shut, and the staff could not find the key.

Count X alleged that Gosnell failed to ensure that one of the patients having an abortion on February 18, 2010, had a private consultation regarding the necessity of her abortion, as required by §29.32. Count XI stated that the clinic failed to report the death of Karnamaya Mongar within 24 hours as required under 40 Pa.C.S.

Section VI: How Did This Go On So Long?

§1303.313(a) (the Medical Care Availability and Reduction of Error, or MCARE, Act).

Count XII spelled out a violation of §29.38(a)(5) of the abortion regulations, which requires doctors to file a "Report of Complication" with DOH any time they treat a patient as a result of a complication from an abortion. The complication that Gosnell treated, but allegedly did not report, was the cardiac arrest suffered by Karnamaya Mongar.

Count XIII accused the clinic of violating §29.38(5), which requires abortion providers to file quarterly reports with DOH, stating the number of abortions performed by the facility in each trimester of pregnancy. The most recent report filed by Gosnell's clinic stated that it had performed 118 first-trimester and 2 second-trimester abortions in the fourth quarter of 2009. But even in the few files that DOH evaluators reviewed in February 2010, there were six second-trimester procedures performed in the last two months of 2009.

The last count in the DOH document—Count XIV—cited the failure to file reports on every abortion performed, as required by §29.38(3). Specifically, DOH stated that Gosnell did not file reports on six of the women whose files DOH reviewed in February 2010. This failure violated the abortion regulations and constituted grounds for revoking DOH approval to perform abortions.

Indeed, each of the violations enumerated by the DOH Order to Show Cause constitutes grounds for revoking the clinic's approval to perform abortions under §29.43(d)—many times over, in fact. Once the DOH inspectors entered the facility in February 2010, they did a thorough job of inspecting Gosnell's clinic and moved quickly to revoke its "approval," based on the clinic's many flagrant violations of law.

BLACKOUT: The Official GOSNELL Grand Jury Report

The travesty, from this Grand Jury's perspective, is that DOH could and should have closed down Gosnell's clinic years before. Many, if not all, of the violations cited in the March 12, 2010, document had been present for nearly two decades. The violations had been apparent when DOH site-reviewers, including Susan Mitchell and Janice Staloski, inspected the facility in 1989, 1992, and 1993. Yet it was not until law enforcement discovered the horrendous conditions inside 3801 Lancaster Avenue that DOH took action to close the clinic.

The state Department of Health monitors other comparable health care facilities to assure quality care.

The Department of Health's decades-long neglect of its duty to ensure the health and safety of women undergoing medical procedures in abortion clinics is in stark contrast to its policies and practices with respect to procedures performed in other types of health care facilities.

DOH's authority and duty to regulate, license, and oversee the operation of various health care facilities arises from the Health Care Facilities Act, 35 Pa.C.S.§448.102 et seq. The purpose of the Act is spelled out in §448.801a:

> It is the purpose of this chapter to protect and promote the public health and welfare through the establishment and enforcement of regulations setting minimum standards in the construction, maintenance and operation of health care facilities. Such standards are intended by the legislature to assure safe, adequate and efficient facilities and services, and to promote the health, safety and adequate care of the patients or residents of such facilities. It is also the purpose of this chapter to assure quality health care through appropriate and nonduplicative review and inspection with due regard to the

Section VI: How Did This Go On So Long?

protection of the health and rights of privacy of patients and without unreasonably interfering with the operation of the health care facility or home health agency.

The Health Care Facilities Act charges DOH with the oversight of health care facilities including hospitals, home health care agencies, nursing facilities, cancer treatment centers, birth centers, and ambulatory surgical centers. The health department regulates, licenses, and monitors each of these types of facilities differently. The type of facility that is relevant to this Grand Jury's investigation is the "ambulatory surgical facility" (ASF).

The Health Care Facilities Act defines an Ambulatory Surgical Facility as:

> A facility or portion thereof not located upon the premises of a hospital which provides specialty or multispecialty outpatient surgical treatment. Ambulatory surgical facility does not include individual or group practice offices of private physicians or dentists, unless such offices have a distinct part used solely for outpatient surgical treatment on a regular and organized basis. For the purposes of this provision, outpatient surgical treatment means surgical treatment to patients who do not require hospitalization, but who require constant medical supervision following the surgical procedure performed.

This is precisely what Gosnell's clinic was—a facility that provided specialty outpatient surgical treatment. And, by definition, so are all freestanding abortion clinics (those not associated with hospitals). The regulations that DOH wrote pursuant to the Abortion Control Act (18 Pa. C.S. §3201 et seq.) are entitled "Regulations for Ambulatory Gynecological Surgery" (28 Pa. Code 29.1, et seq.). Section 29.33(13) expressly requires:

BLACKOUT: The Official GOSNELL Grand Jury Report

> Each patient shall be supervised constantly while recovering from surgery or anesthesia, until she is released from recovery by a registered nurse or a licensed practical nurse under the direction of a registered nurse or a physician. The nurse shall evaluate the condition of the patient and enter a report of the evaluation and orders in the medical record of the patient.

The plain language of the Health Care Facilities Act mandates that abortion clinics should be regulated, licensed, and monitored as Ambulatory Surgical Facilities. DOH licenses many types of facilities as ASFs, including endoscopy centers, where colonoscopies are performed; offices where plastic surgery procedures such as liposuction, facelifts, and breast augmentation are performed; and eye surgery centers. Under the regulations written by DOH, such facilities must be inspected and licensed yearly. In addition, DOH inspectors are expressly authorized to inspect ASFs, at any time, announced or unannounced, to investigate any complaints (28 Pa. Code §§ 551.31 through 551.51).

The regulations for Pennsylvania ASFs — which run over 50 pages — provide a comprehensive set of rules and procedures to assure overall quality of care at such facilities. They include, for example, measures for infection control (28 Pa. Code. §567.3 lists 17 specific actions that ASFs have to take to control infection); a requirement that linens be sterile (§567.21-24); and a requirement that the premises and equipment be kept clean and free of vermin, insects, rodents, and litter (§567.31).

The ASF regulations devote three pages to anesthesia protocols alone. They not only spell out the equipment a facility must have, but also require that the equipment actually be used to monitor patients under anesthesia. "At a minimum," 28 Pa. Code §555.33(6) requires:

Section VI: How Did This Go On So Long?

 (i) The use of oxygen saturation by pulse oximetry.
 (ii) The use of End Tidal CO [2] monitoring during endotracheal anesthesia.
 (iii) The use of EKG monitoring.
 (iv) The use of blood pressure monitoring.

And §555.33(5) requires:

 (5) A patient receiving anesthesia shall have an anesthetic record maintained. This shall include a record of vital signs and all events taking place during the induction of, maintenance of and emergence from anesthesia, including the dosage and duration of anesthetic agents, other drugs and intravenous fluids.

These and other ASF regulations set out basic, minimum standards of care that any patient having a surgical procedure should expect to receive when anesthesia is involved. They are the standards that DOH came up with when charged by the legislature to assure safe, adequate, and efficient facilities and services and to promote the health, safety, and adequate care of patients.

The law exists. The regulations are clear. Why does DOH not apply or enforce these standards for abortion facilities?

The state Department of Health inexplicably allows abortion clinics, alone, to go unmonitored.

The Grand Jury asked several DOH employees, attorneys as well as those charged with overseeing abortion facilities, why the department does not treat abortion clinics as ASFs when the language of the Health Care Facilities Acts is so clear. Their unsatisfactory answers left us bewildered.

The two attorneys closest to the issue—Senior Counsel Kenneth Brody, who advises the Division of Home Health, which currently oversees abortion clinics; and Senior Counsel James Steele, who advises the division that oversees ambulatory surgical facilities—both testified that they believe that abortion clinics such as Gosnell's fit within the law's definition of an ambulatory surgical facility. Their boss, Chief Counsel Christine Dutton, refused to acknowledge that the ASF definition would cover abortion clinics, but could not explain why it did not. She said she "would have to research that to determine if that were the case."

Dutton, however, before becoming chief counsel, was assigned to advise the DOH division that licenses ambulatory surgical facilities. As such, she had to be very familiar with what constitutes an ambulatory surgical facility. In fact, she was senior counsel to the division when DOH was dealing with the aftermath of the death, in 2001, of a 19-year-old girl following liposuction performed in a plastic surgeon's office. When the girl's parents complained to DOH, an immediate investigation revealed that the office of the surgeon, Dr. Richard Glunk, should have been licensed as an ASF, but was not.

As a result of the Glunk case, DOH initiated a campaign to encourage compliance with ASF licensure requirements. Chief Counsel Dutton would have been in the middle of that effort in 2002 when she was senior counsel. Yet she testified that she never considered treating abortion clinics—facilities where, according to the abortion regulations, "ambulatory gynecological surgery" is performed—as ambulatory surgical facilities.

It was clear to us after hearing these witnesses testify that the decisions not to inspect abortion clinics or to license them as ASFs

Section VI: How Did This Go On So Long?

were not based on any serious interpretation of statutes or legal research. These lawyers were simply twisting and reinterpreting the law to explain policy decisions that changed with administrations, even though the laws did not. Dutton admitted in her testimony that the decision not to inspect was a policy decision, not one grounded in the law:

> Q: Does it surprise you to know that some of the reasons cited for the failure to go out and do these inspections is that they believed that they didn't have the legal authority to do so?
> A: That would surprise me, yes. ... To me, I would believe that they didn't go out to do them because some policy had been set in the department at some point in time in the past that we were not going to do regular inspections of abortion facilities.

Dutton's failure to recognize and treat abortion clinics as ASFs, and her silence as DOH shirked its duty to protect women and infants at abortion clinics, reflect a blatant refusal to enforce the law.

The DOH attorneys offered multiple explanations to attempt to justify why the department does not license abortion clinics in the same manner as any other ASF. None of their explanations comports with the law or with common sense.

Two of their "justifications" are barely worth comment. One lawyer told us that there is always "push-back" from doctors who do not want to be licensed as ASFs. Not only is this argument irrelevant to any legal analysis, it is unpersuasive. We learned that there are fewer than 30 abortion providers in the entire state. These doctors should not be able to exert that much push-back. Moreover, the legitimate abortion providers who testified before the Grand Jury told us that they already comply with standards as demanding as those for ASFs. Abortion rights advocates told us the same thing—that licensing abortion clinics as ASFs would not be burdensome because clinics that are members of NAF, or associated with Planned Parenthood, already comply with the highest standards of care.

A second reason proffered by DOH attorneys for not licensing abortion clinics—that abortion is "controversial"—is just insulting. Abortion is a legal medical procedure. Any controversy surrounding the issue should not affect how the law is enforced or whether the Department of Health protects the safety of women seeking health care.

Finally, Dutton, Brody, and Steele asserted that a provision of the abortion regulations—one that gives DOH the authority to approve facilities as abortion providers—somehow precludes any other health care law from applying to abortion clinics. The provision of the abortion regulations that DOH relies on to exempt abortion clinics from the requirements of the Health Care Facilities Act reads:

> Facility approval
> **(a) Every medical facility which performs abortions within this Commonwealth shall be approved by the Department.**
> (b) All medical facilities except hospitals may become approved facilities upon submission of an application to the Department from a person authorized to represent such facility and, at the discretion of the Department, satisfactory completion of an onsite survey.
> (c) Every hospital licensed or approved by the Department, which has filed with the Department the Abortion Facility Registration form, and which meets the standards set forth in this title, will be deemed to be an approved facility by virtue of its hospital license or approval ...
> (d) Notwithstanding this section, facility approval for performance of abortions may be revoked if this subchapter is not adhered to.
> —28 Pa. Code § 29.43 *(emphasis added).*

Section VI: How Did This Go On So Long?

On its face, this explanation is nonsensical. The cited provision requires not only clinics, but also hospitals, to obtain DOH approval before abortions can be performed. This added approval requirement certainly does not exempt hospitals from all other applicable licensing requirements. Indeed section (c) assumes and refers to the licensing of the hospitals. This provision can no more remove abortion facilities from the regulations covering ASFs than it can remove DOH oversight responsibilities for hospitals.

If one were to accept DOH's interpretation of its duties with respect to overseeing the quality of care in abortion facilities, those duties would be limited to granting or denying approval based on a single piece of paper—the "Abortion Facility Registration Form," which contains the name and mailing address of a facility and a couple of check marks. Brody said that it is DOH practice to conduct an on-site survey of facilities before granting approval, but acknowledged that even that feeble effort at oversight is discretionary under the regulations. Then, once the initial approval is given, DOH—according to the rules that it wrote and interprets—never has to do anything else to monitor what happens in the abortion clinic.

Dutton, the chief counsel, testified that DOH's only role with respect to abortion clinics is to collect certain reports from them:

> Q: So which department of the Commonwealth of Pennsylvania is responsible for enforcing the Abortion Control Act?
> A: Primarily the Department of State and the District Attorney's Office and other law enforcement.
> Q: What about the Department of Health?
> A: We have a role in enforcing it if certain reports are not filed and we become aware of the fact that that they're not filed.
> Q: And that's it?
> A: Uh-huh.

Q: So it's just a paper thing?

* * *

A: Yes...When you read the act, that is what it unfortunately says.

The DOH attorneys all complained similarly about how little authority the Abortion Control Act, and the accompanying regulations that DOH wrote, gives to the department to inspect, license, or monitor abortion clinics. But it is these lawyers who are responsible for allowing their department to ignore the plain language of the Health Care Facilities Act.

That act gives DOH all the power it needs to assure safe abortion clinics. Yet, instead of applying the law as it is written, and counseling DOH to license abortion clinics as ASFs, these lawyers have used illogical arguments to evade the Health Care Facilities Act. They have insisted that a criminal statute, the Abortion Control Act, provides DOH's only authority to protect the health and safety of women and premature infants aborted alive within abortion clinics. Essentially, they have tied their own hands and now complain that they are powerless.

The Secretary of Health has, since the February 2010 raid, ordered the department to start inspecting abortion clinics regularly. Nevertheless, the larger point remains: Women who go to abortion clinics and premature babies born alive at them deserve the same DOH protection as patients at other health care facilities. Abortion is legal, and political agendas should not influence how DOH carries out its responsibility to ensure the health and safety of medical patients at all facilities.

Section VI: How Did This Go On So Long?

Pennsylvania's abortion regulations, written by the Department of Health, are totally inadequate to protect the health and safety of women at abortion clinics.

The abhorrent conditions and practices inside Gosnell's clinic are directly attributable to the Pennsylvania Health Department's refusal to treat abortion clinics as ambulatory surgical facilities.

But even if DOH's position with respect to whether abortion clinics are ASFs were reasonable—which it is not—that interpretation would not excuse the department's abdication of its duty to afford women who go to these clinics the same types of safeguards that plastic surgery patients receive. This is because—whether a facility is called an ambulatory surgical facility, a hospital, or a freestanding abortion clinic—the legislature with the Abortion Control Act has charged DOH with the duty to write and enforce regulations that protect the health and safety of women undergoing abortion procedures.

DOH's position is that one subsection of the abortion regulations—28 Pa. Code §29.33—contains all of the rules necessary to ensure that women will be protected. But patients at any other ASF are protected by 30 pages of rules and regulations. 28 Pa. Code §§ 51.1 et seq. Gosnell's clinic, which operated for decades with impunity, constitutes more than sufficient proof that one subsection of regulations, without monitoring, licensing, or inspections, offers inadequate protection.

Given that DOH is capable of writing and enforcing regulations that are comprehensive and enforceable, such as those governing ASFs, we question whether DOH officials have even tried over the decades to protect women who go to clinics for abortion procedures.

The ASF regulations, for example, require that patients undergoing every other kind of ambulatory surgery be monitored with high-tech equipment while under anesthesia. The abortion regulations, on the other hand, require that the facility have the high-tech equipment, but do not require that it be used (28 Pa. Code § 29.33(1) and (2)). There is not a single provision in the abortion regulations relating to infection control (nothing to prohibit Gosnell from eating cereal while doing procedures, for example, or from reusing single-use instruments, or from allowing sick, flea-infested cats in the procedure rooms), whereas several pages of rules cover infection control at ASFs.

Most importantly, the abortion regulations include no requirement for DOH ever to inspect or monitor abortion providers. The Grand Jury was astonished to discover that abortion clinics in Pennsylvania, unlike any other health care facility, are apparently supposed to operate on the honor system.

Many abortion clinics deliver quality care because that is their mission. But what if a particular doctor's mission is to maximize profits by cutting corners? He may hire unqualified staff, reuse instruments, administer expired drugs, tolerate unsanitary facilities, and use obsolete and broken equipment—until one or more of his patients dies. Then, after law enforcement gets involved, DOH might take action.

This is what happened in Gosnell's case. It is not a workable system for regulating health care facilities that perform one of the most common surgical procedures, or for assuring safe medical care for the women of Pennsylvania.

Section VI: How Did This Go On So Long?

The laws and regulations designed to protect viable late-term fetuses and infants aborted alive can only be effective with Department of Health oversight.

In contrast to the provisions of the abortion regulations that are supposed to protect women's health at abortion facilities, those designed to protect late-term fetuses and infants born alive should have been sufficient to accomplish that purpose. Late-term fetuses, because of their advanced gestation and likely viability, are accorded certain legal rights. Pennsylvania's Abortion Control Act strictly prohibits abortions "when the gestational age of the unborn child is 24 or more weeks." The only significant exception is to prevent the pregnant woman's death or the "substantial and irreversible impairment of a major bodily function of the woman." 18 Pa.C.S. §3211(b)(1).

Pennsylvania law also requires medical practitioners to resuscitate babies that are born alive. The Abortion Control Act states: "All physicians and licensed medical personnel attending a child who is born alive during the course of an abortion or premature delivery, or after being carried to term, shall provide such child that type and degree of care and treatment which, in the good faith judgment of the physician, is commonly and customarily provided to any other person under similar conditions and circumstances." 18 Pa.C.S. §3212(b).

Gosnell routinely performed abortions beyond the 24-week limit. He was ruthless in severing the spinal cords of viable babies outside their mothers' wombs. This conduct clearly constitutes prosecutable criminal behavior. In order for district attorneys to be able to prosecute, however, the crimes must first be detected. This is DOH's job—to ensure that violations of Pennsylvania health care laws are detected. Its inspectors must review files as part of their inspections. They must look at ultrasound tests and pathology reports on second-trimester fetuses. They must make sure that informed and parental consent forms have been signed and that abortions have been reported to DOH.

Instead, Pennsylvania officials have created what amounts to an honor system, a system conspicuously lacking in regulatory oversight or enforcement. If DOH abdicates its responsibility to monitor and inspect abortion clinics, the protections that the Abortion Control Act provides to prematurely born infants and unborn post-24-week fetuses become meaningless to those willing to break the law. The wrongful death of a viable fetus is deemed a homicide. DOH must ensure that the law is applied to protect those least able to protect themselves.

Assuring safety at abortion clinics has been a low priority for Pennsylvania's Department of Health for decades.

No one from DOH was able to tell us who decided to exclude abortion clinics from meaningful oversight that would protect patient safety, or why such a decision was made. Nor did the jurors get a satisfactory answer as to why abortion clinics are under DOH's Division of Home Health (which oversees agencies that provide care in people's houses), rather than the more appropriate Division of Acute and Ambulatory Care. Or why, on DOH's website, even on the page that lists the types of facilities overseen by the Division of Home Health, abortion clinics are not even mentioned.

The website states:

Section VI: How Did This Go On So Long?

The Division of Home Health establishes and enforces quality care and safety standards for Health Care Facilities in Pennsylvania. We conduct state licensure, Medicare certification, and complaint investigations for the following health care providers:

- Birth Centers
- Comprehensive Outpatient Rehabilitation Facilities (CORFs)
- Home Health Agencies
- Home Care Agencies/Home Care Registries Hospice Agencies
- Kidney Dialysis Centers - End State Renal Disease Centers (ESRD)
- Outpatient Physical/Speech/Occupational Therapy Clinics Rural Health Clinics

In addition to demonstrating the low priority that DOH has assigned to patient care in abortion clinics, the invisibility of abortion facilities on the website makes it next to impossible for clients or others who want to make complaints to do so. The website publishes phone numbers to call for various types of complaints: the Division of Acute and Ambulatory Care for ambulatory surgical facilities, the Division of Home Health's "hotline" for home health agencies, hospices, and End State Renal Disease facilities. There is no mention, however, that DOH even oversees abortion facilities, or that it accepts complaints about them.

In light of this, the policy that DOH would inspect facilities only in response to complaints (leaving aside that even this policy was not followed) goes beyond bad management. It appears to reflect purposeful neglect. It raises the question—as does the failure to act on the serious complaints against Gosnell—whether DOH ever intended to exercise its responsibility to protect the health and safety of women seeking abortions in Pennsylvania.

BLACKOUT: The Official GOSNELL Grand Jury Report

No matter why or when or by whom the decision not to license or monitor abortion facilities was made, the practice has continued for roughly two decades and through several administrations. We have no idea how many facilities like Gosnell's have remained out of sight, out of mind of DOH for decades—since they were first "approved."

The only thing DOH seems to have consistently concerned itself with during this time is collecting reports that the Abortion Control Act requires abortion providers to file with the department and the department, in turn, to report to the Legislature—forms for every abortion performed and quarterly reports stating how many first, second, and third trimester abortions the facility performed. This responsibility is clearly meaningless, since providers' information is not verified. Gosnell simply made up the information, and DOH never audited or checked the reports. As long as the department received some paperwork, that apparently was sufficient.

The forms that Gosnell filed between 2000 and 2010—the ones DOH then relied on to compile its reports to the Legislature—recorded only one second-trimester abortion and no complications. His false entries, alone, make DOH's reports to the Legislature worthless. Instead of using its manpower to inspect facilities and protect women's health, DOH has devoted its resources to collecting and publishing inaccurate and meaningless data—data that mislead the legislature and the public.

> **State Department of Health inspectors refused to share information with law enforcement.**

Darlene Augustine testified that she was instructed by senior attorneys for DOH, Kenneth Brody and James Steele, that she

Section VI: How Did This Go On So Long?

should not reveal anything about Karnamaya Mongar's death to law enforcement when she accompanied them on the raid in February 2010. The lawyers told her that if she were asked about it, she should refer the agents to legal counsel. The reason the attorneys gave for their instruction was that information received by the department pursuant to the MCARE law is strictly confidential.

The MCARE law does provide some degree of confidentiality for materials obtained by DOH solely for the purpose of complying with MCARE's reporting requirement:

> § 1303.311. Confidentiality and compliance
> (a) PREPARED MATERIALS.-- Any documents, materials or information solely prepared or created for the purpose of compliance with section 310(b) or of reporting under section 304(a)(5) or (b), 306(a)(2) or (3), 307(b)(3), 308(a), 309(4), 310(b)(5) or 313 which arise out of matters reviewed by the patient safety committee pursuant to section 310(b) or the governing board of a medical facility pursuant to section 310(b) are confidential and shall not be discoverable or admissible as evidence in any civil or administrative action or proceeding. Any documents, materials, records or information that would otherwise be available from original sources shall not be construed as immune from discovery or use in any civil or administrative action or proceeding merely because they were presented to the patient safety committee or governing board of a medical facility.

The act does not, however, preclude disclosures of information necessary for criminal prosecutions. There are several reasons that this provision should not have prevented Darlene Augustine from sharing information about Karnamaya Mongar's death with law enforcement. First, two laws required that Gosnell inform DOH of Mongar's death—not only the MCARE Act, but also the Abortion

Control Act. Second, according to DOH witnesses, Gosnell had not complied properly with the MCARE reporting requirement when the raid took place. Third, the clear purpose of this provision is to preclude the use of self-reported materials against the reporter in malpractice cases. Nothing in the language prohibits sharing information on a death with law enforcement, even if it had come in solely as a report under MCARE.

Had DOH investigated Mrs. Mongar's death, as it should have—and had it discovered, as it would have, that an unlicensed employee had administered the fatal anesthesia—it would have been incumbent on the department to report these criminal circumstances. Someone should have shared what DOH had learned about Mrs. Mongar's death with law enforcement agents conducting a search of the facility.

There could be many similar situations in which DOH would learn information that could be crucial to law enforcement—where crimes might go undetected without DOH's cooperation. To the extent DOH believes that the MCARE Act precludes sharing information in criminal investigations, that situation needs to be addressed.

PENNSYLVANIA'S DEPARTMENT OF STATE NEGLECTED ITS DUTY TO DISCIPLINE A DOCTOR ENGAGED IN UNPROFESSIONAL CONDUCT.

The Department of Health was not the only state agency that could and should have shut down Gosnell decades ago. The State Board of Medicine (the Board) is one of 29 boards overseen by the Department of State's Bureau of Professional and Occupational Affairs. The Board's attorneys had ample notice of Gosnell's illegal and reckless abortion practices, and of the damage he had done to patients. Eight

Section VI: How Did This Go On So Long?

years before Karnamaya Mongar died, a former Gosnell employee told the Department of State about the illegal practice that resulted in Mrs. Mongar's death: Gosnell had unlicensed workers anesthetizing patients when he was not at the clinic. Yet, despite receiving that report and several other serious complaints over the years, the Board took no action to suspend or revoke his license.

Attorneys for Pennsylvania's Department of State disregarded notices that numerous patients of Gosnell were hospitalized—infected, with fetal remains still inside them; and with perforated uteruses, cervixes, and bowels. Incredibly, in 2004, Department of State attorneys closed—without investigation—a case reported to the Board involving the death of 22-year-old Semika Shaw.

Between 2002 and 2009, Board of Medicine attorneys reviewed five cases involving malpractice and other complaints against Gosnell. (The Grand Jury also received records of three older complaints—from 1983, 1990, and 1992—one of which resulted in a reprimand.) None of the assigned attorneys, or their supervisors, suggested that the Board take action against the deviant doctor. In fact, despite serious allegations, three of the cases were closed without any investigation. The other two were investigated and then closed—without any action being taken.

> **Pennsylvania Department of State attorneys failed to investigate a 22-year-old patient's death caused by Gosnell's recklessness.**

In all this inaction, one failure to investigate stands out. On October 9, 2002, the Professional Underwriters Liability Insurance Company reported to the State Board of Medicine that it had paid a $400,000 settlement to the family of Semika Shaw, the 22-year-old mother of two who died following an abortion procedure at Gosnell's clinic in March 2000. (In January 2003, the Pennsylvania Medical Professional Liability Catastrophe Loss Fund reported to the Department of State that it had paid an additional $500,000 toward a $900,000 award to the family.) The October 9 report is logged in as "received" by the Department of State's "Complaints Office" on December 6, 2002. The file turned over to the Grand Jury shows no further activity until over a year later — January 2, 2004 — when a one-page printout of Gosnell's license information is stamped "received" by the complaints office.

The next action recorded in the file is a one-paragraph "Prosecution Evaluation," dated April 29, 2004, in which Mark Greenwald, a prosecuting attorney for the Board of Medicine purportedly summarizes the case and concludes: "Prosecution not Warranted." Here is the paragraph:

> **Brief Factual Summary:** The file was opened as a result of a Medical Malpractice Payment Report. The underlying malpractice case involved the death of a 22 year old female following the termination of her 5th pregnancy. Following a seemingly routine procedure on 3/1/02, the patient was taken to the ER at the University of Pennsylvania with complaints of pain and heavy bleeding. The patient underwent surgery but the surgeon was unable to locate any perforation and the patient died from infection and sepsis. Although the incident is tragic, especially in light of the age of the patient, the risk was inherent with the procedure performed by Respondent [Gosnell] and administrative action against respondent's license is not warranted.
>
> **RECOMMENDATION:** Z-02, Prosecution not Warranted

Section VI: How Did This Go On So Long?

In fact, all the information in this single paragraph is taken entirely—including incorrect dates—from the insurance company's original paragraph-long report sent to the Board in October 2002. And yet, while Greenwald included the irrelevant, but pointed, assertion that this was the patient's fifth pregnancy that was being terminated, the Department of State prosecutor omitted from his summary the most important information that the insurance company had provided: "Autopsy report indicated perforation of cervix into uterus. Heirs alleged our insured improperly performed the termination procedure and failed to diagnose post-op uterine perforation resulting in sepsis and death."

Greenwald's supervisor, Charles J. Hartwell, the Senior Prosecutor-in-Charge at the Department of State's Bureau of Professional and Occupational Affairs, purportedly reviewed Greenwald's "evaluation" and approved it on May 14, 2004. Hartwell did so, ostensibly, knowing nothing beyond the bare facts that Semika Shaw died from infection and sepsis two days after Gosnell perforated her uterus and cervix during an abortion procedure. (Greenwald also omitted from his evaluation that the insurance carrier had settled the case for $900,000, the majority of which had to be disbursed by a Pennsylvania catastrophic expense fund.)

Aside from the absence of facts to support the prosecutors' recommendation, logic, too, is missing. Abortion in the hands of decent, caring doctors is an extremely safe procedure for patients. Even if it were not, that does not mean that the death in this case was not actionable by the state. If prosecutors are going to forgo investigations every time someone dies during a medical procedure, with the excuse that death is always a possible risk with any kind of surgery, there is no point in pretending that they are investigating and prosecuting cases against doctors.

> **Before Department of State prosecutors decided not to investigate the 22-year-old patient's death, they had been told of Gosnell's many illegal practices.**

What makes these prosecutors' inaction even more astonishing is that they did know more than the bare facts included in the Board attorney's evaluation of the case. On the same day in 2004 that they decided not to do anything about Semika Shaw's death, these same two prosecutors also closed the investigation into the complaint brought to the Department of State more than two years earlier by Marcella Stanley Choung. That was the complaint that had alerted the Board of Medicine—eight years before Karnamaya Mongar died—to almost all of the same violations revealed by this Grand Jury's investigation.

In December 2001, Marcella Stanley Choung had filed a detailed, written complaint with the Pennsylvania Department of State. Although she wanted to remain anonymous, she provided her name and her phone number, and participated in a follow-up interview on March 4, 2002. She informed the department investigator that Gosnell was using unlicensed workers (including herself) to give IV anesthesia to patients when he was not at the clinic; that his facility was filthy; that two sick, flea-infested cats roamed freely in the procedure rooms, vomiting throughout; that Gosnell ate in the procedure rooms; that the autoclave used to sterilize instruments was broken; that he reused single-use curettes; that there were no licensed nurses at the facility when IV anesthesia was administered;

Section VI: How Did This Go On So Long?

that Gosnell allowed one patient to use her cousin's insurance card to pay for an abortion; that Gosnell performed abortions on "underage children" against their will if their mothers asked him to; and that he performed other abortions without consent forms.

Choung told the Department of State investigator that she thought a second-trimester patient had died at a hospital after Gosnell performed an abortion on her. And she said that she had seen patient files in which he prescribed 90 Percocet tablets (a narcotic combining oxycodone and acetaminophen) for a patient one week and then, again, 90 more tablets the next week. She gave very detailed information about the files, what she saw, and when. She provided the name of at least one patient, and suggested that the investigator look at her file. Choung wrote that any of the other clinic workers—except one named Jonathan—would be willing to confirm her information.

But the investigator with the Department of State did not question any of the other unlicensed workers. And the Board of Medicine did not use its subpoena power to obtain files to substantiate Choung's complaint. No one even asked to see the facility or its files. The investigation consisted of three interviews—one with Gosnell; one by telephone with another doctor, Dr. Warren Taylor, who said he performed abortions at the clinic in 2001; and one with a pharmacist two blocks from the clinic on Lancaster Avenue.

Dr. Taylor confirmed some of what Choung said. He said that he remembered one case where he had refused to perform a procedure on an underage girl, but that he did not know if Gosnell had then done it. He claimed to know nothing more. The pharmacist said he had not detected a pattern of Gosnell over-prescribing narcotics.

(However, by the time an investigation was finally conducted in 2010, that pharmacy had stopped honoring Gosnell's prescriptions.)

Gosnell, according to the investigator's report, did not directly contradict many of Choung's allegations, but made excuses instead. He also told outright lies that could easily have been disproved. He said the clinic was licensed as a surgical facility — which it was not and is not. This fact could have been confirmed by a simple call to the Department of Health, or by an internet search. Gosnell claimed that he did not use Schedule II controlled substances for anesthesia, even though he did.

Gosnell asserted that he always administered the anesthesia, something any of the clinic workers would have refuted. He acknowledged that he let his patients choose their own anesthesia from mixes entitled "heavy," "twilight sleep," and "custom sleep" — names that should have been a tip-off that someone at the clinic was heavily sedating patients. Gosnell declined to provide a written response to Choung's allegations.

Still, no one at the Department of State probed further to see if one of Choung's most serious contentions — that unlicensed employees were administering the anesthesia with no medical professional present — was true. The investigator did not request to see any files. His notes indicate that he "visited the area of Women's Medical Society," but there is no indication that he asked to go in. He conducted his interview of Gosnell at a regional office in King of Prussia rather than at the doctor's office where he could have confirmed many of Choung's allegations first hand.

Even with this superficial inquiry, the investigator recommended further action. He concluded his report by suggesting that the

Section VI: How Did This Go On So Long?

Department of Health be notified of Choung's complaint, which, he wrote, "alleges health issues at Women's Medical Society that may be detrimental to staff and the public." The investigator made it clear that he had not notified the Department of Health when he submitted his report. His investigation was completed by August 26, 2002.

According to the files turned over to the Grand Jury by the Department of State, no further action was taken until April 29, 2004 — nearly two years later — when Greenwald, the same prosecuting attorney who recommended against following up on Semika Shaw's death, also recommended closing the case on Choung's allegations. With serious allegations that Gosnell was allowing unlicensed workers to administer IV anesthesia, that he was over-prescribing Percocet, and that he was violating many provisions of the Abortion Control Act, Greenwald did not subpoena any records from the clinic. He did not send the investigator back to talk to the other unlicensed workers, as Choung had recommended. He simply concluded that the allegations had not been confirmed and recommended no prosecution. And Hartwell, the Senior Prosecutor-in-Charge, agreed.

Even though the alleged violations were ones that the Department of State was charged with enforcing, Greenwald seconded, in 2004, the recommendation that the investigator had made in 2002 — to send the case off to the Department of Health for "review and investigation." Records subpoenaed by the Grand Jury from both the Department of State and the Department of Health fail to show that even this shirking of responsibility — the simple act of handing off of the case to someone else — was ever carried out.

The Department of State had supposedly been investigating Marcella Choung's alarming allegations since December 2001 —

long before the department and the Board of Medicine received the report of Semika Shaw's death as a result of an abortion procedure at Gosnell's' clinic. It is incomprehensible to us how state officials could decide not to investigate the 22-year-old's death after having heard Choung's complaints. Especially since an insurance carrier and the State of Pennsylvania's catastrophic loss fund had already agreed to settle with Ms. Shaw's heirs for nearly a million dollars.

There can be no claim of a communication gap or of a case simply falling through the cracks: A single Board of Medicine prosecutor and his supervisor disposed of both the Choung allegations and the Shaw case at the same time. The Board has the authority to impose disciplinary sanctions or take other corrective measures if it finds that a doctor has practiced negligently. 40 P.S. §905. If nothing else, the Board prosecutors should have contacted the insurance company to find out what its investigation had revealed that prompted it to settle the malpractice suit in the Shaw case.

Even without a minimal effort at investigation, there was possibly one prosecutable violation apparent from the day the insurance carrier reported its settlement payment. Gosnell had not reported the Shaw civil suit to the Department of State. Depending on when the suit was filed, Pennsylvania's MCARE (Medical Care Availability and Reduction of Error) Act would have required him to report any malpractice action to the Board of Medicine within 60 days of the filing. The Board of Medicine has the authority to fine doctors up to $10,000 for this violation.

With a call to the Department of Health, the Board's attorneys could have known immediately of at least one other prosecutable offense: Gosnell violated the Abortion Control Act by not reporting

Section VI: How Did This Go On So Long?

Ms. Shaw's death to the Department of Health. For this offense, the Board of Medicine had the authority to suspend or revoke Gosnell's license. The state prosecutors, however, clearly had no interest in investigating Gosnell, much less holding him accountable for the crime spree that he called a medical practice.

Other Department of State prosecutors also failed to act against Gosnell.

Greenwald and Hartwell were not the only state Board of Medicine attorneys who failed to take appropriate action against Gosnell. In September 2005, a plaintiff's attorney sent a copy of a malpractice complaint he had filed against Gosnell to the Department of State. The case involved a patient we will call "Alice." She had suffered a seizure after Gosnell administered anesthesia to her in a procedure room as he prepared to perform an abortion in March 2005. Alice had notified clinic staff that she was undergoing methadone treatment and that she had received her daily methadone dose before the procedure. The lawsuit alleged that, despite this warning, Gosnell gave her a medication that was clearly contraindicated for people on methadone, triggering a seizure.

According to the complaint, Alice told Gosnell to stop the medication when she started to have a reaction, but Gosnell ignored her and continued the IV injection. Alice began to convulse and fell off of the procedure table, striking her head. A companion who had accompanied Alice to the clinic was summoned to the procedure room to assist. He found the patient naked and convulsing on the floor and asked that someone call 911.

BLACKOUT: The Official GOSNELL Grand Jury Report

When Gosnell denied his request, the companion attempted to leave the clinic to summon help. The complaint alleges that the doors were locked and the staff refused to let him out. As a result, Alice convulsed for an hour while Gosnell and the staff refused to allow her companion to leave the clinic to get help. Finally, Gosnell permitted the companion to go get some methadone to administer. The additional methadone stopped the convulsions.

On May 4, 2006, David Grubb, another prosecuting attorney for the Board of Medicine, recommended closing the file without any investigation or prosecution. Grubb closed the case without interviewing Alice, her companion, Gosnell, or any of his staff members. Grubb apparently ignored altogether a suggestion contained in the plaintiff's attorney's letter that Gosnell was not insured at the time of the procedure—a clear violation of law. The plaintiff's attorney pointed out that Gosnell had answered the complaint himself, without benefit of a lawyer, which was not customary if the doctor had insurance. Grubb's supervisor, Senior Prosecutor-in-Charge Andrew Kramer, approved of closing the case without investigation on May 16, 2006.

On June 9, 2006, Grubb wrote to Gosnell informing him that the Department of State had decided that no further investigation was warranted. The prosecutor thanked Gosnell "for forwarding a copy of the complaint" to the department, even though the only copy of the complaint in the file had been provided by the plaintiff's attorney. The documents turned over to the Grand Jury suggest that Gosnell once again violated the MCARE law by failing to report Alice's lawsuit. But, again, the prosecuting attorneys with the Board of Medicine either did not notice or did not care.

Section VI: How Did This Go On So Long?

Aside from the obvious reporting violation, had Grubb simply checked to see if Gosnell was insured in March 2005, he would have found out that he was not. Grubb would also have discovered that a colleague at the Bureau of Professional and Occupational Affairs, Prosecuting Attorney William Newport, had been handling another complaint about Gosnell's lack of insurance coverage. On August 2, 2005, a "Compliance Coordinator" for the MCARE Fund had notified the Department of State that Gosnell was not in compliance with the MCARE law's requirement that doctors carry liability insurance. On September 28, 2005, and again on July 5, 2006, Prosecuting Attorney Newport wrote to Gosnell, requesting that the doctor respond to the complaint that he was non-compliant with MCARE's liability insurance requirements.

On July 20, 2006, Gosnell's insurance agent sent a response to a Department of State paralegal, asserting that Gosnell was covered from 1998 through 2003. For the next two years, the paralegal, at Newport's request, kept checking with various compliance officers at the MCARE Fund to ascertain whether Gosnell was compliant. The answer was always no. Nevertheless, on September 5, 2008, the paralegal followed Newport's instructions and recommended closing the file. The file was closed without any meaningful investigation.

Had Newport conducted a real investigation, or subpoenaed documents, he would have discovered what Sherilyn Gillespie, the Department of State investigator, found out in 2010 — that Gosnell was not insured at all between July 15, 2004, and April 18, 2005. Thus, had either of two Board of Medicine prosecutors investigated the complaint made by Alice's attorney, they would have discovered Gosnell's blatant violation of the MCARE law. They would have learned, as Gillespie did in May 2010, that Gosnell was operating without insurance when Alice had gone to him for an abortion in March 2005, and that Gosnell had told his insurance agent that he was practicing only in Delaware at the time Alice had her seizure at his clinic.

Unfortunately, like the other prosecuting attorneys working for the Department of State's Board of Medicine, neither Grubb nor Newport investigated or resolved the complaints that continued to pile up against Gosnell.

> **In 2009, another Department of State prosecutor closed—without any investigation—a complaint that Gosnell acted recklessly in perforating another woman's uterus, cervix, and bowel.**

When Gosnell applied to renew his medical license in December 2008, he indicated, as he was required to, that a civil malpractice lawsuit had been filed against him in November 2008. He had not sent a copy of the complaint to the Board of Medicine, as required by MCARE, but he eventually did so after it was requested.

The lawsuit was brought by Dana Haynes, who had gone to Gosnell for an abortion on November 11, 2006. The complaint alleged that Gosnell had performed the abortion in a reckless manner, tearing Haynes's cervix, uterus, and bowel. It asserted that after performing the botched abortion, Gosnell failed to call an ambulance and, instead, kept her waiting at the clinic for four hours, bleeding and in severe pain. Haynes accused Gosnell of placing her life in jeopardy in order to cover up his negligence.

The complaint stated that Haynes bled extensively for a long time and had to be hospitalized. At the hospital, doctors discovered

Section VI: How Did This Go On So Long?

that Gosnell had not completed the abortion and had left fetal parts inside Haynes. Her injuries required extensive surgery.

On April 20, 2009, a prosecuting attorney for the Department of State, Juan Ruiz, recommended closing the file without "intensive review"—in fact, without reviewing anything but the complaint. With no other facts, and no attempt to determine any other facts, Ruiz concluded: "The important allegation is that referenced above [Plaintiff contends she suffered permanent injuries due to respondent lacerating her small intestine during an abortion.]. Barring a pattern of conduct—which does not exist in this case—this would be, at most, considered simple negligence or incompetence, as this would be a case of surgical site injury."

Ruiz testified before the Grand Jury. He insisted that "everything of substance gets investigated." Yet he ordered no investigation of Dana Haynes's complaint. No one even talked to Ms. Haynes—until investigator Gillespie did after the February 2010 raid. Ruiz wrote that no "pattern of conduct" existed in this case. But how could he possibly know that? He did not look at Gosnell's history. A simple database search conducted by the evaluator from the National Abortion Federation, before she visited the clinic in December 2009, showed that at least five women before Haynes had successfully sued Gosnell for perforating their uteruses. Private settlements do not show up on the database, so there could be many more. Gosnell, or his insurers, had paid over $1.7 million to these women or their families. One, Semika Shaw, had died from her injuries—as Ruiz should have been aware.

Ruiz claimed that he had no way to find this information. If that is true, it is appalling. The database used by the abortion federation's evaluator—the National Practitioner Data Bank (NPDB)—is designed for use by state boards of medicine to assist them in quickly and easily identifying and disciplining medical providers who engage in unprofessional behavior. The database was established by the U.S. Congress and is administered by the U.S. Department of Health and Human Services. It lists the names of complainants, their allegations, and the amount of the settlements. The basis for Ruiz's decision—that Gosnell had no history of perforating uteruses—would have been quickly dispelled had he simply checked the NPDB's information.

Even if the prosecuting attorney did not have access to the NPDB database, Ruiz should have been alarmed by the information in the Department of State's own records. Semika Shaw had died from the same injuries alleged by Ms. Haynes. Marcella Choung, who had no monetary interest, had spelled out essentially all of Gosnell's criminal practices to the department. The woman we have referred to as Alice and her companion had accused Gosnell of locking the companion in the clinic to prevent him from getting medical help for Alice. Accordingly, when Ms. Haynes alleged that the doctor did not summon help for her, but left her for four hours, bleeding and in pain, that should have warranted at least a phone call to Ms. Haynes.

Yet Ruiz, apparently, did not even read the complaint carefully. He claimed before the Grand Jury that no one investigated the allegation that rescue was not called for four hours because it was not contained in the legal filing in Ms. Haynes's medical malpractice suit. In fact, it was. The complaint stated:

Section VI: How Did This Go On So Long?

22. The negligence and gross negligence, recklessness and carelessness of Defendant Gosnell, included, but is not limited to:

* * *

(j) Allowing the patient to wait four (4) hours in severe pain and bleeding before calling an ambulance to take the plaintiff to receive proper care for the injury caused to her;

(k) Placing plaintiff's life in jeopardy in order to cover up his own negligence; ...

Prosecuting Attorney Ruiz testified that it was unfortunate that Haynes's attorney "did not lay out all of the facts in that complaint." Even leaving aside the erroneous claim that the complaint did not include an allegation about failing to call an ambulance in a timely fashion, the prosecutor's testimony points out a serious flaw in the Department of State's procedures. The department's disciplinary responsibilities should not depend on the quality of a plaintiff's representation. At least some independent fact-finding should take place. At a minimum, the complainant should be interviewed.

Had the prosecutor asked an investigator to call Ms. Haynes, he would have learned what inspector Gillespie did a few months later — that in Ms. Haynes's case, Gosnell had locked her family members out of the clinic, preventing them from discovering that she was bleeding profusely after a bungled procedure and from summoning help. He would also have learned that Gosnell was violating the Abortion Control Act.

When interviewed, Ms. Haynes, age 38, told Gillespie that she was nearly 17 weeks pregnant when Gosnell performed a two-day, second-trimester abortion. Gosnell inserted laminaria on November

10, 2006, and she returned the next day for the procedure. She said that no one counseled her about the abortion—and that no one had counseled her before three other abortions performed at Gosnell's clinic. She arrived in the afternoon on November 11 and was given some valium and medicine to help her dilate. At 7:45 p.m., when she was taken to the procedure room, she called a cousin to tell her that she would be ready for pickup shortly.

In the procedure room, one of Gosnell's sons inserted an IV and administered anesthesia. Ms. Haynes said she remembered Gosnell entering the room, and talking to his son, but then "everything else is a blur." When she woke up, she was in the hospital with her family around her. Ms. Haynes told the investigator that the clinic staff refused to let her two cousins come inside the building when they arrived around 8:00 p.m. to pick her up.

This one interview established at least two serious violations that should have prompted disciplinary action by the Board of Medicine—Gosnell's routine failure to counsel abortion patients in violation of the Abortion Control Act, and the use of unlicensed employees to perform work for which they were unqualified. The evidence that clinic staff locked Ms. Haynes's cousins out of the facility to cover up the fact that Gosnell had seriously injured the patient—and thereby prevented getting her help—was even more serious. It clearly warranted an investigation and disciplinary action.

Investigator Gillespie's interviews with Ms. Haynes's cousins confirmed that they had been purposefully locked out of the facility for over four hours. When they first arrived at 8:00 p.m. to pick up Ms. Haynes, they rang the buzzer on the clinic's front door, but were told that she was not ready and that they could not come inside to

Section VI: How Did This Go On So Long?

wait. The cousins went across the street to get pizza and returned an hour later. Again, the clinic staff refused to admit them. This went on for several hours as the cousins watched a continuous flow of people enter and leave the building.

Finally, sometime after midnight, the cousins threatened to call the police if they were not allowed into the building. A clinic employee then told them to wait a minute and eventually admitted them. Once inside, the cousins declined the worker's request that they wait to speak to Gosnell and demanded to see Ms. Haynes. The worker escorted them to the back of the building where they found Ms. Haynes by herself, lying on a recliner, with no supervision, no monitoring equipment, and no pants. She was covered with a throw blanket and there was blood on the floor around her. She was slumped over and was completely unresponsive when they tried to arouse her.

Gosnell appeared about five minutes later. He told them she was heavily sedated because she had just had the procedure — which they knew was false because of Ms. Haynes's phone call at 7:45, when the procedure was about to start. He told them that there had been complications and that he had been unable to remove the entire fetus. He insisted there was no need to call an ambulance, but they demanded that he do so.

At the hospital, Ms. Haynes was told that Gosnell had left most of the fetus inside her, and that he had cut holes in her cervix and bowel. She required a large blood transfusion and remained hospitalized for five days.

Had investigators from the Department of State pursued Ms. Haynes' complaint and spoken to Kareema Cross, she could have told them what she told the Grand Jury—that Gosnell did not call an ambulance because he wanted to keep trying to complete the abortion. He had already removed the patient from the room once, performed other procedures, and brought her back to try again. Cross knew that the doctor had punctured something. Had the cousins not threatened to involve the police, Gosnell would undoubtedly have brought Ms. Haynes back into the procedure room, for at least the third time, rather than summon an ambulance.

In the end, none of this mattered as far as the Department of State was concerned. No one there thought Ms. Haynes' complaint was worth investigating.

The problems with the Board of Medicine and Department of State go beyond individual prosecuting attorneys.

The Grand Jury is convinced—based on the number of state prosecutors who failed to take action against Gosnell, on the fact that the prosecutors' supervisors uniformly approved recommendations not to take action, and on the testimony of Prosecuting Attorney Ruiz—that the problem does not lie just with the individual attorneys. There are clearly problems with procedures, training, management, and motivation within the Department of State's Bureau of Professional and Occupational Affairs.

It seems obvious that, in order to evaluate a complaint against a doctor, a prosecutor should look at the doctor's history, including other complaints, lawsuits, and their outcomes. Yet the various prosecuting attorneys who handled the complaints against Gosnell seemed either unaware of or unconcerned about the content—or even the existence—of previous complaints. Ruiz, for example, when asked how many

Section VI: How Did This Go On So Long?

complaints against the doctor had come in, said that the department had been notified of only two lawsuits involving Gosnell. These, he said, were Alice's in 2005 and Dana Haynes's in 2008. He also acknowledged that the Board had received Marcella Choung's complaint.

Ruiz's supervisor, Kerry Maloney, apparently shared the same misunderstanding regarding the number of complaints. Maloney is quoted in a March 3, 2010, Philadelphia Inquirer article, stating: "In my experience, two cases in eight years is not a lot." Both Ruiz and Maloney seemed to be unaware of the other complaints that Department of State attorneys had reviewed since 2002, including the case of Semika Shaw, whose death was reported to the department by Gosnell's insurance carrier, pursuant to the MCARE law.

The Department of State turned over seven complaint files on Gosnell to the Grand Jury. (One was from 1990, and another from 1992; no file was produced for an eighth complaint—an allegation from 1983 that Gosnell had no malpractice insurance.) Our review of the files showed that some prosecutors were aware of all previous complaints against Gosnell. These files included printouts listing the file numbers for the earlier complaints.

Clearly, Greenwald, who handled Semika Shaw's case, also knew of Marcella Choung's allegations—he was assigned to that case as well—though this did not stop him from closing the Shaw case without investigation. Other prosecutors, however, seem not to have even looked for prior complaints. Ruiz's account of "prior history" includes only the complaint from 1992, for which Gosnell received a reprimand. Grubb's file shows that, when he handled the 2006 complaint from Alice, he knew there was another open complaint at the time, but he chose to ignore it.

BLACKOUT: The Official GOSNELL Grand Jury Report

The department's prosecuting attorneys never put the pieces together about Gosnell because they did not bother to consider prior complaints. Had every subsequent prosecutor been aware of Marcella Choung's complaint, perhaps at least one of them would have looked more carefully at the case in front of him and recognized that the injuries inflicted by Gosnell were not caused by temporary negligence. Had any prosecutors properly investigated, perhaps they would have understood the magnitude of Gosnell's recklessness. When one prosecutor gets a complaint that the doctor has no insurance, and another prosecutor has been looking into a similar complaint for over two years, some form of coordination or collaboration should be required to ensure proper action is taken.

The testimony of the one prosecutor who appeared before the Grand Jury revealed a lack of knowledge about certain aspects of state law and Department of State procedures that indicates a lack of training. For example, Ruiz said he was unaware that insurance companies had to report medical liability settlements to the department, even though Gosnell's file contained just such a report relating to Semika Shaw. This is significant because it is an obvious way for state officials to check to make sure that doctors are reporting all of the lawsuits filed against them as required by MCARE. Had anyone cross-checked, it would have been discovered that Gosnell did not report Ms. Shaw's lawsuit to the Department of State, or her death to the Department of Health.

This lack of training is apparent in all of the departmental attorneys who did nothing to investigate the mayhem at Gosnell's clinic.

Section VI: How Did This Go On So Long?

The Department of State only pursued allegations aggressively when the case was very public, or when the complainant knew somebody.

Given the inaction by Pennsylvania Department of State attorneys on seven of the eight recorded complaints against Gosnell, the Grand Jury questions how aggressively the prosecutors are protecting the public from bad doctors. The complaints relating to Gosnell's abortion practice were serious, the harm he inflicted on patients was substantial, and his routine included the wanton killing of babies outside the womb.

Yet even a 22-year-old woman's death did not warrant an investigation, according to the Board of Medicine. It is curious, therefore, that the only complaint against Gosnell that did lead to any kind of disciplinary action by the Board involved a non-certified physician's assistant who treated a child for pink eye in 1990. As it happens, the child's grandmother, the complainant, worked for the Bureau of Professional and Occupational Affairs.

The next time state officials acted was 20 years later, when Gosnell was in the news. After law enforcement asked the Department of State to participate in the February 18, 2010, raid on Gosnell's clinic, Gosnell and his facility received extensive newspaper and television news coverage. With the spotlight on them, state officials finally conducted a thorough investigation.

Prosecuting Attorney Ruiz went back through the complaints that had come in over the years. He had Sherilyn Gillespie interview Dana Haynes, Marcella Choung, and Marie Smith, a patient who had sued Gosnell, but whose suit was never reported to the department. Gillespie conducted an impressive investigation and produced abundant evidence of Gosnell's criminal activities and his unfitness to practice medicine.

We are concerned, however, about the patients whose doctors do not end up in the news—doctors who may be unethical, reckless, or unprofessional every day with impunity. We want to know that the Department of State is protecting the public from dangerous doctors even if they do not happen to treat someone with a connection to the department, and even if they do not end up in the news. We do not have that confidence after this investigation.

The Departments of Health and State do not work together to protect the public.

One might think that two state agencies regulating heath care providers would offer twice as much—or at least more—protection of the public's health and safety than one. But from what we have observed in this investigation, that does not seem to be the case. We found that, rather than two departments taking responsibility, the Department of State and the Department of Health evaded their duties by asserting that the other department has clearer jurisdiction over the matter, and neither took action to protect the public.

We found that the departments do not share information or coordinate to make sure that a problem is addressed. Instead, they seem to use the other's existence in order to justify doing nothing. We saw this in the way the Department of State handled Marcella Choung's complaint. While it contained significant allegations that the Department of State could and should have prosecuted— for example, Gosnell's practice of allowing unlicensed workers to administer anesthesia, and his routine failure to counsel or obtain

Section VI: How Did This Go On So Long?

consent from abortion patients—the prosecuting attorney instead recommended referring the case to the Department of Health, which apparently he did not actually do.

Meanwhile, when the Department of Health was contacted by plaintiffs' attorneys complaining about Gosnell or seeking records, officials in that department did not heed or act on the information conveyed. Instead, they told the attorneys that their records were privileged and referred them on to the Department of State. On hearing of Semika Shaw's death, for example, Janice Staloski, the director of home health who had responsibility for overseeing abortion clinics, did not order an investigation or even an inspection of the clinic. She failed to perform even the simple task of checking to see if Gosnell had reported her death as the Abortion Control Act mandated. She did refer Ms. Shaw's attorney to the Department of State.

Similarly, her predecessor, Robert Bastian, ignored the substance of a complaint by the attorney for the 19-year-old who had to have a radical hysterectomy after Gosnell perforated her uterus. After consulting with Senior Counsel Brody, Bastian cited several statutes and regulations to explain why the department could not provide records. And he referred the attorney to the Department of State. More to the point, Bastian, like Staloski, did not order an investigation or inspection of the clinic that it was his duty to monitor. Even when Ms. Shaw's heirs were awarded $900,000, and when the 19-year-old recovered $500,000, no one at DOH seemed to think it was worth taking a look at the clinic.

Semika Shaw's case is just one example of how the lack of communication between the departments hampers enforcement. In October 2002, Gosnell's insurance carrier reported to the Department of State that it had paid its $400,000 share of the $900,000 settlement for her death. Gosnell, however, did not report Ms. Shaw's death to DOH even though he was required to do so under the Abortion Control Act. 18 Pa. C.S. §3214(g). Even after learning of Ms. Shaw's death from her estate's attorney, Staloski ignored the information.

The Department of State prosecutors, who are charged with enforcing the reporting requirement of the Abortion Control Act (18 Pa. C.S. §3214(i) and §3219), could not know that Gosnell failed to report Ms. Shaw's death to DOH unless DOH informed them. On the other hand, DOH might not know that Ms. Shaw died. That information was, however, known to the Department of State prosecutors because the insurance company told them.

The obvious solution to this problem is to have procedures whereby the Department of State prosecutor, before closing the file on Ms. Shaw's death, would contact DOH to make sure Gosnell had complied with reporting laws. Conversely, Staloski, on learning of Ms. Shaw's lawsuit from the plaintiff's attorneys, should have checked with the Department of State to make sure that Gosnell had reported the suit as mandated by the MCARE law.

As it happened, none of the state officials who testified before the Grand Jury shared or requested information that was necessary to carry out their duties. Frankly, their demeanor during their testimony indicated that they were content to use their self-imposed lack of knowledge as an excuse for inaction. Proper supervision and accountability for performance, in addition to new procedures, clearly are required.

Section VI: How Did This Go On So Long?

Patients and groups that were aware of Gosnell's reckless practices found it hard to file complaints with the state.

We have learned during our investigation that Gosnell's reckless ways were not unknown to people in the community. Some pro-choice and women's health groups learned from Gosnell's patients of their frightening experiences. Patients reported that they were put totally to sleep for long periods of time, that they were treated badly, and that the facility was dirty. The community groups tried to help women file complaints. They were unsuccessful, however, in part because the complaint form used by the Department of State—the same form that one would use to complain about a barber or a car salesman—is difficult to fill out, especially if the complainant is not well educated or does not speak English. It demands considerable personal information, and it does not guarantee confidentiality for medical records.

Women who had undergone abortions were generally not willing to send all of this information to Harrisburg. When representatives of one of the organizations tried to file a complaint with the Board of Medicine on behalf of the women, they were allegedly told that they could not file a third-party complaint.

Ruiz, the prosecuting attorney, told us that the Department of State has always accepted complaints from any source—third parties, local, state, and federal agencies, newspaper stories, basically anyone who wants to file a complaint. He further testified that the complaints can be conveyed by telephone and do not have to be made on the formal complaint form. He said that any complaint would be logged in and considered.

Our review of records subpoenaed from the Department of State, however, reveals that the only complaints recorded or acted on — even if the action was only to close the file without investigation — were those where a formal, written complaint was sent to the department. We saw no record of a complaint from any women's health organizations. Indeed, according to the department's records, no one over two decades ever conveyed a complaint over the phone.

> **A Department of State witness complained that the department does not have more law enforcement powers, but failed to use the ones that it has.**

Prosecuting Attorney Ruiz repeatedly mentioned the Pennsylvania Department of State's desire to be considered a law enforcement agency. He suggested to the Grand Jury that the department could have done a better job of investigating complaints against Gosnell if it had had the full powers of law enforcement. We are unconvinced. The Board of Medicine already has subpoena powers that could and should have been used to obtain files and documents that could have substantiated the complaints received. Yet it did not use this power.

The Department of State witness suggested that the power to inspect would have been useful in investigating the complaints against Gosnell. But this does not require law enforcement powers. As Ruiz noted in his testimony, many of the other boards he works for, other than the Board of Medicine, do have the power to inspect the establishments that they license, without having law enforcement authority. We agree that the Board of Medicine should have the same inspection power possessed by other state boards, such as the board that oversees cosmetologists. In this case, however, there is no

Section VI: How Did This Go On So Long?

suggestion that anyone from the Department of State asked—or even wanted—to inspect Gosnell's clinic. No evidence indicates that any state official even sought to interview Gosnell in his office.

Finally, the Board prosecutor mentioned that Pennsylvania's Criminal History Record Information Act prevents law enforcement from sharing investigative information with the department. He contended that this somehow hampered the department's own investigations. Again, we did not see that in this case. Indeed, it was the Department of State that possessed the crucial information, provided by Marcella Choung in 2001, that could have been used to stop Gosnell's illegal practice years ago—long before Karnamaya Mongar was killed.

If anything, it was the confidentiality and privilege claimed by the Departments of State and Health that threatened to impede the criminal investigation. The Department of State initially claimed that its complaint files were confidential and could not be turned over to the Grand Jury.

The problem with the Departments of State and Health is not that they lacked authority to end the crime spree that Gosnell and his staff passed off as practicing medicine. The problem is that the state overseers preferred not to exercise their authority. They chose to look the other way.

> **THE PHILADEPHIA DEPARTMENT OF PUBLIC HEALTH ALSO IGNORED ALARMING WARNINGS ABOUT GOSNELL'S PRACTICE.**

Marcella Choung was not the only person to report Gosnell's appalling medical practice to health officials. An employee of the Philadelphia Department of Public Health alerted her bosses—

twice—that things were seriously wrong at Gosnell's clinic. The last time she did so was one month before Karnamaya Mongar died. Records produced by the city department reveal that employees in at least two different divisions within the department missed red flags that should have led to investigation and action.

Supervisors in the Division of Disease Control ignored a nurse's disturbing report about conditions in Gosnell's clinic in 2008 and 2009.

The City of Philadelphia employee who did notice and report the abysmal conditions she observed at Gosnell's clinic was a registered nurse named Lori Matijkiw. Matijkiw conducted what the Health Department calls an "AFIX" visit, or vaccine inspection, in July 2008.

Using the name "Family Medical Society," Gosnell purported to be a provider of children's vaccines under a program administered by the Philadelphia Health Department's Division of Disease Control. The doctor's history with the program, however, was rocky. Emails going back to August 2001 reveal that he was suspended from the program repeatedly for failing to maintain logs and for storing vaccines in filthy, unsuitable refrigerators, and at improper temperatures.

Health department employees who visited the clinic between 2001 and 2007 recorded that they dealt with "Drs." O'Neill and Massof, but never Gosnell. These inspectors noted problems with the refrigerator, the clinic's record-keeping, and expired vaccines. They were apparently oblivious, however, to other obvious deficiencies that did not relate directly to vaccines.

Section VI: How Did This Go On So Long?

On July 16, 2008, at 1:30 p.m., Matijkiw made a vaccine inspection visit to Gosnell's clinic. Unlike the inspectors before her, she did not simply stick to her narrow, assigned task of inspecting vaccines and their storage units. She took seriously her broader duty to protect public health. Following her visit to Gosnell's facility, she reported on a multitude of deficiencies she found.

In an email to her superiors at the Philadelphia Department of Public Health—whom we have identified as Program Manager Lisa Morgan and Medical Director Dr. Barbara Watson—Matijkiw reported that she had trouble even scheduling an appointment. No one answered the phone at the clinic, and when they finally did, they told her that "Dr. Massof" was on leave. After she finally scheduled an appointment, neither Gosnell nor the office manager was at the facility when she arrived. The two women who were there, she wrote, were "clueless."

While Matijkiw waited for the women to try to contact Gosnell, she noticed signs taped to the front desk. One was a price list for abortions detailing the costs for different gestational ages, with a price list for four different levels of anesthesia [Appendix C]. A third sign announced: "If you have the pre-procedure blood tests and work up done, and change your mind, you are still responsible for the costs of the tests." Matijkiw wrote down everything she observed. She noted that the office was "not clean at all, and many areas of the office smell like urine." She reported a "dark layer of dust" on the baseboards and described the "enormous" fish tanks, filled with murky water. In the refrigerator, she found expired vaccines—one with an expiration date of March 2006, another 2005. The temperature log, which was supposed to record the refrigerator temperature every day, had not been marked since the second day of June—a month and a half earlier. On top of the refrigerator, she found a stack of temperature logs, already filled out, showing readings twice a day, with no initials, time, or month.

Matijkiw wrote that Tina Baldwin showed her to a freezer in a "lab" (quotation marks are in the original email) on the second floor. Inside she found "3-4 large plastic containers with blood-colored frozen contents, wrapped in blue chux." She described a "red fluid spilled/frozen on the floor of the freezer." Chicken pox vaccines were stored in an ice tray above the containers of bloody fetuses.

The clinic staff told Matijkiw that "Dr. Massof" had left abruptly in June and that Gosnell was unfamiliar with the program. When Matijkiw asked to see files showing vaccines administered, the staff told her they had none. She reported to her bosses that she looked up Gosnell on the state website and found that he had been disciplined in the past.

Based on Matijkiw's report, the city health department suspended Family Medical Society—once again—from the vaccine program, but took no further action. In fact, a little over a year later, the department was considering re-enrolling the clinic in the program. A note by one employee in August 2009 recorded: "Site was told they need to purchase a new unit to store their vaccines completely SEPARATE from all other medical products"—an apparent reference to the containers filled with fetuses. Other than assuring that vaccines were not placed in the same freezer, the city health department showed no concern about the stored fetuses or the dripping frozen blood observed by Matijkiw.

On October 7, 2009, Matijkiw returned to the clinic. Again she

Section VI: How Did This Go On So Long?

wrote a scathing report, addressed, again, to her supervisor, Lisa Morgan. In it Matijkiw described a two-hour meeting with "(Dr.) O'Neill" (the parentheses were in her original email). During the visit, Matijkiw learned that O'Neill had no understanding of the vaccine program. O'Neill reportedly believed that the free children's vaccines could be given to adult patients and to those with private insurance. Matijkiw noticed that one of the free vaccines was given to Gosnell's daughter.

In addition, Matijkiw noticed that the clinic listed 20 children on Keystone Mercy, a Medicaid health plan. Matijkiw wrote that three of the "children" were almost 19 years old, and one had private insurance through Aetna. She wondered if any of them had ever been in the clinic. She also said that O'Neill was improperly trying to count abortion patients as vaccination patients.

In response to questioning by Matijkiw, O'Neill admitted that she was not licensed in Pennsylvania. She falsely claimed to have had a Delaware license, which she said she let lapse. When Matijkiw asked who in the practice treated children, O'Neill replied: "They don't come in." Yet Gosnell and O'Neill claimed to be providers of children's vaccines.

Again Matijkiw documented the dirtiness of the facility, the murky fish and turtle tanks, the expired vaccines, and the lack of temperature logs. In addition, this time, she reported seeing patients being escorted into the procedure area when Gosnell was not in the clinic. Matijkiw concluded her report to her boss: "If Dr. Gosnell was out of the office and [O'Neill] had to call the other physician's assistant on his cell phone and leave a message for his MA#, why were patients in the procedure area?"

BLACKOUT: The Official GOSNELL Grand Jury Report

Matijkiw's email to Morgan should have resulted in immediate action. Just like her report the year before should have triggered a response. If nothing else, Matijkiw's supervisors should have passed her information about the unsanitary conditions and the fetuses in the freezer to another division within the city health department with jurisdiction over such matters.

They should also have reported Gosnell and O'Neill to the Department of State's Board of Medicine, based on the evidence apparent to Matijkiw that patients were being treated in Gosnell's absence and that O'Neill was practicing without a license. Yet the city health department did nothing.

A month after Matijkiw's second visit to the clinic, Mrs. Mongar died. A month after that, in December 2009, a notation in Philadelphia Department of Public Health records stated: "Site will not be enrolled in [the Vaccine for Children program] after Matijkiw's visits. We will pick up any wasted vaccines in January. Jim is reporting Dr. to state licensing."

But "Jim," an apparent reference to Immunization Program Director Jim Lutz, never did report Gosnell. And no one else at the city health department did either.

> **The Philadelphia Health Department's Environmental Engineering Section failed to follow through after receiving a complaint in 2003 about aborted fetuses stored in an employee refrigerator.**

Years earlier, in August 2003, another branch of the city's health department had received an anonymous complaint about Women's Medical Society. Mandi Davis, a sanitation specialist in the environmental engineering section, wrote a memo to a colleague at

Section VI: How Did This Go On So Long?

the department, Ken Gruen, with a copy to then-Assistant Health Commissioner Izzat Melhem. She informed them that she had received a "rather disturbing" complaint of aborted fetuses stored in paper bags in an employee refrigerator at Gosnell's clinic.

Davis requested that a site visit be conducted to assure that proper infectious-waste handling and disposal practices were in place. Davis further instructed Gruen: "I am not expecting a 'wild goose chase' for aborted fetuses." Current Philadelphia Health Commissioner Donald Schwarz testified that notations on the memo seem to indicate that a site visit was, in fact, made.

The city health department, however, could not produce any report of that site visit. Nor is there evidence that the department took any action against Gosnell for his dangerous handling of medical waste, or for his failure to have an approved infectious waste plan, as is required by the city Health Code.

A year later, Gosnell still had no approved disposal plan. On March 28, 2004, Davis sent Gosnell a letter stating that a "plan" he had submitted was "incomplete." In fact, it was completely blank, except for the name and address of the clinic, some contact information, and an indication that it was a medical facility. On May 3, 2004, Davis sent another letter. This one was a form letter. Davis wrote:

> Several years ago all Doctors practicing in Philadelphia received a letter from former Health Commissioner Estelle B. Richman explaining the need for the Department to have an infectious waste handling and disposal plan from your practice. The Commissioner's letter explained the necessity for infectious waste to be properly containerized, stored, transported, and disposed in a manner to preclude any hazard to you, your staff, and patients, the community or the environment.

BLACKOUT: The Official GOSNELL Grand Jury Report

The letter noted that the city had never received a plan or a fee from the clinic.

On May 7, 2004, a city health department inspector was sent to the clinic. His report stated that proper labels were missing from areas where waste was stored; that red bag containers for infectious waste were not lidded; that marked boxes of infectious waste were sitting on the basement floor—not raised as they should be; that red bags for pick-up were not properly stored in the basement; and that the clinic did not provide a contract with a disposal company.

Gosnell subsequently produced some more paperwork, including a copy of a contract for disposal. However, he never paid his fee. The city never approved his medical waste plan. And he never cleaned up the infectious waste. Yet five years later, he was still operating. When the Grand Jurors toured the facility in 2010, boxes of waste were still sitting on the basement floor. Gosnell still stored aborted fetuses in plastic containers in the freezer. Employees described a stench emitted by bags of fetal tissue that piled up in the clinic.

Commissioner Schwarz tried, unsatisfactorily, to explain why the city never enforced the regulations that purport to protect staff, patients, the community, and the environment. Protection of the public, according to Dr. Schwarz's testimony, was not the real intent behind the regulations. The impetus for requiring doctors to have infectious waste plans approved by the city was not public health; it was revenue.

The city regulations required the city's 10,000 providers to pay $100 for individuals, $250 for clinics, and $500 for institutions such as hospitals, schools, and nursing homes. But the regulations provided

Section VI: How Did This Go On So Long?

no guidance as to what the health department was supposed to do to enforce the plans once submitted. Dr. Schwarz related to the Grand Jury what he heard from people who were in the health department at the time:

> The department was told, apparently, to collect the money, make sure the plan came in, get the fee, and not enforce, that is don't take action against people but remind them. This is a revenue generating activity.

The department would only inspect or take action when there was a complaint about a provider's infectious waste handling or disposal.

Then, according to what Dr. Schwarz was told, sometime in 2004 or 2005—shortly after Davis sent to the clinic the form letter reminding delinquent medical providers to submit their waste plans and pay their fee—the department stopped trying to enforce the regulation against those who had not complied.

The health commissioner's testimony might explain why the department did not pursue Gosnell for his failure to submit an adequate infectious waste plan or pay his fee. But it does not explain the department's inaction after an inspector observed and reported Gosnell's perilous storage and disposal of infectious waste in May 2004 (and probably in 2003, though we did not see that report).

There is no record to indicate that the health department ever checked to see if the dangerous conditions in the clinic had been remediated. It is clear from our investigation that they never were.

BLACKOUT: The Official GOSNELL Grand Jury Report

Philadelphia's Health Commissioner told the Grand Jury that he is taking steps to improve the department's procedures.

Dr. Schwarz, Philadelphia's health commissioner since January 2008, testified twice before the Grand Jury. He expressed appropriate regret for his department's inaction. And he personally took responsibility. We found refreshing his acknowledgement of fault, his candor, and his evident efforts, at least since being called before the Grand Jury, to find out how and why his agency failed to protect the West Philadelphia community from a notoriously dangerous doctor.

But while he accepted responsibility personally, Dr. Schwarz seemed to excuse department employees who ignored the serious — and obvious — threat to public health posed by Gosnell's clinic, and he provided feeble excuses for their inaction. We saw no evidence that the city health department had initiated an internal assessment to determine how Gosnell fell through the cracks — either in November 2009, when the Medical Examiner performed an autopsy on Mrs. Mongar's remains, or in February 2010, after publicity surrounding the raid made the horror at 3801 Lancaster Avenue known to all.

When Dr. Schwarz testified the first time before the Grand Jury, he should have known that many department employees were well aware of Gosnell's operation. He should have known this because professionals within the department who had information about the dangerous conditions in Gosnell's clinic should have told him.

The health commissioner assured the Grand Jury that the department is now taking steps to address problems that prevented the department from responding as it should have. He identified

Section VI: How Did This Go On So Long?

structural problems—and a corresponding mentality among health department employees—that contributed to the city health department's ineffectual handling of complaints about Gosnell. The department has several very different responsibilities. The tasks it oversees range from conducting autopsies to testing for sexually transmitted diseases to dog-catching. Each function is handled by a different division with different staff.

The department's involvement with Gosnell's clinic touched several divisions and sections. One unit, the Division of Disease Control's STD Control Program, tested lab samples from Gosnell's clinic, collected data for sexually transmitted diseases, and followed up to make sure infected patients were treated. Kareema Cross testified that employees from the city health department came to the clinic to pick up specimens and blood to check for STDs. The Grand Jury received no evidence that any of these employees informed others at the health department about what they saw during their visits to the clinic.

Another part of the Division of Disease Control has responsibility for the children's vaccine program, Matijkiw's unit, which provides vaccines to clinics and conducts inspections. Investigating infectious waste complaints is the responsibility of the Environmental Engineering Section. The Medical Examiner, whose office is also part of the city health department, performed the autopsy on Karnamaya Mongar and examined fetal remains seized from the clinic's freezer.

Thus, when Matijkiw, who worked in the vaccine program, discovered infectious waste in a freezer, that information was never conveyed to the environmental engineering people who could have done something about it. Dr. Schwarz recognized that, at the least, the department should have electronic records that can be shared among divisions. Employees in any unit would then be able to search for all of the department's records on a particular provider and see the reports of other divisions.

The city health commissioner also identified a more troubling problem. Although he phrased it more diplomatically, what he was describing was an "it's-not-in-my-job- description" mindset displayed by many department employees. When asked why Matijkiw's superiors had not reported Gosnell to the Pennsylvania Department of State for action against his license, Dr. Schwarz tried to explain:

> I would say that I think what happens is people have a narrowly defined job and I don't think there has been an expectation that people would report to the state as professionals. So I think that is wrong and we are going to figure out a way to change that.

The same narrow view of their job responsibilities was displayed when Matijkiw's superiors failed to share her report with other divisions within the city health department that could have acted.

Some of Dr. Schwarz's explanations for health department employees' lapses were not entirely convincing. For example, he testified that the Director of Disease Control, Dr. Caroline Johnson, told him that one reason "Jim" did not report Gosnell to the Department of State in December 2009, was that "the program people apparently knew something was happening at the site and they didn't call the state."

It is highly unlikely, however, that anyone at the city health department knew that something was "happening" to Gosnell in

Section VI: How Did This Go On So Long?

December 2009. Mrs. Mongar's death had triggered no investigation by the state Department of Health. And there is no evidence that the Department of State was doing anything either.

Dr. Schwarz also told the Grand Jury that the city health department is limited in what it can do in response to complaints about medical providers. He gave examples of the kinds of complaints the department can do something about:

> I could send somebody out if they have rats. I could send somebody out if someone got diarrheal disease. I could send somebody out if there was an animal, but I can't send someone out if a person's injured.

We understand that the city health department did not have the authority to investigate all of the things that were wrong in Gosnell's clinic. If a patient called up to complain that they were treated badly at Women's Medical Society, or that Gosnell was violating the Abortion Control Act in some way, the health department would not have jurisdiction. But it could certainly submit complaints to the Pennsylvania Department of State and demand that they be investigated. Furthermore, some issues were directly within the department's purview—such as the infectious waste problems and the circumstances of Mrs. Mongar's death.

The latter gave the Medical Examiner's office authority to inspect the facility and to ask questions in order to investigate the manner of death. At the very least, the department's overall mission—to protect public health in Philadelphia—ought to have prompted more responsiveness and sharing of information about the reckless doctor in West Philadelphia.

Regarding the responsibilities of his department, the city health commissioner displayed a very different attitude from that of the state officials who testified. He did not, for the most part, try to evade accountability—or work—by claiming that his agency lacked authority to do certain things. In fact, he suggested ways to fill gaps in responsibility that Gosnell fell through. He expressed an interest in increasing accountability, responsiveness, and communication among the various local and state agencies.

Even though the city lacks the authority to regulate doctors or abortion clinics, Dr. Schwarz recognized that the Department of Public Health should have a system in place, which it now does not have, to handle calls made by Philadelphia residents to complain about Philadelphia medical providers. When asked if the health department had ever received calls about Gosnell, the commissioner frankly acknowledged: "if someone called, I'm embarrassed to say, I don't know what would happen."

Dr. Schwarz testified that he sees a role for the city health department in cataloging complaints and helping patients of Philadelphia doctors refer complaints to the proper authorities. Complaints about individual doctors would be forwarded to the Department of State, which licenses doctors and is responsible for investigating complaints and imposing sanctions. Complaints about health care facilities, such as Gosnell's clinic, would be forwarded to the state Department of Health, which has the authority and duty to license, inspect, and sanction them.

The health commissioner told the Grand Jury that his department is already considering ways to help callers register their complaints with the proper authority. The process, he said, should include

Section VI: How Did This Go On So Long?

a response to the individual who filed the complaint, letting them know that it was received and what is being done about it.

Dr. Schwarz suggested the health department might fill another gap by conducting routine sanitation and safety inspections of doctors' offices and clinics. Neither the state nor the city currently inspects them. The city health department does inspect some institutions, such as day care centers, prisons, and schools. It inspects the food services at hospitals, though not the hospitals themselves. Dr. Schwarz acknowledged that the city health department probably could step into that role, although not without hiring more inspectors.

The Grand Jurors hope the health commissioner follows through on his suggestions. We also wish state officials showed as much eagerness to address the bureaucratic deficiencies and neglect that, for decades, allowed someone like Gosnell to wantonly break laws, harm and endanger women, and kill viable babies in the secure knowledge that no official overseer would intervene to stop him.

FELLOW DOCTORS WHO OBSERVED THE RESULTS OF GOSNELL'S RECKLESS AND CRIMINAL PRACTICES FAILED TO REPORT HIM TO AUTHORITIES.

Pennsylvania's Abortion Control Act requires any doctor who treats a woman because of a complication arising from an abortion to make a report to DOH. Willful failure to do so constitutes "unprofessional conduct" and subjects the treating doctor to sanctions by the Board of Medicine. Clearly, this law is being violated, if not willfully, at least consistently.

We learned of at least five of Gosnell's patients who were treated for serious complications at the Hospital of the University of Pennsylvania (HUP) or Presbyterian Hospital, the two closest emergency rooms to the Women's Medical Society clinic. We heard evidence of many more women, whose names we did not learn, who also had to seek emergency care after undergoing abortions at Gosnell's facility. Yet we received no complication reports when we subpoenaed documents from DOH.

The attorney representing HUP doctors before the Grand Jury was able to produce only one confirmed report ever made (which raises the question why DOH did not turn over this report). That one report was for Semika Shaw, who died at the hospital in March 2000. Documents turned over to the Grand Jury show that, following Shaw's death, another hospital attorney, Mary Ellen Nepps, distributed a memo to doctors at HUP and Pennsylvania Hospital. The memo reminded the physicians, "in light of some recent reports of abortion complications and maternal deaths," that they were responsible for filing reports with DOH in such cases.

Yet, when Karnamaya Mongar died at HUP nine years later, no report was made. Nor did the Grand Jury receive evidence of reports made, other than in Shaw's case, for any of the serious complications that other patients of Gosnell suffered. Dana Haynes went straight to the HUP emergency room from Gosnell's clinic with a perforated cervix and bowel and most of a fetus still in her uterus. She required surgery and was hospitalized for five days. Another 19-year-old patient of Gosnell's had a hysterectomy performed at HUP after Gosnell perforated her uterus. And Marie Smith arrived at Presbyterian Hospital, unconscious, with fetal remains still inside her.

Another patient, who was approximately 29 weeks pregnant, had laminaria removed at HUP after she changed her mind about

Section VI: How Did This Go On So Long?

terminating her pregnancy. The doctor who performed that procedure had to know that Gosnell was breaking the law by starting to abort a 29-week fetus. And this is just the tip of the iceberg. Latosha Lewis testified that she was told by personnel in HUP's emergency room that they treated a lot of women who came from Gosnell's clinic with problems.

We are very troubled that almost all of the doctors who treated these women routinely failed to report a fellow physician who was so obviously endangering his patients. We understand that in emergency rooms more than one doctor may treat a patient; it might be unclear who should do the reporting. In that case, the hospital should have an established policy, which HUP apparently did not. One of the HUP doctors told us that a procedure is now in place to assure proper reporting. Among the documents turned over by the attorney for HUP was a memo to HUP personnel reminding them that they are required to report abortion complications and maternal deaths and advising them of the procedure for doing so. The memo was dated September 3, 2010, shortly before the first HUP doctor testified before the Grand jury—and 10 years after the doctors had received the same instructions in an earlier memo.

The issue, however, goes beyond simple compliance with the Abortion Control Act's reporting requirement. Based on the evidence we heard regarding state officials' procedures and practices, it is doubtful that reporting under that act would actually have triggered any kind of action from the state. Staloski, the DOH director in charge of abortion facilities, told us that she did not even get—or ask for—complication reports. It seems that they were treated as statistical information rather than as a means to uncover problem facilities.

BLACKOUT: The Official GOSNELL Grand Jury Report

We would like to believe that the dozens of complication reports doctors should have submitted to DOH would have spurred the department into action against Gosnell. However, even perfect compliance with that provision of the Abortion Control Act would not address the bigger issue of rooting out bad doctors.

The doctors at HUP should have reported Gosnell to the Department of Health and to the Board of Medicine years ago. Not just because the Abortion Control Act requires them to, but also because reporting a doctor who harms his patients and breaks the law is the right thing to do.

WHO COULD HAVE PREVENTED ALL THIS DEATH AND DAMAGE?

Had state and local officials performed their duties properly, Gosnell's clinic would have been shut down decades ago. Gosnell would have lost the medical license that he used to inflict irreparable harm on women; to illegally abort viable, late-term fetuses; and to kill innumerable babies outside the womb.

Had DOH treated the clinic as the ambulatory surgical facility it was, DOH inspectors would have assured that the staff were all licensed, that the facility was clean and sanitary, that anesthesia protocols were followed, and that the building was properly equipped and could, at least, accommodate stretchers. Failure to comply with these standards would have given cause for DOH to revoke the facility's license to operate.

If inspectors had looked solely for violations of Pennsylvania's abortion regulations, there would have been ample grounds to revoke the approval of Gosnell's clinic as an abortion provider—as was demonstrated when DOH inspectors finally entered the facility in February 2010.

Had state inspectors reviewed patient files, they would inevitably have noticed that Gosnell was routinely performing abortions without informed consent from patients or signed consent from parents. His files revealed that he was performing numerous illegal abortions at "24.5 weeks," in itself a confession of criminality. Gosnell, moreover, almost never had the required pathology reports for second-trimester abortions.

BLACKOUT: The Official GOSNELL Grand Jury Report

Had DOH inspectors spoken to the workers, they might well have discovered that Gosnell's procedure included severing the spinal cords of babies born alive. Revoking his approval to perform abortions would have been simple. But no one from DOH set foot in Gosnell's clinic for over 16 years.

The Department of State prosecutors did not even need to go looking for reasons to revoke Gosnell's medical license. Complaints came to them. Marcella Choung, the former Gosnell employee, spelled out his entire criminal operation for them. Complaints of perforated uteruses and bowels; of a patient's death from a botched procedure that resulted in a $900,000 settlement; and of family members physically barred from summoning emergency help, were all sent to Department of State attorneys. Yet the department considered none of these complaints serious enough to take action against Gosnell.

Had the Philadelphia Department of Public Health reported to state officials all that its employees knew or suspected about filthy facilities, fraud, the unlicensed practice of medicine, anesthesia chosen by patients based on cost, infectious waste improperly handled and stored, and vaccines stored next to medical waste, perhaps state authorities would have taken action against Gosnell and Women's Medical Society.

And had fellow doctors, the ones who treated the women after Gosnell butchered them, demanded the attention of DOH and the Board of Medicine, that too might have made a difference.

We don't know. We only know what happened when none of these people did what they should have.

SECTION VII:
CRIMINAL CHARGES

Gosnell and his staff showed consistent disregard not only for the health and safety of their patients, but also for the laws of Pennsylvania. After reviewing extensive and compelling evidence of criminal wrongdoing at the clinic, the Grand Jury has issued a presentment recommending the prosecution of Gosnell and members of his staff for criminal offenses including:

- Murder of Karnamaya Mongar
- Murders of babies born alive
- Infanticide
- Violations of the Controlled Substances Act
- Hindering, Obstruction, and Tampering
- Perjury
- Illegal late-term abortions
- Violations of the Abortion Control Act
- Violations of the Controlled Substances Act
- Abuse of Corpse
- Theft by Deception
- Conspiracy
- Corrupt Organization
- Corruption of Minors

Specifically, the Grand Jury recommends that the Philadelphia District Attorney's Office bring the following criminal charges:

BLACKOUT: The Official GOSNELL Grand Jury Report

MURDER IN THE DEATH OF KARNAMAYA MONGAR

Gosnell's contempt for the law and his patients cost Karnamaya Mongar her life. Her death was the direct result of deliberate and dangerous conduct by Gosnell and his staff. They consciously disregarded the unjustifiable risk that their conduct would cause death.

Under Pennsylvania law, the voluntary commission of an act that results in the victim's death, where the offender acts with legal malice, express or implied, is murder, even if the resulting death is unintentional or accidental. "Malice" is a legal term meaning, for example, hardness of heart, wanton conduct, recklessness of consequences, or a mind regardless of social duty. If someone consciously disregards an unjustified and extremely high risk that his or her conduct might cause death or serious bodily injury, he or she has acted with malice, and may be convicted of murder.

Gosnell, Williams, and West acted with malice when they consciously disregarded the extremely high risk that administering high doses of Demerol to Karnamaya Mongar could kill her. The overmedication of Mrs. Mongar was more than careless. It was consistent with the routine practice at Gosnell's clinic of keeping patients subdued and sedated by giving them whatever medication Gosnell's workers deemed appropriate. Gosnell set up his practice this way, and delegated to his unlicensed and unsupervised staff the responsibility to inject patients with potent drugs.

Despite warnings from his other employees about Williams and West and their overmedication of patients, and even though the doctor knew that neither West nor Williams was trained, authorized, or

Section VII: Criminal Charges

licensed to dole out controlled substances, Gosnell recklessly allowed them to drug patients.

West told the FBI that she and Williams mixed medications for various levels of anesthesia and administered these drug mixtures to patients. According to Ashley Baldwin, Williams would medicate patients "whenever Sherry told her to." West also medicated patients "a lot," Baldwin said. When West and Williams called Gosnell on November 19, 2009, reporting that Mrs. Mongar was in pain, Gosnell directed them to "med her up."

Demerol is a drug known to have cardiac and respiratory side effects. Its sedating effect is enhanced when it is given with other medications such as promethazine, another ingredient in Gosnell's routine sedation formula. This "synergistic effect" can depress respiration. But these hazards were of no concern to Gosnell.

The Philadelphia medical examiner found that the cause of Mrs. Mongar's death was "acute anoxic encephalopathy following resuscitation from cardiopulmonary arrest due to meperidine intoxication." In other words, despite resuscitative efforts, her brain ceased to function after her heart and breathing stopped as a result of the overdose of Demerol. The medical examiner concluded that the manner of death was homicide.

Another expert, the Delaware County medical examiner, concurred, explaining that to give potent drugs "willy-nilly" — without tailoring the administration of the drugs to the patient, without monitoring the patient, and without the doctor even being on the premises — was grossly negligent, reckless, and, in his opinion, homicide.

The gross negligence, recklessness, and disregard of life-threatening risks displayed by Gosnell and his staff cost Karnamaya

Mongar her life. Their actions demonstrated a hardness of heart, wanton conduct, recklessness of consequences, and a mind regardless of social duty, establishing legal malice. **We recommend that Kermit Gosnell, Lynda Williams, and Sherry West be charged with third-degree murder,** pursuant to 18 Pa.C.S. § 2502(c).

Drug delivery resulting in the death of Karnamaya Mongar

The evidence also supports a murder charge for drug delivery resulting in death.

> A person commits murder of the third degree who administers, dispenses, delivers, gives, [or] prescribes … any controlled substances … in violation of section 13(a)(14) or (30) of the … Controlled Substance, Drug, Device, and Cosmetic Act, and another person dies as a result of using the substance.18 Pa.C.S. § 2506.

The Controlled Substances Act prohibits delivery of a controlled substance such as Demerol by any unlicensed practitioner, or the dispensing of any controlled substance by or at the direction of a practitioner other than "in accordance with treatment principles accepted by a responsible segment of the medical profession." 35 P.S. §§ 780-113(a)(14), (30).

Gosnell, Williams, and West violated these provisions when they gave Mrs. Mongar the excessive medication that killed her. **We recommend prosecuting Kermit Gosnell, Lynda Williams, and Sherry West for Drug Delivery Resulting in Death.**

West and Williams were not remotely qualified to tend to patients, much less to be injecting narcotics into patients, yet this

Section VII: Criminal Charges

is precisely what Gosnell had them do, regularly and without any medical supervision, in violation of the law. The administration of high doses of Demerol to anesthetize the diminutive Mrs. Mongar was well outside any "treatment principles accepted by a responsible segment of the medical profession."

Responsible medical care also requires sedated patients to be monitored. This is particularly important, and indeed obvious, when a drug has known cardiac and respiratory side effects, as Demerol does. The anesthesiology expert testified that the standard of care for ambulatory surgical facilities and outpatient clinics requires monitoring of no less than blood pressure, heart rate and rhythm, and breathing, by electrocardiogram and pulse oximeter. Sedating without monitoring, the expert said, "is offensive to me as a physician." In Mrs. Mongar's case, it constituted murder.

BLACKOUT: The Official GOSNELL Grand Jury Report

MURDER OF BABIES BORN ALIVE

As a result of Gosnell's regular practice of terminating pregnancies beyond the 24-week legal limit, viable babies were often born alive at his clinic. And when they were, he would kill them, by severing their spines with scissors. He told his staff that this barbaric conduct was standard medical practice. It was not. It was criminal behavior.

A medical expert with 43 years of experience in performing abortions was appalled. This expert told us, "I've never heard of it [cutting the spinal cord] being done during an abortion." The expert explained, "I'm not aware of any basis within which a physician would cut the neck of a fetus." Describing the practice as "bizarre," he said, "it would be the same thing as putting a pillow over the baby's face, that the intention would be to kill the baby."

Although no one could place an exact number on the instances, Gosnell's staff testified that killing large, late-term babies who had been observed breathing and moving was a regular occurrence. Based on seven identifiable victims, **we recommend murder charges against Kermit Gosnell, Lynda Williams, Adrienne Moton, and Steven Massof. We also recommend that Gosnell, Williams, Moton, and Massof be charged with conspiracy to commit murder.**

In addition, **Gosnell should be charged with three counts of solicitation to commit murder.** We also recommend charges of conspiracy to commit murder generally, with respect to the standard practice, testified to by employees who observed it countless times, of killing viable babies born alive.

Section VII: Criminal Charges

Kareema Cross and Ashley Baldwin testified about one baby, whom we are calling "Baby Boy A," born in July 2008. **We recommend that Kermit Gosnell be charged with murder for killing Baby Boy A.** According to an ultrasound, the 17-year-old mother, "Sue," was 29.4 weeks pregnant. Gosnell induced labor and sedated the mother, who delivered a baby boy. Cross saw Baby Boy A breathe and move. Cross told us the baby was 18 to 19 inches long and nearly the size of her own newborn daughter, who was six pounds, six ounces at birth. Even Gosnell commented on Baby Boy A's size, joking "this baby is big enough to walk around with me or walk me to the bus stop."

Cross testified that she saw "the doctor just slit the neck" and place the remains in a plastic shoebox for disposal. Employees Adrienne Moton and Ashley Baldwin also were present. All three workers were so startled by Baby Boy A's size that they each took a photograph. Cross explained,

> Q. Why did you all take a photograph of this baby?
> A. Because it was big and it was wrong and we knew it. We knew something was wrong.

Adrienne Moton gave an FBI agent consent to search her cell phone for the photograph that she took. The FBI lab was able to find the picture on her cell phone; we saw this photograph, introduced as Exhibit 57. Moton told FBI Agent Jason Huff that she took this picture because Baby Boy A was born alive.

A neonatologist viewed Exhibit 57, the photograph of Baby Boy A. Based on his size, hairline, muscle mass, subcutaneous tissue, well-developed scrotum, and other characteristics, the neonatologist opined that the gestational age was at least 32 weeks.

BLACKOUT: The Official GOSNELL Grand Jury Report

The Grand Jury was able to identify this baby because Kareema Cross remembered the mother, "Sue," who came in with her great-aunt. The aunt testified before the Grand Jury that Gosnell demanded an extra $1,000 because Sue's pregnancy was so advanced.

We recommend a murder charge against Kermit Gosnell in the death of "Baby Boy B," whose frozen remains were discovered during the February 2010 raid. The search team discovered red biohazard bags containing the remains of 47 fetuses, which were turned over to the Philadelphia medical examiner. One was "Baby Boy B," found frozen in a plastic spring-water jug (labeled by the medical examiner as 1B). The medical examiner determined that this baby had a gestational age of at least 28 weeks. According to the medical examiner's report and testimony, the baby was viable and intact, except for a "surgical defect" at the base of his neck.

We recommend murder and conspiracy charges against Kermit Gosnell and Lynda Williams for the murder committed by Lynda Williams in 2006 or 2007 of "Baby C." Cross testified that she saw Williams cut the neck of the infant we have named Baby C, who had been moving and breathing for approximately 20 minutes. Gosnell had delivered the baby and put it on a counter while he suctioned the placenta from the mother. Williams called Cross over to look at the baby because it was breathing and moving its arms when Williams pulled on them. After touching the baby, Williams slit its neck.

When asked why Williams had killed the baby, Cross answered:

> Because the baby, I guess, because the baby was moving and breathing. And she see Dr. Gosnell do it so many times, I guess she felt, you know, she can do it. It's okay.

Section VII: Criminal Charges

The evidence of an intentional killing and an implicit agreement to kill a newborn supports charges of murder and criminal conspiracy against Williams and Gosnell for killing Baby C.

There is sufficient evidence to charge Adrienne Moton and Kermit Gosnell with murder and conspiracy in the death of "Baby D." Kareema Cross testified that a woman had delivered this large baby into a toilet before Gosnell arrived at work for the night. Cross said that the baby was moving and looked like it was swimming. Moton reached into the toilet, got the baby out, and cut its neck.

Cross said the baby was between 10 and 15 inches long and had a head the size of a "big pancake." Cross could not pinpoint the year that this happened, but testified that this killing occurred while Steven Massof was still working at the clinic. (Massof left in July 2008.) Moton herself admitted to Agent Huff that she had severed the spinal cords of living babies. According to her statement, Gosnell trained and instructed her to do this. The charts that the neonatology expert provided us indicate that the size of Baby D was consistent with viability.

This evidence of an intentional killing by Moton and an implicit agreement with Gosnell to kill babies as he instructed supports the charges of murder and criminal conspiracy against Moton and Gosnell for killing Baby D. **We recommend charging Kermit Gosnell with Criminal Solicitation of Adrienne Moton.**

We recommend that a murder charge be filed against Kermit Gosnell for the murder of "Baby E," a baby that Ashley Baldwin heard crying before Gosnell killed it. Ashley testified that she heard the baby cry in the large procedure room, the one used for later-term abortions, and saw the baby moving. She said Lynda Williams summoned Dr. Gosnell, who then went into the procedure room where the baby was.

Kareema Cross testified that Ashley had called her over, and that she heard this baby "whine" once while Dr. Gosnell was alone in the procedure room with the baby. Ashley confirmed that Gosnell was the only person in the room with Baby E. When he came out of the room, the baby was dead. Gosnell put the baby's remains in a waste bin. Ashley saw an incision in Baby's E's neck.

We recommend murder and conspiracy charges against Kermit Gosnell and Steven Massof for killing "Baby F."

Massof testified that he was assisting Gosnell with an abortion when he saw the baby's leg "jerk and move." The neonatology expert testified about the significance of movement in determining gestational age, and explained that the muscle tone and neurological development for a baby to pull back a limb exist "definitely in the bigger preemies like above, you know, 25, 26, 27 weekers."

After Massof observed this movement of Baby F outside the mother's womb, Gosnell severed the baby's spine with scissors. We believe that the evidence supports charges of murder and conspiracy against Gosnell and Massof.

Steven Massof also testified about the killing of a baby whom he observed breathing. We refer to this baby as "Baby G." Massof said that he was again helping Gosnell in the large procedure room when he saw the fully expelled baby exhibit what he called "a respiratory excursion," meaning a breath. According to Massof, Gosnell then "snipped the cervical part of the vertebra."

Section VII: Criminal Charges

The evidence supports charges of murder and conspiracy against Kermit Gosnell and Steven Massof for the killing of Baby G.

These seven murders were not isolated incidents. Severing the spinal cords of moving, breathing babies outside their mothers' wombs was, according to Massof, "standard procedure." Gosnell encouraged his staff to kill babies born alive; Lynda Williams, Adrienne Moton, and Steven Massof all followed his barbaric example. Massof testified that Gosnell taught him and showed the scissors-in-the-neck technique to "ensure fetal demise." **The evidence warrants three charges of criminal solicitation against Kermit Gosnell.**

Gosnell's students parroted his grisly techniques. Massof himself admitted to us that, of the many spinal cords he cut, there were about 100 instances where he did so after seeing a breath or some sign of life. The shocking regularity of killing babies who were born alive, who moved and breathed, as testified to by Gosnell's employees, demonstrates that these murders were intentional and collaborative. In addition to the specific murder charges identified above, **we recommend that Kermit Gosnell, Lynda Williams, Sherry West, Adrienne Moton, and Steven Massof be charged with conspiracy to commit murder.**

BLACKOUT: The Official GOSNELL Grand Jury Report

INFANTICIDE

Failure to provide care to any baby born alive during an abortion or premature delivery constitutes the crime of infanticide under Pennsylvania law. 18 Pa.C.S. § 3212. The legal duty to provide care extends to any newborn "born alive" where such care is "commonly and customarily provided ... under similar conditions and circumstances." According to the neonatology and obstetric experts that we consulted, care is routinely provided, and resuscitation is routinely attempted, at 22 or 23 weeks.

At Gosnell's clinic, no steps were ever taken to attend to these babies, according to his employees. Every time that Gosnell failed to provide appropriate care and treatment to a child born alive, he committed infanticide, under Pa.C.S. § 3212. We were surprised to learn, however, that infanticide is subject to a two-year statute of limitations. That means we are unable to recommend charges for any of the many instances of infanticide that we heard about that occurred before January 2009.

Instead, based on the following specific instances, **we recommend that Kermit Gosnell be charged with two counts of infanticide:**

A 28-week-old male, found frozen in container 1B with a surgical incision at the base of the neck, discovered in the February 2010 raid, and determined by the medical examiner to have been viable.

A 26-week-old female also found in the February 2010 raid, determined by the medical examiner to have been viable. Her frozen remains were in a distilled water container labeled by the medical examiner as 1C.

Section VII: Criminal Charges

VIOLATIONS OF THE CONTROLLED SUBSTANCES ACT IN RELATION TO THE DEATH OF KARNAMAYA MONGAR

Violations of the Controlled Substances Act, in addition to forming the basis for murder charges, constitute separate criminal offenses. Neither Williams nor West was licensed to dispense Demerol, yet Williams injected Karnamaya Mongar multiple times, and West assisted her. West told the Department of Health that she called Gosnell, and that he directed her and Williams, in his absence, to give Mrs. Mongar more medication, including Demerol.

As Gosnell, West, and Williams all knew, neither Williams nor West was licensed to dispense any controlled substance. And, as discussed above, the dispensing of excessive amounts of Demerol to Mrs. Mongar was not remotely consistent with accepted or reasonable medical practice. **We recommend that Kermit Gosnell, Lynda Williams, and Sherry West be charged with felony drug offense under the Controlled Substances Act.**

Also, because Gosnell, Williams, and West together agreed to commit these violations of drug laws, and acted in concert with their criminal objective being the unlawful dispensing of Demerol, **we recommend that Kermit Gosnell, Lynda Williams, and Sherry West be charged with conspiracy.** And because Gosnell instructed Williams and West to drug Mrs. Mongar, **we recommend that Kermit Gosnell be charged with two counts of criminal solicitation.**

BLACKOUT: The Official GOSNELL Grand Jury Report

HINDERING PROSECUTION, OBSTRUCTION OF JUSTICE, TAMPERING WITH EVIDENCE, AND PERJURY IN RELATION TO THE DEATH OF KARNAMAYA MONGAR

Gosnell and some of his staff attempted to cover up their criminal activity and mislead investigators. On November 19, 2009, when emergency personnel arrived at the clinic long after Karnamaya Mongar had stopped breathing, Sherry West snatched the victim's file. On the way to the hospital, she evidently made misleading notations, indicating that Mrs. Mongar had received minimal Demerol—only two "local" (10-mg.) doses.

She did so despite being fully aware that, having received Gosnell's instructions over the telephone a few hours before, Williams had actually given Mrs. Mongar far more Demerol. West thus withheld from emergency personnel trying to save Mrs. Mongar's life the crucial fact that the victim had received massive amounts of Demerol.

Emergency room records reflect that someone from the clinic—and West was the only person from Gosnell's clinic to go to the emergency room—provided false information about the circumstances preceding Mrs. Mongar's cardiac arrest. The records state "that the patient had an uneventful vacuum abortion and was in the recovery room watching TV when she suddenly became unresponsive." As Dana Kuzma, one of the EMTs who treated Mrs. Mongar testified, "that is just a complete lie." Ashley Baldwin agreed, "That is a lie." Mrs. Mongar's family members testified that they had not provided this information—not only did they not speak English, but they had no idea what happened at the clinic.

Section VII: Criminal Charges

After Mrs. Mongar was rushed to the hospital, West told coworkers, including Ashley Baldwin, that Mrs. Mongar "took some pills, because she was trying to get rid of it at home." This, too, was pure invention. Liz Hampton testified that the Mongar family had told her this, in English, which she claimed they spoke "very well." But the Grand Jurors heard the testimony of the family members through an interpreter, and thus know this to be untrue.

The toxicology expert confirmed there was no evidence that Mrs. Mongar had taken any abortifacient or other medication. Moreover, West's and Hampton's attempt to misdirect blame at the victim was discredited by the expert testimony establishing that it was the overdose of Demerol, not some mystery pill, that killed Mrs. Mongar.

West later lied to homicide detectives by telling them that Williams had given Mrs. Mongar only a "local," (10-mg Demerol) dose. West subsequently told the FBI that Williams had given her a "local" (10 mg.) and then a "custom" (75 mg.) dose of medication. The toxicology analysis established that this account also was false.

Gosnell tried to mislead investigators as well. FBI Agent Huff, DEA Investigator Stephen Dougherty, and District Attorney's Detective James Wood interviewed Gosnell at the clinic on February 18, 2010. Gosnell claimed to have been at the clinic when Demerol was given to Mrs. Mongar. Agent Huff then spoke to Williams, who confirmed that Gosnell was not at the clinic at any time when drugs were given to Mrs. Mongar. Agent Huff returned to Gosnell who told him, again, that any medication given to Mrs. Mongar was administered was while he was at the clinic.

Gosnell stated that he had given one dose to Mrs. Mongar and that a "nurse" may have medicated her at his direction and while he was present at the clinic. Gosnell's fabricated account not only was self-serving, in that he claimed to have been supervising his employees, but it also served to hinder apprehension of Williams and West for their involvement in Mrs. Mongar's death. **We recommend that Kermit Gosnell be charged with the crime of hindering.**

Because West also actively sought to minimize Williams's and Gosnell's culpability for Mrs. Mongar's death by providing false or misleading information, **we recommend that Sherry West be charged with tampering with or fabricating physical evidence, tampering with records, and hindering apprehension or prosecution. We recommend charging Liz Hampton with perjury** in light of her patently false testimony to the Grand Jury about events surrounding the death of Mrs. Mongar.

Section VII: Criminal Charges

ILLEGAL LATE-TERM ABORTIONS

Pennsylvania law generally prohibits abortions when a woman is 24 or more weeks pregnant. **We recommend that Kermit Gosnell be charged with 33 counts of performing illegal abortions.** From the testimony and the evidence we have reviewed, we believe that Gosnell performed scores more such abortions. Violation of this law, however, is subject to a two-year statute of limitations. And investigators to date have been able to locate only a portion of Gosnell's files from the past two years.

Gosnell's staff consistently told us that he regularly performed abortions after the 24-week limit. Latosha Lewis saw patients who were as much as 26 weeks pregnant "very often." Kareema Cross testified, "our clinic was the clinic that it doesn't matter how many weeks you are, he'll do it." Steve Massof estimated that 40 percent of supposed second-trimester abortions were actually greater than 24 weeks.

Gosnell's employees told us that when an ultrasound indicated that a woman was more than 24 weeks pregnant, Gosnell would conduct another ultrasound, manipulating the transducer to distort the image and produce a false reading of an earlier pregnancy. Williams explained to the FBI that Gosnell "dummies" the paperwork. Cross told us, "If it's a big baby, he [Gosnell] never tell us the truth." She testified that when Gosnell manipulated ultrasounds to disguise late abortions, "He'll always say the baby was 24.5." Latosha Lewis told us the same thing.

This testimony was corroborated by numerous patient files showing woman after woman to be precisely 24.5 weeks pregnant before Gosnell performed an abortion. In many of these files there were multiple ultrasounds, including those showing that the woman was more than 24 weeks pregnant.

Ironically, in falsifying gestational ages, Gosnell routinely designated late-term pregnancies as 24.5-week pregnancies, yet 24.5 weeks is too late. Pennsylvania law prohibits abortions "when the gestational age of the unborn child is 24 or more weeks," 18 Pa.C.S. § 3211(a); the legal limit is thus 23 weeks and 6 days. Even accepting at face value the remarkable coincidence of so many supposed 24.5-week pregnancies, every single one of those terminations was an illegal abortion.

In the presentment, we have listed 31 instances where, based on our examination of patients' files, we found that Gosnell performed illegal late-term abortions; we recommend felony charges for each of these instances. In addition, we recommend that Gosnell be charged with two counts of performing illegal abortions on 28-week-old Baby Boy B and 26-week-old Baby Girl A, discussed in an earlier section.

We recommend that Lynda Williams and Sherry West be charged with performing illegal late-term abortions, and that Kermit Gosnell, Williams, and West be charged with conspiracy to perform abortions beyond 24 weeks. We have specific evidence that Williams assisted Gosnell in 13 of the 31 illegal abortions listed in the presentment, and that West assisted Gosnell with one of these cases.

We recommend prosecuting Pearl Gosnell for performing, and conspiring with her husband to perform, illegal abortions, based on testimony that she assisted him on Sundays. That was the day, according to the other staff, that very late-term abortions were done. Pearl testified that she alone assisted on Sundays, and that her

Section VII: Criminal Charges

role was to "help do the instruments" in the procedure room and to monitor patients in the recovery room. Lewis testified that Pearl assisted with late-term abortions "on Sundays or days we were closed [to] do special cases."

We heard testimony about one Sunday patient, a 14-year-old girl who was almost 30 weeks pregnant, far beyond the 24-week limit. She said she was scheduled to undergo the abortion procedure on Sunday, July 13, 2008. At home at 3:00 a.m. Sunday, however, her membranes ruptured after several hours of labor and she went instead to Crozer-Chester Hospital. There, she delivered a stillborn baby girl. The medical examiner of Delaware County determined that the baby girl was at least 29 weeks old, and possibly as old as 34 weeks.

BLACKOUT: The Official GOSNELL Grand Jury Report

VIOLATIONS OF THE ABORTION CONTROL ACT

Under Pennsylvania's Abortion Control Act, a doctor must counsel a patient and obtain her written consent at least 24 hours before performing an abortion. The physician must inform the patient at least 24 hours before an abortion of:

> (i) The nature of the proposed procedure or treatment and of those risks and alternatives to the procedure or treatment that a reasonable patient would consider material to the decision of whether or not to undergo the abortion.
> (ii) The probable gestational age of the unborn child at the time the abortion is to be performed.
> (iii) The medical risks associated with carrying her child to term.

In addition, at least 24 hours before an abortion, the physician or an assistant must provide the patient with certain state-mandated information. The patient must certify, in writing, that she has received the required information.

Gosnell did not bother with these requirements. He did not counsel patients as required by law — he usually did not meet or even speak to them before completing their abortions. Mrs. Mongar's sole contact with Gosnell, for example, was while she lay unconscious on the procedure table. According to Kareema Cross, in the four years she worked at the clinic, "we never did it," referring to the state-required counseling. Instead patients were given a piece of paper to sign. That was it for "informed consent."

Gosnell ignored the 24-hour waiting period, and instead offered some patients same-day procedures. Latosha Lewis told us:

Section VII: Criminal Charges

They would be able to come in 10 [a.m.] to 4 [p.m.], do an ultrasound and blood work . . . [and] we would ask them, did you want to stay today, have your procedure done, even though by state law, we were supposed to give them 24 hours.

FBI agent Catherine Carter testified that Lynda Williams explained that, at an abortion patient's initial visit, a staff member has her sign the consent form. We found 243 instances in which the patient then had an abortion on the same day that she signed the consent form. We also found files where there was no consent form, the consent form was not signed, or the consent form was not dated. All of these constitute violations of the law. **We recommend that Kermit Gosnell be charged with 310 counts of violating the Abortion Control Act.**

BLACKOUT: The Official GOSNELL Grand Jury Report

ABUSE OF CORPSE

We heard evidence that Gosnell often mutilated dead babies and fetuses by cutting off their feet, which he, weirdly, kept in specimen jars in the clinic. During the February 2010 raid, investigators were shocked to see a row of jars on a shelf in the clinic containing fetal parts. Kareema Cross showed us several photographs that she took in 2008 of a closet where Gosnell stored jars containing severed feet of fetuses. Ashley Baldwin testified that she saw about 30 such jars.

None of the medical or abortion experts who testified before the Grand Jury had ever heard of such a disturbing practice, nor could they come up with an explanation for it. The medical expert on abortions testified that cutting off the feet "is bizarre and off the wall." The experts uniformly rejected out of hand Gosnell's supposed explanation that he was preserving the feet for DNA purposes should paternity ever become an issue. A small tissue sample would suffice to collect DNA. None of the staff knew of any instance in which feet were ever used for this purpose.

It is a crime for a person to treat "a corpse in a way that he knows would outrage ordinary family sensibilities." We were as outraged as the medical experts at this practice.

The following severed feet and a fetus without feet were discovered in the 2010 raid:

> The feet of a 22-week fetus in specimen containers that the medical examiner referred to as 4C-1 and 4C-2. These containers were labeled with the same name and the date 12/5/09. Each foot was in a separate container. The medical examiner found with respect to each foot that "the distal portion of the leg has been sharply transected 2.5 cm above the sole of the foot."

Section VII: Criminal Charges

A 21-week fetus, gender indeterminate, found in a plastic bleach bottle, wrapped in red biohazard bag 3F. The medical examiner discovered that "Both feet have been severed at the level of the distal leg and are not present in the container."

The left foot of a 19-week fetus in specimen container 4B. According to the medical examiner, "The distal portion of the leg has been sharply transected 2.7 cm. above the sole of the foot."

The feet of a 19-week fetus in specimen containers 5B-1 and 5B-2. As to the left foot, the medical examiner found, "The distal portion of the leg has been sharply transected 2.5 cm. above the sole of the foot in an oblique fashion." As to the right foot, "the distal portion of the leg has been sharply transected 1.9 cm. above the sole of the foot in an oblique fashion."

We also heard evidence that, after cutting the spinal cords of live babies, Gosnell would put the babies in cut-off milk jugs, water containers, and juice cartons. The intact body of one 28-week-old male, which we previously referred to as Baby Boy B, was discovered in a bag in the clinic's freezer during the February 2010 raid. It was in a plastic water container with the top cut off, along with the placenta and gauze pads. The baby had a surgical incision at the base of the neck and was determined by the medical examiner to have been viable.

The Medical Examiner testified:

> But certainly things like drink containers, milk containers, water containers, this is not something we do in medical practice. ... What I do does not deal with living patients, and I would not put something in a plastic drink container. It just— it feels wrong I guess is what I'm saying. It feels wrong.

Based the evidence, we recommend that Gosnell be charged with five counts of abuse of corpse.

BLACKOUT: The Official GOSNELL Grand Jury Report

THEFT BY DECEPTION

Gosnell hired unqualified staff because he could pay them low wages, often in cash, "under the table." These staff members included two medical school graduates, Steven Massof and Eileen O'Neill, who testified that they never had valid Pennsylvania medical licenses while working for Gosnell.

According to the testimony of other workers, "Dr. O'Neill" and "Dr. Steve" held themselves out to be doctors. Gosnell hired them knowing that they were not licensed to provide medical care and, as Massof and O'Neill testified, paid them a pittance to treat patients in his absence. Kareema Cross told us that both acted and practiced like doctors, and that she and other workers believed them to be doctors.

Patients were duped as well. Massof testified that he wrote prescriptions for patients on pads pre-signed by Gosnell. Della Mann, a registered nurse and former clinic employee, was a long-time patient of O'Neill's who said she was shocked to discover recently she was not a licensed physician.

We reviewed Della Mann's file. It contains 14 faxes sent by Ms. Mann addressed to "Dr. Gosnell, Dr. O'Neill" and 3 addressed solely to "Dr. O'Neill." A fax dated June 18, 2007 reads: "Dear Dr. Please call Rite-Aid Coreg problem Metforman needed Rite-Aid 215-438-5167." There is a handwritten note, "Done" on this fax, signed "E" and dated 6/18/07. A fax addressed only to Dr. O'Neill and sent on 2/17/08 with the subject line "Carvedilol 6.25mg bid," reads: "out of medication please call in Rite aid 215-438-5167." This fax also contains a handwritten notation, "done — need BP ??," followed by a signature "E" and the date, 2/18/08.

Section VII: Criminal Charges

We found forms in Ms. Mann's file showing that on 1/30/07, 3/8/07, 6/4/07, and 6/7/07, Dr. O'Neill signed as the clinician for office visits. On each date she observed and treated symptoms and made diagnoses. We also found prescriptions that were written for Ms. Mann on 3/8/07, 6/7/07, 8/10/07, and 12/1/07; these appear to be in the same handwriting as on the patient visit information and the handwritten notes on the faxes signed "E." Two of these prescriptions are for "Coreg" and one is for "metformin." Our examination of Ms. Mann's file shows that two $80 claims were submitted to Independence Blue Cross for Ms. Mann's March and June 2007 visits.

Della Mann was not the only patient who was deceived. We found 10 other examples of patients who paid Gosnell's clinic for examination and treatment by a doctor, but were instead treated by "Dr. O'Neill" or "Dr. Steve." **We recommend that Kermit Gosnell, Eileen O'Neill, and Steven Massof be charged with theft by deception and conspiracy to commit theft by deception.** Based on patient dates within the past five years in the cases listed above, and the testimony and evidence provided by Della Mann, summarized above, we recommend nine counts of theft against O'Neill, one count against Massof, and 10 against Gosnell.

BLACKOUT: The Official GOSNELL Grand Jury Report

PERJURY IN RELATION TO THE UNAUTHORIZED PRACTICE OF MEDICINE

Eileen O'Neill testified before the Grand Jury under oath that she did not treat patients at Gosnell's clinic. She testified that she would "see" patients if Gosnell asked and when he was present, but "I never decide what treatment is." She claimed she did not see patients alone, that Gosnell would at least "st[i]ck his head in," and that everyone knew she was not a licensed doctor.

But Della Mann testified that she had no idea that her long-time "doctor," O'Neill, was not a licensed doctor. Employees testified that they believed she was a legitimate doctor. And the patient files we reviewed showed that, contrary to her sworn testimony, O'Neill examined and treated patients. She performed medical abortions. She wrote out prescriptions.

O'Neill also testified that she did not work on Wednesdays. But our review of patient files shows that she did see patients on Wednesdays. The Wednesday patient visits are significant because Gosnell was not present at the clinic to treat patients on Wednesdays; O'Neill thus would have treated these patients without supervision, notwithstanding her testimony that Gosnell was always present when she saw patients. Randy Hutchins testified that on Wednesdays, O'Neill was at the clinic by herself. He also told us that other days she came in "an hour or two before [Gosnell] did" and upon her arrival there were "patients waiting to see her."

Based on this evidence **we recommend charging Eileen O'Neill with false swearing and perjury.**

Section VII: Criminal Charges

VIOLATIONS OF THE CONTROLLED SUBSTANCES ACT IN RELATION TO THE ILLEGAL ADMINISTERING AND PRESCRIPTION OF DRUGS

Steven Massof testified that when Dr. Gosnell was not present, he would administer drugs to patients. Kareema Cross confirmed that "in the procedure room he [Massof] did the IV's, he did patient medications." Massof also testified that Gosnell left him pre-signed prescription pads, allowing him to prescribe medicine for patients, even though he was not authorized to write prescriptions.

Based on this evidence **we recommend that Kermit Gosnell and Steven Massof be charged with conspiring to violate the Controlled Substances Act.**

CORRUPT ORGANIZATION

We recommend charging Kermit Gosnell, Lynda Williams, Sherry West, Eileen O'Neill, Steven Massof, and Tina Baldwin with violating the corrupt organization statute, 18 Pa.C.S. § 911, based on a pattern of racketeering activity. **We recommend that these same six individuals as well as Pearl Gosnell and Maddline Joe be charged with conspiring to commit racketeering activity.**

"Racketeering activity" includes violations of chapter 25 of the Crimes Code (homicide), chapter 39 (theft), section 13 of the Controlled Substances Act, and conspiracy to commit any of these violations. A "pattern of racketeering activity" means "two or more acts of racketeering activity." It is "unlawful for any person employed by or associated with any enterprise to conduct or participate, directly or indirectly, in the conduct of such enterprise's affairs through a pattern of racketeering activity." 18 Pa.C.S. § 911(b)(3).

Gosnell ran a corrupt organization. He performed illegal late-term abortions that resulted in babies born alive, whom he killed, or had others kill; he directed his workers to sedate patients with narcotics in violation of the controlled substances act; and he employed bogus doctors to treat unsuspecting, paying patients. Maddline Joe, his office administrator, collected the money that came in from these criminal activities. Williams, West, O'Neill, Massof, Tina Baldwin, and Pearl Gosnell all actively participated in various aspects of Gosnell's corrupt organization.

The Grand Jury received evidence of multiple violations of Chapter 25. These included not only the specific murders discussed earlier in this report, but also the ongoing pattern of killing babies born alive by Gosnell, Massof, Williams, and Moton. Patient files show that Tina Baldwin assisted with these late abortions. So did Pearl Gosnell. By aiding very late-term abortions, they conspired with Kermit Gosnell to kill living babies delivered by their unconscious mothers.

We heard ample evidence, summarized earlier in this report, regarding recurrent violations of the Controlled Substances Act. Steven Massof, Lynda Williams, Sherry West, Tina Baldwin, and Adrienne Moton, as part of their duties for which Gosnell hired them, conspired with him to violate the drug laws by agreeing to illegally administer narcotics to patients.

Gosnell's corrupt enterprise also involved theft. Gosnell employed bogus doctors, deceiving patients who thought they were being treated by, and paying for treatment by, bona fide physicians.

Section VII: Criminal Charges

O'Neill and Massof each conspired with Gosnell to commit thefts by deception, as we explained above. These thefts were integral to Gosnell's corrupt enterprise. As numerous witnesses testified, he largely ran his practice in absentia and hired the fake doctors to treat patients in his absence.

Maddline Joe worked for Gosnell for more than 20 years, most recently as the office administrator. She testified that in that role she ordered and paid for Demerol. As many employees testified, it was a long-standing, established practice at Gosnell's clinic that this drug was to be given to patients by unlicensed workers and without medical supervision. Joe also testified that she paid Gosnell's workers and that she handled the money paid to the clinic by patients. She said she also saw patient files. We did too, and we saw that non-doctors Massof and O'Neill treated and examined many patients. Gosnell, with the assistance of Maddline Joe, received the fees collected from duped patients.

We have concluded there is probable cause to believe that each of these persons knowingly agreed with Gosnell to participate in his corrupt organization. **We recommend that charges of conspiracy to violate the corrupt organizations statute be brought against Kermit Gosnell, Pearl Gosnell, Lynda Williams, Sherry West, Adrienne Moton, Steven Massof, Eileen O'Neill, Tina Baldwin, and Maddline Joe.**

BLACKOUT: The Official GOSNELL Grand Jury Report

OBSTRUCTION OF JUSTICE AND TAMPERING WITH EVIDENCE IN RELATION TO THE DESTRUCTION OF FILES

Between the time that law enforcement officials raided Gosnell's office in February 2010 and the time that investigators returned with a warrant to seize patient files, many files disappeared. We viewed a videotape of the raid and saw files on shelves outside the procedure rooms. Latosha Lewis and others told us that these were recent second-trimester abortion files. The shelves were bare when investigators returned.

Tina Baldwin testified that "second trimester charts, usually those real big ones, they didn't stay in the office." Other employees corroborated her observation. Gosnell took those files home, Baldwin said, "if there were difficult cases or some cases where he thought they shouldn't be in there." A subsequent search of Gosnell's home and car turned up only some of these files. Massof told us that Gosnell always took files home, so "I think he has them. If he hasn't destroyed them, he has them."

We also learned from the state Department of Health that sometime after the February 2010 raid, Gosnell suddenly filed numerous reports of abortions, including previously unreported second-trimester abortions. To complete the detailed health department forms, Gosnell would have had to have the patient files. We have reviewed these forms and, for the most part, the corresponding patients files are missing. In a letter accompanying his March 2010 submission to the Department of Health, Gosnell advised that the information came "from patient charts [that] have been removed from the facility."

Section VII: Criminal Charges

Based on this evidence, we believe that Gosnell, aware he was under investigation, intentionally destroyed or disposed of patient files. This constitutes intentional obstruction of "the administration of law or other governmental function by ... physical interference or obstacle." 18 Pa.C.S. § 5101 (obstruction). It also constitutes tampering with physical evidence. 18 Pa.C.S. § 4910 (tampering). **We recommend that Kermit Gosnell be charged with obstruction and tampering.**

CORRUPTION OF THE MORALS OF A MINOR

Gosnell hired high school student Ashley Baldwin to medicate patients, in violation of the Controlled Substances Act, and to assist with illegal abortions, in violation of the Abortion Control Act. Ashley's mother had worked at the clinic for years, assisting Gosnell with abortions, including illegal late-term abortions, and with medicating patients, in violation of the Controlled Substances Act.

Ashley was only 15 when she began working for Gosnell. He subsequently trained her, as he had trained her mother, to assist with abortions and give medications to patients. Tina Baldwin and Ashley Baldwin both testified that Gosnell would keep Ashley at the clinic, assisting with abortions, sometimes until well after midnight, even though Ashley was still in high school. Tina Baldwin knew her daughter was being directed to perform tasks that she was not authorized to do.

We recommend charging Kermit Gosnell with corruption of a minor. We also recommend that Tina Baldwin be charged with the same crime. Tina worked for Gosnell for several years before recommending her daughter for employment. As Ashley's involvement in Gosnell's illegal practices became deeper—at one point she was working 50-hour weeks and well past midnight, while trying to complete high school—Tina did nothing to curtail her minor daughter's exploitation by Gosnell.

We also reviewed evidence that Gosnell did not obtain parental consent, as required under the Abortion Control Act, before performing abortions on minors. The law bars such patients from obtaining abortions without parental consent or judicial approval, but Gosnell went ahead and performed the abortions. Based on two files from the past two years, in which we found there was no parental signature, we recommend two additional charges against Kermit Gosnell for corruption of a minor.

SECTION VIII: RECOMMENDATIONS

This Grand Jury's responsibilities are not limited to recommending criminal charges against those directly responsible for the death of Karnamaya Mongar, the killing of babies born alive, and other criminal activity at the Women's Medical Society clinic. The jurors assume, as well, the task of proposing institutional and legal reforms—to address the systematic flaws exemplified by this case, and to reduce the likelihood that similar crimes will recur.

1. There should be no statute of limitations for infanticide.

We recommend that the legislature amend the statute of limitations so that infanticide is treated as what it is—homicide. It is important to extend the statute of limitations not only because of the seriousness of the offense, but also because the crime is hard to discover. Gosnell, we are convinced, committed hundreds of acts of infanticide. He got away with them for decades because they all took place inside his clinic. We are disappointed that we can charge him for only the babies he let die in the past two years. Homicide has no statute of limitations, and neither should infanticide.

2. The statute of limitations for illegal abortions beyond 24 weeks should be extended to five years.

Like infanticide, illegal abortions can go undetected for years, or forever. There is no one to complain and, most often, no witness to testify. Again, the jurors were frustrated that we could not recommend charges against Gosnell for scores of crimes we know he committed. We recommend that the statute of limitations for illegal post-24-week abortions be extended to five years.

3. Impersonating a doctor should be a crime.

We were surprised to find out that impersonating a doctor in Pennsylvania is not a crime. There are civil sanctions for those who practice medicine without a license, but not criminal sanctions. Pretending to be a doctor is a serious offense. The fake doctors at Women's Medical Society were employed by Gosnell to probe women's bodies. Worse still, he had these unlicensed phonies administering dangerous drugs to unsuspecting patients. We recommend making impersonation of a doctor a crime.

4. The Abortion Control Act should be amended to prohibit the mutilation of fetal remains.

One of the most bizarre things about this case is Dr. Gosnell's fetal foot collection. He cut the feet off the fetuses he aborted and kept them in a row of jars. No civilized society can accept such an abomination, whether the fetuses in question were viable or not.

Section VIII: Recommendations

Although current law prohibits abuse of corpse, there may be some question about how that law applies in the case of fetal remains.

To remove any such question, we recommend an amendment to the Abortion Control Act. The act contains a provision addressing fetal experimentation. Criminal penalties are provided, however, only for "experimentation" on a fetus that is as yet unborn, or on a fetus that is born alive. We believe that the statute should be changed to prohibit the mutilation of any fetal remains, whether or not viable or born alive.

5. The Pennsylvania Department of Health should license abortion clinics as ambulatory surgical facilities.

Under the plain language of the Health Care Facilities Act, abortion clinics should be regulated, licensed, and monitored as Ambulatory Surgical Facilities. Had the state Department of Health not inexplicably declined to classify abortion clinics as ASFs, Gosnell's clinic would have been subject to yearly inspection and licensing.

The department's inspectors could have inspected at any time, announced or unannounced, to investigate any complaints. The sight of unlicensed employees sedating patients in Gosnell's absence would presumably have triggered action. Given the clinic's filthy conditions, it surely would have been shut down long ago if DOH had merely taken a look.

The regulations for Pennsylvania's ambulatory surgical facilities—which run over 30 pages—provide a comprehensive set of rules and procedures to assure overall quality of care at such facilities. The effect of the Department of Health's reluctance to treat abortion clinics as ASFs was to accord patients of those facilities far less protection than patients seeking, for example, liposuction or a colonoscopy.

Those clinics, unlike abortion facilities, must implement measures for infection control (28 Pa. Code. §567.3 lists 17 specific procedures that ASFs must follow to control infection). They must use sterile linens (§567.21-24). They must keep premises and equipment clean and free of vermin, insects, rodents, and litter (§567.31). The regulations devote three pages to anesthesia protocols (28 Pa. Code §555.33).

Gosnell's facility fell far below the basic, minimum standards of care that any patient having a surgical procedure should expect to receive. There is no justification for denying abortion patients the protections available to every other patient of an ambulatory surgical facility, and no reason to exempt abortion clinics from meeting these standards.

The inspection of abortion facilities is too important a responsibility to be left to the discretion of the Department of Health, subject to the whim of bureaucrats and lawyers who have abdicated their duty to uphold the law. As ASFs, abortion providers would be subject to mandatory annual inspections. If a facility failed to meet the standards required for all ambulatory surgical facilities, it would lose its license.

Section VIII: Recommendations

6. The state Department of Health should update the regulations for abortion providers.

Officials from the Pennsylvania Department of Health complained that the regulations that it wrote do not give it the authority needed to carry out its duty to protect the health of women having abortions and of premature babies delivered alive. We recommend that the department amend its regulations so that it is not only able to carry out its responsibilities, but is required to do so. The regulations, which have stood essentially unchanged since 1988, should also be updated to reflect changes in abortion practices and medical advances.

Crucial to state health officials' ability to ensure quality care and compliance with the law is the authority to inspect facilities and their records regularly and thoroughly. The abortion regulations should be amended to require annual inspections and to allow unannounced inspections.

Even if the Department of Health licenses abortion clinics as ASFs, there is still a need to inspect for compliance with laws and regulations that do not apply to other ASFs — safety measures that are specific to childbirth and protections for premature infants aborted alive. Inspections for compliance with the Abortion Control Act and its regulations could be conducted at the same time as the ASF inspections to minimize intrusion and maximize resources.

The abortion regulations should specify that annual inspections of abortion providers include, at a minimum:

- Verification of necessary certifications and licenses of all staff. A clinic must also provide a list of all employees, including any unpaid externs, interns, residents, or volunteers.
- Certification that all medical staff are CPR-trained.
- A review of patient files to determine that they are properly maintained, secure, and current.

File inspection should include, at a minimum, a review of:

- *Consent forms.* The form should be signed at the time counseling is provided by a physician, if counseling is in person. If the counseling occurs over the telephone, the form should acknowledge this, and state the time of the counseling.
- *Ultrasounds.* They should be signed by a certified technician, and must include the accurate date and time when the ultrasound was performed.
- *Anesthesia records.* They should include what drugs were administered and by whom.
- *Pathology reports.* These should be required for second-trimester abortions after the 20th week of gestation. The doctor must certify that the fetus is not viable and send the fetus to a pathologist for confirmation.
- *Recovery room records.* They should be signed by the attending nurse.
- *Report forms.* Clinics must file a report with the state for every abortion. These should be cross-checked against

Section VIII: Recommendations

monthly and quarterly reports that clinics must also file with the state.
- *Inspection of all equipment*, to be sure it is in working order.
- *Inspection of medications* for expiration dates.

The Department of Health might draw additional standards for inspection from protocols published by the National Abortion Federation, Planned Parenthood, and CHOICE, a Philadelphia non-profit that offers information, education, and referrals related to women's and children's health care. These groups conduct inspections of abortion facilities before approving them or referring women to them. Their standards are, in many ways, more stringent and more protective of women's safety than are Pennsylvania's abortion regulations.

The revised abortion regulations should specify procedures to be followed when deficiencies are found, and consequences for when the deficiencies are not remedied. We recommend requiring that identified problems be corrected within 30 days, with a clinic subject to unannounced re-inspections to check remediation.

Loss of license or approval to operate should be the sanction for failure to take adequate remedial action. The Department of Health should give itself the power to take immediate action to revoke approval of a facility if deficiencies present an immediate danger to women or to viable fetuses beyond 24 weeks, whom the law protects.

In order to deter providers like Gosnell from attempting to elude detection for multiple crimes by simply failing to report second and third-trimester abortions, the sanction for willful and repeated failure to report should be made more severe, including permanent revocation of the facility's approval as an abortion provider.

We recommend that the state Department of Health's inspection reports be sent to the Philadelphia Department of Public Health. Failure to remedy deficiencies should also to be reported to the city health department and to the Department of State for action by the Board of Medicine.

In addition, we recommend the following amendments to Pennsylvania's abortion regulations:

Require that all abortions past 18 weeks be performed or supervised by a board certified obstetrician/gynecologist. The current regulation, requiring only that a clinic have a certified obstetrician/gynecologist available for consultation, clearly was ineffective in this case. The name of the supervising obstetrician/gynecologist should be on the paperwork for every abortion the doctor supervises or performs.

Give the Department of Health the authority and duty to investigate all reports of maternal death arising from pregnancy, childbirth, or abortion. Require that such maternal deaths be investigated by DOH as quickly as possible, but in no case later than 60 days of the report. The results of the investigation should be conveyed to county health departments, to the state Board of Medicine, and to law enforcement.

Section VIII: Recommendations

7. Pennsylvania's Departments of Health and State should make their process for filing complaints against doctors and facilities simpler and more responsive.

The Pennsylvania Department of Health makes it next to impossible to file a complaint concerning abortion providers. We could find no mention on its website that the department was even responsible for regulating or overseeing abortion clinics. When persistent lawyers, like Semika Shaw's; and doctors, such as Dr. Hellman, the Medical Examiner from Delaware County, and Dr. Schwarz, Philadelphia's Health Commissioner, have registered complaints anyway, they have been uniformly ignored. DOH did not inspect Gosnell's clinic even after Karnamaya Mongar died.

We applaud the current Secretary of Health for reinstituting regular inspections of abortion facilities. But the department must also develop an effective, easy, and responsive complaint process. Complaints should be accepted by telephone (a toll-free 800 number should be instituted), online, or in writing—in any manner, that is, in which a citizen might choose to complain. Every complaint should be logged in and investigated. The complainant should be informed that the department has received the complaint and should be provided with a means of following up to check its status. When fellow doctors, public health agencies, or law enforcement agencies file complaints, they, obviously, should be taken seriously and should trigger immediate investigations, including unannounced inspections.

The **Department of State** has a complaint process, and a complaint form, for filing complaints against doctors. The complaint process should be made easier and more responsive. Complaint forms to health care-related boards should be tailored to medical concerns and assure confidentiality of patients' records. Forms should be available in common foreign languages and should be simple to understand and fill out. Complaints should also be accepted by telephone and internet, with the phone number published online. Patients should be allowed to remain anonymous, but third-party complainants should be identified. Hearings, if necessary, should be offered locally.

All complaints should be acknowledged and logged in. Complainants should have a way of tracking their status. If a complaint comes in that properly belongs with the state Department of Health or local health agencies, the Department of State should be responsible to make sure that it gets to the right place and is investigated appropriately.

8. Philadelphia's Department of Public Health should develop a hotline to assist residents in filing complaints with the proper state and local authorities.

The Philadelphia Department of Public Health does not regulate doctors or medical facilities. It should, however, play an active role in assuring that Philadelphia doctors and facilities are providing safe and competent services to its citizens. We recommend that the department devise and implement a hotline system along the lines suggested by Dr. Schwarz. It should log in complaints and assure that they are forwarded to the proper state agency, whether it is the Department of Health for complaints about facilities, the Department of State for complaints about individual doctors, or the city health department for issues under its authority. Among the three departments, a way

Section VIII: Recommendations

should be devised to track complaints and respond to the medical consumers. The city health department should also track complaints so that it can identify providers that have a particularly large number of complaints.

We recommend that Philadelphia City Council pass a law requiring that medical facilities post the city health department hotline number at their front desks.

9. The Pennsylvania Departments of Health and State need to share information they receive that is pertinent to each other's responsibilities.

It was clear from the testimony of witnesses from both agencies that there is inadequate coordination between the two departments that should serve a common purpose — to protect public health and safety. Although the need to coordinate functions obviously exists, given that the Department of State is charged with licensing and regulating doctors, while the Department of Health is charged with licensing and monitoring the health care facilities where they practice, no system is in place now that makes this happen.

Coordination between the two departments is especially crucial because different laws require different information to be reported to different agencies. Both departments could carry out their duties better if they shared this information and the results of their investigations. For example, the Abortion Control Act requires doctors to report maternal deaths and complications resulting from abortions to the Department of Health, but not the Department of State (18 Pa.C.S. §3214(g) and (h)).

The Medical Care Availability and Reduction of Error (MCARE) law also requires health care facilities to report "serious incidents" to the Department of Health (40 P.S. §313), which is required to investigate the incidents (40 P.S. §306). But lawsuits are reported to the Department of State (40 P.S. §903). Insurance companies likewise report settlements to the Department of State under the MCARE act (40 P.S. §746).

The Abortion Control Act gives the Department of Health the job of regulating and monitoring abortion clinics (18 Pa.C.S. §3207). But enforcement of many of the act's provisions is left to the Department of State (18 Pa.C.S. §3219).

These two departments have to devise a system so that the agency that has the authority and the responsibility to take action also has the necessary information.

10. The Department of State should train its prosecutors and provide the necessary tools so they can more effectively investigate complaints against doctors.

Our review of the Department of State's handling of complaints filed against Gosnell revealed many problems. Some of the prosecutors seemed to be unaware of the full history of complaints against the doctor. Others seemed not to coordinate with a colleague who was working on a similar complaint. Prosecutor Ruiz said that he had no way to find out about malpractice suits filed against a doctor, unless they were reported to the department. And some Board of Medicine attorneys simply used terrible judgment—closing an "investigation" of a death with no apparent investigation.

Section VIII: Recommendations

If the National Practitioner Data Bank is not accessible to prosecutors and investigators for the Department of State, it should be. If it is available, all prosecutors should be instructed to use it. Had Ruiz known that Gosnell's insurers and a State of Pennsylvania insurance fund had paid $1.7 million to five women whose uteruses, cervixes, and bowels he had perforated, he might have viewed Dana Haynes's case differently. If he had noticed that, in 2007, Gosnell paid $10,000 to settle a civil lawsuit for performing an abortion on a minor without parental consent, Ruiz could have charged Gosnell with a violation of the Abortion Control Act.

The NPDB database also provides another way that the Department of State can check that doctors are reporting their malpractice suits under MCARE. The prosecutors who handled Gosnell's complaints seemed unconcerned about MCARE reporting. But the effectiveness of the entire system contemplated by the MCARE law — which was designed to enhance patient safety — rests largely on self-reporting by doctors. To make it work, there has to be enforcement of the reporting requirements.

Reporting by doctors should be checked against public records and the NPDB database whenever there is a complaint or an application for license renewal.

Most importantly, Department of State prosecutors should be instructed that their job is to suspend and revoke the licenses of doctors who are incompetent, unethical, or criminal. Failure to do so should be grounds for termination.

11. The Pennsylvania Departments of Health and State should be required to share with law enforcement information relevant to criminal investigations.

The jurors are aware that the Department of State initially asserted some type of privilege with respect to the confidentiality of its investigative files. We also heard evidence that Department of Health investigators were instructed by department lawyers not to share information about Karnamaya Mongar's death with law enforcement. And, in fact, DOH did not share with law enforcement the letter that Gosnell sent to the department notifying it of Mrs. Mongar's death. That letter, in which Gosnell admitted what drugs were administered, but lied about how much medication was given and by whom, would have been helpful to have before the February 2010 raid.

We do not believe the MCARE act or any other statute protects the department's records from subpoena by a grand jury or law enforcement. If the Department of State or Health insists on interpreting any statute to have that effect, we recommend that such law be changed to clarify that the department's records should be made available for criminal investigations.

We believe the departments not only are able to share relevant information with law enforcement — they should be required to do so. If either the Department of State or the Department of Health learns of criminal activity during investigations, or even an inspection, there should be an obligation to report it to law enforcement.

Section VIII: Recommendations

12. A task force including the Medical Examiner's Office, the District Attorney's Office, and the Police Department should work to improve protocols for investigating suspicious deaths.

We are troubled that Mrs. Mongar's death might have gone unnoticed if not for the drug raid three months later. The city must improve protocols for investigating suspicious deaths that require investigation before they can be labeled homicide. We recommend that a task force be formed to develop protocols for cases such as this one—where a patient dies from an overdose of drugs at a medical facility as well as others where the manner of death requires substantial investigation, including gathering facts and evidence possibly outside the expertise of the Medical Examiner.

13. The City of Philadelphia should enforce medical waste disposal plans that it requires from providers.

Commissioner Schwarz testified that the city instituted a program to require medical providers to submit infectious waste disposal plans simply as a revenue measure. We recommend that the city actually enforce compliance with those plans. At the very least, the department should respond more effectively than it did in this case when a complaint is made. If the department enforces compliance with fines, it can continue to generate revenue and offset the cost of additional inspectors.

14. We recommend that the National Abortion Federation reconsider the inclusion of Atlantic Women's Medical Services in Delaware in its membership.

We recommend that NAF reassess the membership of Atlantic Women's Medical Services, the Delaware abortion clinic where Gosnell worked part-time before losing his license in that state. We learned that at least six patients were referred from Atlantic to Gosnell's clinic in Philadelphia for illegal late-term abortions. These patients paid Atlantic for late-term procedures performed by Gosnell in his Lancaster Avenue clinic. We heard evidence that Gosnell would insert laminaria in patients in Delaware and then have them come to his Philadelphia office for the abortion procedure itself. The director of Atlantic Women's Medical Services, Leroy Brinkley, was unconcerned. He did not properly supervise the doctors he hired as "independent contractors" to assure that they were complying with the law. Remarkably, despite Gosnell's long time association with Atlantic, Brinkley only produced three files for patients seen by Gosnell at Brinkley's clinic.

Section VIII: Recommendations

15. The authorities responsible for overseeing, monitoring, or licensing Gosnell or his operation should conduct serious self-assessments to determine why their departments failed to protect the women and babies whose lives were imperiled at Gosnell's clinic. Employees who failed to perform their jobs of protecting the public should be held accountable.

The employees of the state and local health departments and the prosecutors for the Board of Medicine are charged with protecting the public health. Very few that we ran across in this investigation came even close to fulfilling that duty. These people seemed oblivious to the connection between their dereliction and the deaths and injuries that Gosnell inflicted under their watch.

Those at the state Department of Health who were responsible for assuring the health and safety of women and infants delivered live at abortion clinics were aggressively passive when it came to inspections or responding to complaints. The department's attorneys were encouraged to misinterpret laws so that the department could evade its duty to protect public health. DOH employees were only too glad to go along with the charade. The prosecutors for the Board of Medicine, who are charged with sanctioning bad doctors, appeared determined not to discipline even one of the worst doctors in the region.

Numerous city health department employees went about their jobs going in and out of Gosnell's clinic, performing some particular task to promote public health, while ignoring the most squalid, unsafe conditions imaginable in a Philadelphia health care facility.

One diligent employee, Lori Matijkiw, who reported what she saw, expected her supervisors to do something. They did nothing.

It is not our job to say who should be fired or demoted. We believe, however, that anyone responsible for permitting Gosnell to operate as he did should face strong disciplinary action up to and including termination. This includes not only the people who failed to do the inspecting, the prosecuting, and the protecting, but also those at the top who obviously tolerated, or even encouraged, the inaction.

The Department of State literally licensed Gosnell's criminally dangerous behavior. DOH gave its stamp of approval to his facility. These agencies do not deserve the public's trust. The fate of Karnamaya Mongar and countless babies with severed spinal cords is proof that people at those departments were not doing their jobs. Those charged with protecting the public must do better.

Appendix A

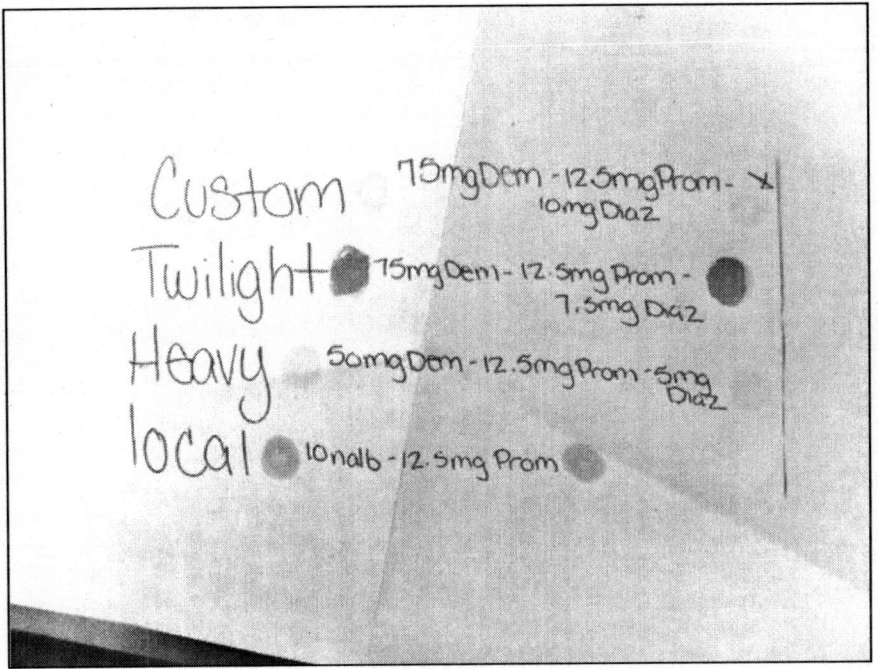

Appendix B

ANESTHESIA FOR SURGERY

You have already decided that a procedure is best for you. Now you need to choose the type of pain relief. It will probably be best to pay the extra money and be more comfortable if some of the following conditions are true for you:
1. The decision to have the procedure is a difficult decision.
2. Medication is usually necessary for your menstrual cramps.
3. Your decision has been forced by your parents or partner.
4. Your family members or friends "don't like pain."

Most women who choose **CUSTOM SLEEP** want to feel <u>**ABSOLUTELY NO CRAMPS OR PAIN**</u> during their procedure. A needle with an anticlotting medication is inserted prior to the procedure and sedation is repeatly administered until the patient is comfortable throughout the procedure.
The additional cost is $150.00

I choose CUSTOM SLEEP _____
(Signature) (Date)

Most women who choose **TWILIGHT SLEEP** want to feel <u>**VERY FEW OR VERY SLIGHT CRAMPS**</u> during their procedure.
The additional cost is $90.00

I choose TWILIGHT SLEEP _____
(Signature) (Date)

Most women who choose **HEAVY SEDATION** feel <u>**SLIGHT TO MODERATE CRAMPS**</u> during their procedure.
The additional cost is $50.00

I choose HEAVY SEDATION _____
(Signature) (Date)

Most women who choose **LOCAL AND PREMEDICATION** feel <u>**NORMAL MENSTRAL CRAMPS TO SEVERE CRAMPS**</u> during their procedure. This level of anesthesia is considered sufficient for most patients and is INCLUDED IN THE BASIC FEE.

I choose LOCAL and PRE MED _____
(Signature) 1/25/2010 (Date)

K.B. GOSNELL, M.D.
FAMILY MEDICAL SOCIETY
a division of
WOMEN'S MEDICAL SOCIETY, INC.
3801 LANCASTER AVENUE
PHILADELPHIA, PENNA.

Appendix C

Family Medical Society
A Division of
Women's Medical Society
3801 - 3805 Lancaster Avenue
Philadelphia, PA 19104
(215) 382-4300 FAX (215) 382-3972

SEPTEMBER, 2005

PRICE LIST FOR ABORTION SERVICES

PRE OPERATIVE EXAM
    (INCLUDING ULTRASOUND) - $ 125

	Insurance, Billing Price	Discount Price* (Medicaid & Cash)	Balance (after pre op fee)
NON SURGICAL TERMINATION (RU 486)			
4-8 weeks	$ 625	$ 450	$ 325
SURGICAL			
6-12 weeks	$ 450	$ 330	$ 205
13-14 weeks	575	440	315
15-16 weeks	675	540	415
17-18 weeks	925	750	625
19-20 weeks	1150	955	830
21-22 weeks	1325	1180	1055
(multi-gravida – 2 day procedure)			
21-22 weeks	$ 1575	$ 1375	$ 1250
(prima-gravida – 3 day procedure)			
23-24 weeks	$ 1850	$ 1625	$ 1500
(almost always, a 3 day procedure)			

SEDATION**
    LOCAL SEDATION & PARACERVICAL BLOCK   no additional charge
    HEAVY SEDATION & PARACERVICAL BLOCK   additional $ 50
    TWILIGHT SEDATION & PARACERVICAL BLOCK   additional $ 90
    CUSTOM SEDATION & PARACERVICAL BLOCK   additional $ 150

* payment by credit card is acceptable but a merchandising fee is added:
    merchandising fee: $ 15 - for maximum of $ 300
                              $ 20 - for maximum of $ 500
                              $ 25 - for maximum of $ 750
                              $ 35 - for maximum of $ 1000
                              $ 45 - for maximum of $ 1500

** twilight or custom is administered at no additional cost for patients 15 to 24 gestational weeks and is provided according to the needs and comforts of the patient.
Procedure days are usually Mondays, Thursdays & Saturdays.
Two day procedures are usually Monday evening insertions for Tuesday
    or Friday late afternoon for Saturday.
Insertion of dilators for 3 day procedures are usually Sunday and Monday for Tuesday
    or Thursday and Friday for Saturday. Specific time must be scheduled!

KBG/bg

Appendix D

inside of folder

10mg dem, 0.6 prom, 2cc diaz @ 10:45 pm
1cc diazpam, 0.6cc prom, 10mg dem
1 local @ 8:14 pm

6:30 L.H.
@ 7:36 pm

NGCO
B/W

Appendix D

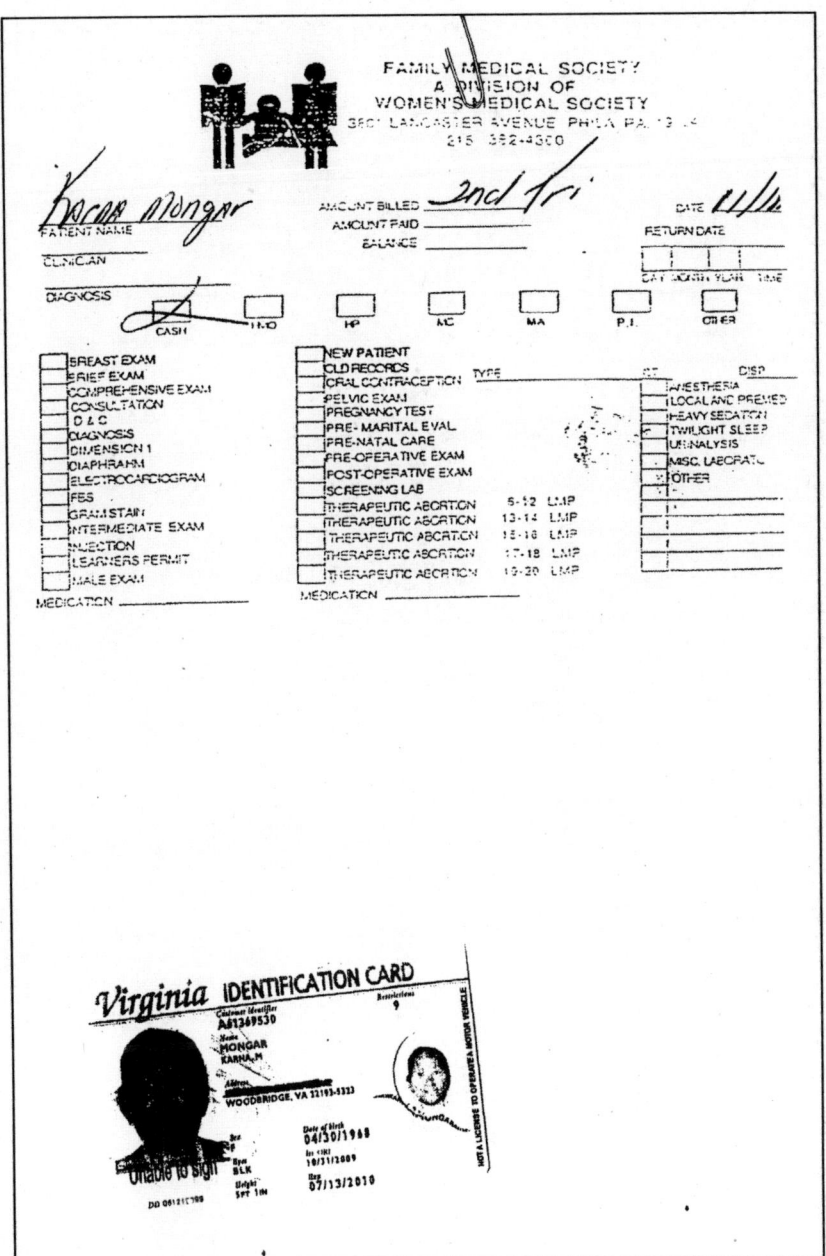

Appendix D

FAMILY MEDICAL SOCIETY
A DIVISION OF
WOMEN'S MEDICAL SOCIETY

PHILADELPHIA, PA 19107
☎ (215) 382-4300

CONSENT TO OFFICE PROCEDURE
ADMINISTRATION OF ANESTHESIA AND RENDERING
OF OTHER MEDICAL SERVICES

I authorize and direct K.B. Gosnell, M.D. and/or his associates and whomever he may designate as his assistant to perform upon

Karna Maya Mongar
(PATIENT NAME)

the following procedure(s):   **Therapeutic Abortion**

If any condition arises during the course of the procedure(s) specified above, which, in the judgment of the above-named Physician or his associates or assistant, calls for surgery, diagnostic or therapeutic procedures, including the administration of blood or blood derivative, I further request and authorize him/her to do whatever is deemed advisable for my health and well-being.

I consent to the administration of anesthesia and supportive measures by or under the direction of one of the staff members at Family Medical Society, a Division of Women's Medical Society, Inc., and use of such anesthetics.

I certify that the risks (bleeding, infection, perforation, ectopic pregnancy and psychological problems), involved in a therapeutic abortion by suction curettage and other procedures of operation, as are named above, have been fully explained to me. Should the complications of bleeding, infection or perforation occur, I understand that medication or additional surgery may be necessary. I further understand the importance and accept the responsibility for follow-up examination(s) as recommended, even in the absence of any problem.

I have been notified that any ectopic pregnancy (pregnancy developed outside the uterus) will not be terminated by the vaginal procedure listed above. A sonogram may be necessary to evaluate the possibility of an ectopic pregnancy and hospitalization may be required.

It is recommended the RHOGAM be administered and will be available within 72 hours after termination of pregnancy, if my blood type is RH Negative.

I hereby release Women's Medical Society, Inc., its Physicians, staff and personnel from any and all claims arising out of the operation and procedure(s) named above, including, without being limited to a therapeutic abortion through suction curettage.

Appendix D

I waive any claim that my consent is not an informed consent.

I have not been coached into having this procedure.

I certify that I have read and fully understand the above consent statement.

_____K,M_____ _____11/18/009_____ _____Yashoda_____ /s/
PATIENT's SIGNATURE   DATE   WITNESS

_____Kim_____ _____11/18/009_____ _____
PARENT/PARTNER SIGNATURE   DATE   VERIFICATION

ARBITRATION AGREEMENT

The patient understands and acknowledges that Women's Medical Society, Inc., is responsible only for the performance of administrative duties. It is agreed between patient and Women's Medical Society, Inc. that any claims of gross and wanton negligence, shall be settled by arbitration as described below.

It is agreed between the patient and the physician that any dispute arising from, growing out of, or in any way connected with the physician's rendition of professional services to patient, including (by way of extension and not limitation) any dispute to: (a) proper fees; (b) proper professional care; and (c) alleged malpractice of the physician, shall be settled by arbitration.

Any claim by the patient against the physician or Women's Medical Society, Inc., shall be decided by a panel of arbitrators established by the American Arbitrate Association for such purposes. The proceedings should be conducted pursuant to the Commercial Arbitration rules of said Association, then in force. The arbitrator(s) shall have the power to assess the expenses and costs of the arbitration as shall appear equitable in the arbitrator(s') judgment upon the award rendered may be entered in any court having jurisdiction thereof.

_____/s/_____   _____K,M_____
DOCTOR's SIGNATURE   PATIENT's SIGNATURE
                                               _____11/18/09_____
_____/s/_____   DATE
CLINIC SIGNATURE

EXAMINATION AGREEMENT

Each patient is required to have a follow-up examination within two (2) weeks to three (3) weeks following the abortion with a physician or agency of her choice. If a patient fails to comply with this agreement, the physician and Women's Medical Society, Inc., will not accept any medical or financial liability for any complications that may occur.

_____11/18/09_____ _____Kim_____ _____Yashoda_____ /s/
DATE   PATIENT's SIGNATURE   WITNESS

Appendix D

CYTOTEC - An important and powerful medication

Cytotec is a medication which can be taken orally but can also be very effective when inserted in the vagina. Cytotec is important because of its effectiveness in reducing complications in termination of pregnancy. In the early first trimester of pregnancy, Cytotec is utilized to empty the uterus after RU - 486 has prevented further development of the fetus. In the second trimester, Cytotec is utilized with cervical dilators (known as laminaria or sterile "seaweed sticks") to enlarge and soften the cervix so that less instrumentation is necessary in the later terminations.

Perforation of the uterus, a serious complication, occurs more frequently when more instrumentation is necessary. As a result of the effectiveness of Cytotec in these pregnancies, the risk of perforation is greatly reduced. However, the responsiveness of any individual to Cytotec can be very difficult to predict. Cytotec softens the cervix and helps to dilate the cervix but it also causes contractions and can start labor. In both first and second trimester terminations, the fetus can be delivered in a complete form. Bleeding problems and rupture of the "water bag" of the pregnancy can occur. It is absolutely essential that transportation to our offices or to emergency services is available to any woman receiving Cytotec. In the absence of adequate transportation and/or reliable support during the period of effectiveness of Cytotec, there are circumstances where the Cytotec can be administered and monitored at the office.

All care of the pregnancy termination will be provided at our offices at no additional charge.

We regret that we cannot be responsible for any services delivered or provided by any other medical facility.

It is our firm policy that there are no refunds after the start of the termination by the insertion of dilators or the administration of medications which may be harmful or toxic to the pregnancy.

My signature certifies that I understand the reasons for Cytotec, the potential complications of Cytotec and that I hereby confirm that I have adequate and appropriate transportation and the support of family and/or friends in case of emergency.

_____   _____
Patient Signature   Date

_____   _____
Parent Signature as appropriate   Date

_____   _____
Witness Signature   Date

KBG/bg

Appendix D

Women's Medical Society, Inc.
3801 Lancaster Avenue
Philadelphia, PA 19104
(215)382-4300

24 Hour Counselling
Certification

In accordance with Section 3205 (a) 1 and 3205 (a) 2 (informed consent) of the Pennsylvania Abortion statute, I hereby attest that:

1. I have been counseled by Dr. Gosnell or by Dr. _____, the referring physician

2. I have been made aware of the probable gestational age of my pregnancy.

3. State printed materials regarding abortion alternatives and basic pregnancy information have been made available to me.

4. I understand that medical assistance may be available to me for prenatal and neonatal care and childbirth.

5. I understand that the father of the pregnancy is liable for child support.

6. I understand that the risks of termination of this pregnancy include **infection, hemorrhage, perforation, psychological problems** and noncompleted termination of an ectopic pregnanacy.

7. I understand that, in addition to the above risks, that the risks of continuing the pregnancy to term delivery adds additional risk including **hypertension, diabetes, blood clots, eclampsia, seizures, pulmonary embolus and coma.**

8. I understand that estimation of the risk of dying is less than one in every 100,000 abortions, and the risk of dying from a full term delivery is less than 10 in every 100,000 deliveries.

9. I hereby attest that my notification of this information is at least 24 hours prior to my scheduled abortion procedure.

X _____ _____ _____
SIGNATURE OF PATIENT   DATE   WITNESS

_____ _____
SIGNATURE OF PARENT   VERIFICATION

Oprional:

I hereby **do / do not** authorize medical photography
(please encircle)
for educational purposes or for the benefit of my personal health care.

X _____ _____ _____
SIGNATURE   DATE   WITNESS

Appendix D

COUNSELOR EVALUATION

Name: Karna Mongar

PMH Ⓝ   meds Ⓝ   reason not ready

Date	Wt.	Ht.	B.D.	Temp	Resp	Pulse	B.P.
11/8/09	165	5'1"	4/30/68	98	17	83	112/74

sedation recommendations: local ☐ heavy ☐ twilight ☐ custom ☐
Comments:
Allergies (N) Y _____   by L Lewis on 11/18/09

REQUIRED:
1. How did you hear...
2. Are you married...
3. How many years of...
4. How many years of... Please circle: 1 2
5. How many abortions
6. How many miscarria...
7. How many living chil...
8. How many of your ch...

Karna Mongar 11/18/09
BPD 43mm Kids

GR 5 PARA 4 0 0 3 0   P.T. ___ by ___ LMP 8/09

Appendix D

```
              OPERATIVE SUMMARY - SURGEON
DILAM     _____                    DILATORS  _____ mm
DILAPAN   _____                    DIGITAL   _____ mm
LAMINARIA _____
                                   DILATATION
ULTRASOUND                           PRATT    HERN    to
  compatible  placenta  lie        FORCEPS
EXAMINATION                          BIERER   SOPHER  HERN
  ant    mid    post               CURETTE
PRE OP DX                            BERKELEY  16/___  Sharp  Y  N
          17 wks
MACRO PATH
  placenta  capsule  cord  fetal: 1 2 3 4 5 6 7   COMMENTS:
CONDITION  F.L. ___ mm
  excel   good   fair
```

Date 11/19/__	Physician	Post Op Dx: 17 wks cpd fpd
Name Larsa Morgan		Precautions: bleeding contraception ectopic fundus sedation other –